THE
REFERENCE
SHELF

ISRAEL
AND THE MIDDLE EAST

edited by Thomas Draper

THE REFERENCE SHELF

Volume 55 Number 1

THE H. W. WILSON COMPANY

New York   1983

THE REFERENCE SHELF

The books in this series contain reprints of articles, excerpts from books, and addresses on current issues and social trends in the United States and other countries. There are six separately bound numbers in each volume, all of which are generally published in the same calendar year. One number is a collection of recent speeches; each of the others is devoted to a single subject and gives background information and discussion from various points of view, concluding with a comprehensive bibliography. Books in the series may be purchased individually or on subscription.

Library of Congress Cataloging in Publication Data

Main entry under title:

Israel and the Middle East.

   (The Reference shelf ; v. 55, no. 1)
   Bibliography: p. ·
   1. Jewish-Arab relations--1973-   --Addresses,
essays, lectures. 2. Israel--Foreign relations--Ad-
dresses, essays, lectures. 3. Near East--Politics and
government--1945-   --Addresses, essays, lectures.
I. Draper, Thomas. II. Series.
DS119.7.I82545 1983   327.5694017'4924 83-1046
ISBN 0-8242-0683-5

International Standard Book Number 0-8242-0683-5

PRINTED IN THE UNITED STATES OF AMERICA

81421

CONTENTS

PREFACE

Is peace possible in the Middle East? Can Israel and her Arab neighbors resolve their differences? Most of the articles in this volume seem to agree that a lasting peace in the Middle East is not likely without resolution of the Palestinian problem. One article, however, holds that even if the Palestinian problem is resolved, discord in the Middle East will continue unabated.

In Arab countries we find disagreement and divisiveness everywhere, stemming from territorial and clan feuding, infighting among Islamic sects, and vast differences in economic and political systems. The commonly held belief that Arabs could be united was shaken by the recent June-August 1982 Israeli invasion of Lebanon. At this crucial time, the Palestinian Liberation Organization (PLO) was alone in its struggle; the Arab countries were united only in their hands-off policy toward the plight of the Palestinians.

Israel, meanwhile, cognizant of Arab instability, seems quick to seize the opportunity to expand its lines of defense and territory into Arab lands.

A third actor in the Middle Eastern drama is the PLO leader, Yasir Arafat, who has striven for recognition of his cause with both terrorism and diplomacy.

Can peace be expected with a mix such as this? Rivalries based on ethnic and economic differences have historically tended to find resolution, but divisions based on religious grounds have been more intractable. Perhaps a revival of the spirit of the Camp David accords will produce some hoped-for steps toward Middle East peace.

Articles in the first section of this book examine Israel's neighbors, most of whom are hostile. The second section provides information on Israel's internal and external problems. The third section concentrates on the problem of finding a homeland for the Palestinian refugees.

Tom Draper

November 1982

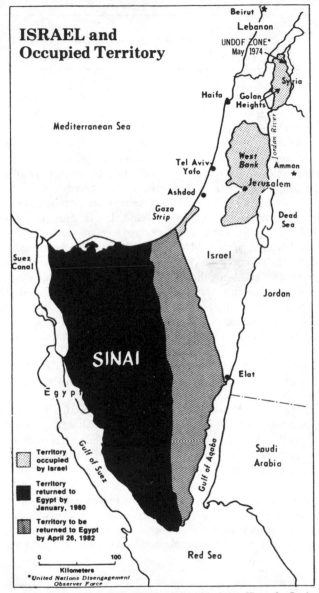

ISRAEL and Occupied Territory

Beirut

Lebanon

UNDOF ZONE*
May 1974

Syria

Haifa

Golan
Heights

Mediterranean Sea

Jordan River

Tel Aviv-
Yafo

West
Bank

Amman

Ashdod

Jerusalem

Gaza
Strip

Dead
Sea

Suez
Canal

Israel

Jordan

SINAI

Egypt

Elat

Gulf of Suez

Gulf of Aqaba

Saudi
Arabia

Territory
occupied
by Israel

Territory
returned to
Egypt by
January, 1980

Territory to be
returned to Egypt
by April 26, 1982

0   100
Kilometers
*United Nations Disengagement
    Observer Force

Red Sea

Source: *Current History*. January 1982. Copyright 1982 by Current History, Inc. Reprinted by permission.

I. THE MIDDLE EAST: DIVIDED
AND INSECURE

EDITOR'S INTRODUCTION

The articles in this section serve not only to increase understanding of the complex territorial rivalries in the Middle East but also to provide a glimpse of the seemingly unreconcilable differences in religion and political persuasion that are ready to shatter the peace.

The first excerpt from *Great Decisions '81,* delineates territorial boundaries of the Middle Eastern countries and touches on some of the many conflicts resulting from historical and cultural differences. Referring to Islam as an "ideology of protest," the Foreign Policy Association editors maintain that today Islam is being revived as a way of life. In the second article, a reprint from the *Nation,* a former Carnegie Endowment for Peace associate, Edward Mortimer, delves deeply into Moslem tenets, with particular emphasis on the Jihad (holy war) against other religions, namely Christianity and Judaism. The next article, from the *Economist,* analyzes population figures of two different and conflicting Islamic sects—the Shias and the Sunnis—in the countries of the Middle East.

The next two articles, reprinted from *Foreign Affairs* and *Current History,* deal with Egypt, the largest Middle Eastern country. In the first, Boutros Boutros-Ghali, Egyptian Minister of State for Foreign Affairs, discusses the history of Egypt, its foreign policy, and its role as peacemaker in the Palestinian crisis. In the second article, Professor John Merriam points out that sectional factionalism in Egypt actually led to the assassination of much-admired Anwar Sadat, initiator of peace in the Middle East. Sadat's ambitious policy of "no religion in politics and no politics in religion" is examined in the context of Egypt's problems, "many seeming to defy resolution."

In speaking to the nation in September 1982, President Reagan noted that Jordan's pivotal role in the Middle East could be instrumental in solving the Palestinian crisis. Adam Garfinkle, author of the sixth article, reprinted from *Current History,* points out that Jordan, having lost both the West Bank and Jerusalem in the 1967 war with Israel is now the home of the largest number of Palestinians in the Middle East. They constitute 50 percent of Jordan's population. Garfinkle describes the Palestinian Arab national movement and the discord among Jordan's factions: Hashemite versus anti-Hashemite, "Palestinians against non-Palestinians, and parts of the PLO against other parts." In the seventh selection, El Hassan Bin Talal, Crown Prince of Jordan, writing in *Foreign Affairs,* states that Jordan is central to any Arab-Israeli settlement and calls for a concerted effort to allow the Palestinians "to freely exercise their national right of self-determination."

A more homogeneous country in the core of the Middle East is Iraq, one of the largest oil producers. Writing in *Current History,* Arthur Turner describes Iraq, with its predominantly Sunni population, as historically one of the most stable and economically successful Middle Eastern countries. He attributes the provocation of war with Iran to territorial claims and religious differences. The next article, also from *Current History,* deals with Iraq's non-Arab neighbor, Iran. James Bill reports that the Iraq-Iran war has hardly affected the internal struggle in Shiite Iran and writes of the continuing internal violence caused by the many warring political factions, from the extreme Right to the extreme Left.

The final article in this section, by *Newsweek* correspondents Angus Deming and Ray Wilkinson, deals with Syria, arch-enemy of Israel. Syria has managed to alienate many of its neighbors and has aligned itself with the Soviets by accepting arms from them. Of particular interest in Syria's inter-Arab feuding is the bitter rivalry between the Syrian Baath Socialist Party and the Iraqi branch of the same party—a rivalry that influenced Syria's siding with Iran against Iraq in the war.

OVERVIEW OF THE MIDDLE EAST[1]

Between Cairo and Kabul lies a part of the world that the first modern Western geographers came to call the Near East and later, the Middle East. Their Western bias showed in the words they chose to distinguish the Far East of China and Japan from these closer lands, yet there was sense in the distinction. China and Japan were unlike anything they had known. But the Middle East, while exotic, was not so completely strange: its great religions, arts and sciences had deeply influenced Western civilizations. In the Westerners' psychological landscape, the Middle East truly was halfway between East and West.

In the post-World War II era, it seemed that the countries of the Middle East were proceeding along a familiar path of modernization comparable with the West's own experience. But the apparent similarities masked deep historical and cultural differences. The mutual incomprehension of the West and the Muslim peoples of the Middle East remains profound, exhibited most starkly in the conflict between the United States and the Islamic Republic of Iran over the fate of the American Embassy personnel taken hostage in Teheran in November 1979.

For Americans, a sound understanding of the Middle East has never been more important. The United States has perceived several key interests there: to limit Soviet influence, to prevent conflict, to develop good relations with the Arab countries of the region, to maintain access to the region's oil, and—most deeply felt—to uphold its moral and political commitment to the security of Israel. These interests would be difficult to reconcile in the best of circumstances. But recent events add up to an awesome challenge to the United States.

One of the first effects of Iran's 1978-79 revolution was a cut in its oil exports, which caused a scramble for oil supplies in a tight global market. OPEC (Organization of Petroleum Exporting Countries) increases pushed the average price of oil from $13

[1] Excerpt from the book, *Great Decisions '81*, by the Editors of the Foreign Policy Association. p 13-14. Copyright, 1981, Foreign Policy Association, Inc. Reprinted by permission.

a barrel in January 1979 to over $30 per barrel in September 1980.

In Iran itself, as *Great Decisions* went to press, the hostage crisis lingered on, and the convulsions of a leadership power struggle left Iran's future international alignment open to question.

Saudi Arabia, our major source of foreign oil, suffered its own internal convulsions. Islamic fanatics seized the Grand Mosque in Mecca on the first day of the Islamic 15th century (November 20, 1979) and it took Saudi troops two full weeks to retake the mosque.

In Afghanistan, Soviet troops invaded massively in December 1979 to install an obedient Marxist regime: the invasion brings Soviet power closer to the Persian Gulf and poses new threats to the entire region.

The Carter Administration's one great achievement in the Middle East, the Egyptian-Israeli peace treaty, threatened to be undone by the lack of progress in the Palestinian autonomy negotiations between Egypt and Israel—a process rejected by the Palestinians and the rest of the Arab world.

The war that erupted in September 1980 between Iraq and Iran caused a halt in oil exports from both countries. In addition, the fierce fighting held the potential of escalating into a struggle over control of the Strait of Hormuz, through which passes 60 percent of the oil in world trade.

Whose interests are served, and whose harmed, by the Iraqi-Iranian war or any other conceivable shooting war in the area is a question with no clear answer. But any conflict could cut the flow of oil or lead to a direct confrontation of the superpowers.

Politics and the Islamic Revival

The current Islamic revival is real—not just in Iran, but throughout the Islamic world, which extends from Morocco to Indonesia. In the Middle East, Islam's birthplace, the revival is evident in the reappearance of beards and veiled women; the growing number who answer the call to the faithful and attend Friday services; the strength of the underground political group, the Muslim Brotherhood, in Egypt, Syria and the Gulf states.

An Islamic revival is nothing new. Westerners have wrongly assumed that because of modernization Islam was a religion in decline. To the contrary, Islam is a vibrant and dynamic faith that has gone through many cycles of decline and renewal. There have been resurgences of the faith in the late 19th century, in the 1920s, in the postwar anticolonial struggle, and again today.

One reason for Islam's resilience is that it is not just a set of beliefs but an entire way of ordering one's life. For this reason, many believe Western political ideologies have failed to take hold in the Middle East. Liberalism, with its notion foreign to Islam of the separation of church and state, and Marxism, with its atheism and hostility to all churches, have made little headway. Even socialism of the pan-Arab variety has failed. Most attempts at emulating the West's political institutions have degenerated into military dictatorship.

But the states of the Middle East are militarily weak. Despite their oil wealth, they still feel powerless and frustrated before American, Soviet and Israeli military power. "Islam has become politically important," says Professor Richard Hrair Dekmejian of SUNY Binghamton, "precisely because the national elites . . . have so dismally failed."

Islam, whether in the revolution against the shah or in the takeover of the Grand Mosque in Mecca, is a powerful ideology of protest. It is a vehicle for the criticism of corruption, disparities of wealth, and leaders who are perceived to compromise their nation or their religious values. It can be expected to remain a political force in this sense. As a Tunisian said, "You can ban student meetings and check the papers of everybody . . . but you can't stop people going to the mosque on Friday and getting together when they come out. And how could the government come out against prayer"

On the other hand, Islam is divided into many sects; and Islamic political unity is likely to remain elusive, except on an issue with strong religious overtones such as Israel's annexation of Arab East Jerusalem.

The adequacy of Islam as an ordering political principle within states is also in doubt. The Koran concerns itself with the relations of family and village groups, not the governance of a modern

society. Koranic guidelines are often vague and, as factional fighting in Iran can attest, open to varying interpretation. But in the
world of Islam, faith and politics are inseparably linked.

IS ISLAM ANTI-SEMITIC?[2]

Is Islam anti-Semitic? Most Jews, and many Christian or ag-
nostic Westerners, assume that it is. That assumption was reinforced last January when the leaders of some thirty Moslem
countries attending a summit conference in Mecca, Saudi Arabia,
pledged themselves to a jihad (usually translated as "holy war")
for the liberation of Jerusalem and other "occupied Palestinian
and Arab territories." Clearly this means a war against Israel, and
a war undertaken on religious grounds. No doubt many Americans take it for granted that the Moslem religion has declared war
on the Jewish religion and all who profess it. The passage in the
conference's declaration affirming "that Islam permits to those
who believe in it and to others [i.e., non-Moslems] only right and
justice, and offers to those who do not fight us in our religion, who
do not drive us out from our homes and do not violate our sancti-
ties only piety and fairness" is either ignored or regarded as empty
rhetoric.

On the level of public relations in the West, the Moslem leaders could hardly have made a greater blunder than to proclaim a
jihad against Israel. In doing so, they incurred the taint of anti-
Semitism and reawakened the feelings of horror that the word itself inspires. It has been used by Moslems in many countries to
describe their resistance to Western imperialism. For the imperi-
alists—and therefore for us, as the inheritors of imperialist culture—a jihad connotes fanaticism, massacre, destruction. When
we hear it, we know instinctively that no white woman is safe. Its
use tells us that Moslems have relapsed into barbarism, if indeed

    [2] Magazine article entitled "Notes on Jihad; Is Islam Anti-Semitic?" by Edward Mortimer, who is on
the editorial desk of *The Times* of London. *Nation*. 233:613-16. Copyright, 1981, by The Nation Magazine.
Reprinted by permission.

they ever emerged from it. Christians and Jews must close ranks, since both will inevitably be in the line of fire. We slip easily and unconsciously into the assumption that anti-Semitism is an inherent feature of Islam, while shrugging it off as no more than an episodic aberration of European culture.

The apologists for Islam argue the exact opposite. For them, anti-Semitism is a peculiarly European phenomenon. One of Islam's special virtues, they claim, is the generous and respectful treatment it accords to minorities, and especially to Christians and Jews—fellow monotheists, "people of the Book." For thirteen centuries, Judaism flourished under Moslem rule. If, in this century, Jews have encountered Moslem hostility, that is the fault of Zionism (another peculiarly European phenomenon), which has sought to turn Jews and Moslems against one another, and to uproot Jews from their Moslem homelands and use them to colonize one particular Moslem country—Palestine—whose Moslem inhabitants the Zionists drove out.

As for the jihad, some Moslems argue today that it was always purely defensive. Others speak of this holy struggle in Marxist terms: its aim is social transformation and justice, and its methods are not necessarily violent. If they are, it is because the adversary inevitably resorts to violence before letting himself be dispossessed of the fruits of oppression. And, this second group adds, neither Christendom nor Jewry has ever suffered under a jihad as Islam did during the Crusades.

Yet the relationship between Islam and Judaism is a complex one. To a certain extent, Islam stands in the same relation to both Judaism and Christianity as Christianity does to Judaism. That is, Islam recognizes the validity of the other two religions but claims to be at a higher stage. As the history of relations between Christians and Jews shows, this makes for a certain ambivalence. Since Christ was a Jew and the Old Testament is sacred for Christians, Christians feel some kinship with the Jews. Yet, since those who are called Jews are by definition those who do not accept Christianity, Christians find themselves in opposition to Judaism. Thus, subconsciously if not consciously, Christians identify Jews with their forebears, who rejected Christ. A committed Christian is virtually bound to believe that Jews have missed the

central point of their own religion. Jews are implicitly blamed by
Christians for not being Christian. Jews had, so to speak, a better
chance than anyone else, and they passed it up.

Mohammed was neither a Jew nor a Christian, but he accepted much of both Jewish and Christian teaching. He accepted the
validity of the Jewish prophets and regarded Christ as the last and
greatest of them before himself. He felt a bond with both Jews and
Christians because he shared their monotheism, but his disap-
pointment was the greater when they did not accept his revelation.

There were several important Jewish clans in Medina at the
time of Mohammed's arrival there in A.D. 622, and he clearly
hoped that the Jews would recognize him as their prophet. The
fact that they instead refuted his claims by pointing to discrepan-
cies between the Koran (the Word of God as revealed to Mohammed) and their own scriptures was a great embarrassment to him.
Consequently, the later passages of the Koran contain a good deal
of polemic against the Jews, as Mohammed received revelations
assuring him that he was right and they were wrong. There is also
some polemic against the Christians, and both groups are accused
of distorting or misinterpreting their own scriptures and failing
to heed the prophets sent to them. But the Christians were not an
organized power in the area near Medina, and some of the Christian holy men may have been early ecumenicists. Thus at one
point the Koran says:

> Thou wilt surely find the most hostile of men to the believers are the
> Jews and the idolaters; and thou wilt surely find the nearest of them in
> love to the believers are those who say "We are Christians."

On the military level, Mohammed moved to eliminate the
powerful Jewish clans as soon as they showed any sign of disloyalty. Two were forced to leave the city, and a third, which had conspired with the pagan Meccans during the siege of Medina in
A.D. 627, had its adult males put to death and its women and children sold as slaves.

Modern biographers of Mohammed emphasize that these
drastic measures did not violate the Arab moral code of the time.
According to W. Montgomery Watt's *Muhammad, Prophet and
Statesman*, "When tribes were at war with one another or simply

had no agreement, they had no obligations toward one another, not even of common decency." That may well be, but it hardly makes it less disconcerting that the man responsible for the Medina massacre is today regarded as a *model* human being by hundreds of millions of people.

That said, it is important to note that the clan was not punished for being Jewish but for a specific act of treason. Other Jews, who did not pose a political threat, remained in Medina and were assured of toleration and protection.

For example, the Jews of Khaybar, an oasis north of Medina that the Moslems conquered in A.D. 628, were allowed to continue cultivating their land as tenants of the Moslem conquerors, to whom they paid half of their produce in rent. This arrangement became the model for the organization of the Islamic empire (although both Jews and Christians were officially banned from Arabia itself after Mohammed's death in A.D. 632). Non-Moslem groups who accepted Moslem political sovereignty received "the protection of God and of his Messenger"; they retained their own governments and in return made a payment, usually in kind, to the Moslem state. They paid two separate taxes, the land tax (*kharaj*) and the poll tax (*jizya*), but were exempt from the poor rate (*zakat*), which was a Moslem religious obligation, and from military service. They kept their own courts and dealt with the Moslem rulers through their own religious leaders.

This was what became known, in the Ottoman Empire, as the *millet* system. On the whole it seems to have worked well. In traditional Arab societies, the prestige of a tribe was judged partly by its ability to protect its minorities, and this was reflected in the attitude of Moslem rulers toward their non-Moslem protégés (*dhimmis*). But as Watt wrote in *Islamic Political Thought:*

> On the whole there was more genuine toleration of non-Moslems under Islam than there was of non-Christians in medieval Christian states. There were exceptions, of course. When times were hard and difficult, non-Moslems would tend to get the worst of it. Occasionally, too, a ruler, in order to divert animosity from himself, would encourage the mob to vent its feelings on the *dhimmis*. On the whole, however, the "protected minorities" had a tolerable existence.

The most striking example of this was Moslem Spain, where the remarkable burgeoning of Jewish art and thought in the fifteenth century was brought to an abrupt end by the Christian *reconquista,* after which both Jews and Moslems were forced either to leave the country or to convert to Christianity (and the Inquisition came into existence to check on the orthodoxy of the converts).

But there are many other examples. From Iran to Morocco and from Central Asia to Yemen, the Moslem world could boast Jewish communities whose members were on average at least as prosperous as their Moslem neighbors, and whose leading citizens were often quite wealthy and influential outside their own sphere. (Many Israelis would deny this—witness the textbooks that present the Jewish experience in Moslem countries as one of squalor and backwardness punctuated by pogroms. These textbooks have provoked vigorous protests within Israel's Sephardic community.)

Islam's treatment of minorities clearly had some shortcomings from the standpoint of twentieth-century liberal humanism. First, the non-Moslem was automatically a second-class citizen. He was tolerated and protected, and he was allowed to regulate his affairs according to his own laws or customs, but he remained wholly dependent on the good will of Moslem rulers over whom he had no control, against whom he had no redress and in whose affairs he had no standing. The state was identified with the community of believers, and the non-Moslem was an outsider even though he lived under the state's power. Disputes between Jews might be settled in a Jewish court, and disputes between Christians might be settled in a Christian court, but any dispute involving a Moslem would be settled according to Islamic law, which always gave preference to the testimony of a Moslem over that of a non-Moslem.

Second, the system assumed that political and religious communities were identical. Moslems were encouraged to think of themselves first and foremost as Moslems, rather than as members of a tribal or national group, and they naturally looked at members of other faiths in the same way. Thus an Egyptian Moslem, for instance, would regard an Egyptian Jew not primarily as a fellow Egyptian but primarily as a Jew. The rise of nationalism in the Moslem world in the nineteenth century divided people along religious lines, rather than along geographical or even linguistic ones.

Arab nationalism, it is true, was taken up enthusiastically (some even say invented) by Arabic-speaking Christians who saw it as a way to escape their second-class status and become equal to their Moslem fellow citizens. But Moslem Arabs have not always seen it that way. With some justification, they tend to regard Islam as the essence of Arab history and Arab civilization, and they therefore assume that the revival of the Arab nation means a Moslem comeback after a period of Christian ascendancy. The rule of the Ottoman Turks was hardly questioned by Moslem Arabs until World War I, and the Arab nationalism since then has been fueled mainly by Moslem resentment of Christian rule and the rise of a Jewish nation in Palestine.

Third, although Jews were by and large well treated by Moslems as long as they remained a submissive minority, it is clear that anyone who wants to arouse Moslem hostility toward Jews can find passages in the Koran and statements by Mohammed that will serve this purpose (just as anyone who wants to incite Christians against Jews can make use of several passages in the Gospel of St. John). Anti-Jewish sentiments in the Koran have been invoked at various times in Moslem history, but in this century, with the appearance of Zionism as a direct challenge to Islam, they have taken on a contemporary relevance. For almost the first time since the conquest of the Khaybar oasis in the seventh century, Moslems find themselves confronted by an organized Jewish power that refuses to recognize the supremacy of Islam.

The creation of a Zionist state in Palestine also resulted in the expulsion of millions of Arabs from their land. In this Islamic exodus was born the "Palestine question."

Let me now attempt to summarize the history of the Palestine question as it has been generally perceived in the Moslem world. A predominantly Moslem territory, Palestine had been under Moslem rule since the first decade after Mohammed's death, with the exception of the brief interlude of the Crusades. It contained, in Jerusalem, the Aqsa Mosque, to which Mohammed is widely believed to have been miraculously transported in his famous

"night journey," and, in Hebron, the tomb of Abraham, who is
thought by Moslems to have built the Ka'ba in Mecca and whose
"true" religion, purged of Jewish and Christian distortions, Mohammed claimed to have revived. (Also in Jerusalem is the Dome
of the Rock, which is said to house the rock on which Abraham,
in a gesture prototypical of Moslem submission to God, prepared
to sacrifice his son.)

Between 1917 and 1948, Palestine was conquered by a Christian power (Britain), and the most fertile and populous part of it
was made into a Jewish state. Most of the Moslem and Christian
inhabitants fled from their homes and became refugees. The attempt by neighboring Arab states to stop the creation of Israel was
ignominiously defeated. In 1967, Israel gained control over the remaining parts of Palestine west of the Jordan River, including the
Old City of Jerusalem with its holy places. In 1969, the Aqsa
Mosque was badly damaged in a fire set by an Australian Christian fanatic. Meanwhile, Jews settled in the Old City and in the
northern, eastern and southern suburbs of Jerusalem (the western
sector had been entirely Jewish since 1948) with the express intention of giving these areas an irreversibly Jewish character.

All of this was interpreted by Moslems as an act of aggression
against the house of Islam in one of its most sacred tenets. That
is what Zionism means to Moslems, and they are against it. This
does not necessarily mean that they are anti-Semitic. One can be
opposed to the implantation of a Jewish state in Palestine without
being systematically hostile to Jews, although it requires a degree
of sophistication. Until the proclamation of the state of Israel in
1948, the Zionist settlers in Palestine were known simply as "the
Jews," and their main spokesmen claimed that they were acting
as the vanguard of a Jewish nation. It was all too easy, therefore,
for Moslems to blame Jews in general for what they saw as the
expropriation of Arab land. And to a certain extent the Islamic
tradition encouraged Moslems to react in that way. Moslems are
accustomed to the idea that a person's political status is determined by his religion, and they are taught by the example of Mohammed to suspect the political loyalty of Jews once an alternative
claim to their allegiance has been put forward.

All but the most sophisticated Moslems, therefore, assumed that the aggressors in Palestine were "the Jews," and many added that this was the sort of thing one must expect from Jews. Perhaps the most passionate devotee of this argument was the late King Faisal of Saudi Arabia. For many years, Faisal supplied his guests with copies of the *Protocols of the Elders of Zion,* and he tried to keep all Jews out of his kingdom (although he was obliged to make an exception for then Secretary of State Henry Kissinger). Faisal also strove untiringly to convince his visitors that Zionism and Communism (both founded by Jews, after all) were but different facets of the same evil.

One could say, therefore, that anti-Semitism is the Islam of fools, just as it was the socialism of fools in nineteenth-century Europe. Anti-Semitism is a convenient weapon for leaders who wish to inflame the Moslem masses, or to direct their anger toward a relatively easy target. In the last half-century the Moslem world, or at least the Arab world, has not been the safest or the most pleasant region for Jews to live in, and the great majority of them have in fact left. Zionism certainly helped to bring that about, both directly and indirectly, but Islam also played a part.

That the Islamic revolution in Iran, which was loudly anti-Zionist, should have provoked an exodus of Iranian Jews is thus not surprising. Some prominent Jews who stayed in Iran have been executed as alleged Zionist agents. Others, like all too many Moslem Iranians, have been arbitrarily arrested or have had their property seized. But it is only fair to add that persecution of Jews has not been encouraged by Iran's religious leaders. Like Christians and Zoroastrians, Jews are officially recognized in the Iranian Constitution as a religious minority; they control their own schools, and they have their own laws and their own representative in Parliament—a modified version of the *millet* system. Their lot is certainly happier than that of the luckless Bahais, members of a sect that began in the nineteenth century as a deviation from Islam and that regards Mohammed as a prophet, thereby denying the finality of his revelation. To orthodox Moslems, the Bahais are guilty of apostasy, a crime traditionally punishable by death. Under the regime of Ayatollah Khomeini, they alone can justly claim to be the victims of *religious* persecution.

What of the jihad? It means "struggle" or "striving." The word derives its sanctity from the frequent references in the Koran to "striving in the way of God," which seems to be a reference to the raids, or *razzias*, carried out by the Moslems against the trading caravans of pagan Meccans. This age-old form of tribal warfare was given a new slant by the Koran, which made it legitimate to use only against non-Moslems. The energies of the Arab tribesmen were thus directed outward and became the driving force of Islam's formidable early expansion.

Clearly the jihad was defensive only in the sense that the best form of defense is attack, and often pre-emptive attack at that. Just as clearly, it could not go on forever. Either the whole world would become Moslem or the expansion of Islam would find its limits and begin to coexist with other religions. The latter occurred, and in this century the jihad has usually been invoked not for the conquest of lands that had never known Islam but for the reconquest or redemption of lands or peoples that had fallen away. Often the idea of internal redemption—the restoration of true religion and social justice in a corrupt and irreligious Moslem society—was paramount. At other times it was the battle against non-Moslem encroachment on Moslem terrain: first the Sikhs and then the British in India; the French in Algeria; most recently the Russians in Afghanistan. In general, success has been proportionate to the commitment of the faithful to a particular struggle and to the credibility of the leaders issuing the call. The biggest flop was the proclamation of a jihad against France, Russia and Britain by the Ottoman government in 1914.

On that basis, the prospects for the jihad proclaimed in Mecca last January do not seem good. Few of the leaders assembled there have the necessary charisma in the eyes of their subjects, and many of them are more absorbed by conflicts with one another than by the question of Palestine. The two regimes that have tried most consistently to base their politics on Islamic militancy—those of Libya and Iran—were conspicuously absent. The hosts of the conference, and the keenest peddlers of the jihad idea, were the rulers of Saudi Arabia, who seem to have adopted it mainly as a smokescreen for their continued close relations with the United States. The Saudis sought to soften the impact of the announcement in Washington by explaining that the jihad would be political and economic, and only in the last resort military.

Most Moslems live a long way from Palestine and are unlikely to take up Yasir Arafat's invitation at Mecca to join his fight ("The ranks of our strugglers are open and welcome all the brothers who seek the afterlife through the present."). According to Arafat, "tens of brother strugglers from the Arab and Islamic countries" were "martyred" last year "for the sake of and in defense of the Palestinian revolution." It seems a fair bet that the number will not be significantly higher this year.

Yet to write off the Islamic summit at Mecca as having no significance and to assume that the Moslem masses are indifferent to the fate of Palestine would be a mistake. Hypocrisy is the tribute vice pays to virtue, and the hypocrites of Mecca would not make such declarations if they did not think they were what the folks back home wanted to hear. Their peoples may not want to die for Palestine, but the failure to liberate Palestine is seem by most Moslems as a reproach to the leadership of the Moslem world. So Moslem leaders must at least appear to be doing something about it, and that will have to be taken into account by Western policy makers until a solution can be found that Moslems will accept as fair to the Palestinians and respectful of Islam's holy places. The jihad in Afghanistan remains a local affair. The jihad for Jerusalem is the big one.

PUTTING THE SHIAS IN THEIR PLACE[3]

The Moslem world is alarmed at the prospect of an onslaught by its Shia minority on its Sunni majority. Yet Shia Moslems number about 85m, only around 11 percent of the estimated 750m Moslems. Ayatollah Khomeini claims, in his more exalted moments, that there are 200m Shias—but then he also claims that there are 1,000m Moslems.

[3] Magazine article from *Economist*. 283:24. Je. 12, '82. Copyright The Economist Newspaper, Ltd., London, 1982. Reprinted by permission.

The Shias are in a majority in only three countries: Iran, Iraq and Bahrain. And though they comprise 94 percent of Iran's 35m people, Iranian Shias are not a single coherent group; only about half of them are Farsi-speaking Persians.

The next largest Shia communities are the 15m in India and the 12m in Pakistan. Sunni-Shia antagonism is probably at its most open in the subcontinent; last year, for instance, the Shia section of Karachi's bazaar was ravaged.

The population statistics for many of these countries are estimates only. The 15 percent of Turks said to be Shias may well be an underestimate. Most of Syria's Shias are the ruling Alawite group. The 200,000 Shias in Saudi Arabia are important since they are located in the oilfield area in the north-east.

The Shias in the part of the Arab world adjacent to Iran are fairly small in number, except in Iraq. Most of them do not want to be "revolutionalized" in Iran's way. The idea that they could become a channel for the export of Iran's intensely Shia revolution is probably less daunting than it is sometimes made out to be.

THE FOREIGN POLICY OF EGYPT[4]

Egypt, for several centuries, has been performing an important function of cultural and political synthesis between Islam and Christianity, the Arab world and Europe, Africa and Asia, and the civilization of the desert and that of the Mediterranean. This reality, together with the perennial character of the citizens of the oldest state in the area, acquired through the ages, constitutes an important factor that conditions the attitudes and behavior of Egypt toward the rest of the world.

However, the foreign policy of a country is the sum of various geopolitical, historical and economic components. From Gamal

[4] Excerpt from magazine article entitled "The Foreign Policy of Egypt in the Post-Sadat Era," by Boutros Boutros-Ghali, Minister of State for Foreign Affairs of the Arab Republic of Egypt. *Foreign Affairs.* 68:769-88. Spring '82. Reprinted by permission of *Foreign Affairs.* Copyright, 1982, Council on Foreign Relations, Inc.

Abdel Nasser to Anwar el-Sadat, from Anwar el-Sadat to Hosni Mubarak, these same components have influenced and shaped the foreign policy of Egypt. Therefore, it is in the nature of things that this policy should have a character of continuity through the various periods, and, consequently, after the tragic death of President Sadat, that this continuity should prevail.

Broadly speaking, Egyptian foreign policy in the last three decades has been directed toward two main challenges: how to contain Israeli ambitions and how to solve the Palestinian problem, the core of the Middle East crisis. This task, difficult in itself and rendered more complex by virtue of the multifaceted nature of the conflict, has been further complicated by the differences among Arabs, and the inability of some to adopt a rational attitude or to discard shortsighted policies toward the problem.

Thus, Egypt's efforts to resolve the contradictions between Palestinian national rights and Israeli national aims had to take place in the framework of an equation that would strike a balance between Egyp's conviction that Arab initiative is an important factor in any peace process and the necessity for her to exercise her traditional leadership in order to break the deadlock that has existed for well over 30 years, a deadlock that was undoubtedly detrimental to the interests of Egypt and all the other Arab states as well as to those of the Palestinian people.

In an interdependent world such as ours, Egypt's initiation of the peace process would no doubt have worldwide implications, particularly concerning her relations with the Arab countries, Africa and the nonaligned countries in general. This essay is an attempt to analyze Egypt's response to that challenge and the impact of that response on her relations with the Arab world, Africa and the Third World at large, in the post-Sadat era.

Egypt's Defense of Palestinian Rights

A review of the history of the region demonstrates that Egypt is the central power in the Middle East. Major developments and events in the area during the nineteenth and twentieth centuries have been, to a great extent, shaped by the role played by Egypt, and major events have never left Egypt indifferent. Ever since the partition of Palestine and the establishment of the state of Israel in 1948, Egypt has been at the forefront of the opposition to the creation of a Jewish state at the expense of the Palestinian people. The Egyptian people were deeply affected by the injustice done to the Palestinian people and the usurpation of their rights. This Egyptian opposition did not in any way stem from any anti-Jewish sentiment, but it was rather based on the dismissal of the violation of the Palestinians' rights to sovereignty and independence, those rights guaranteed by the U.N. Charter and recognized with regard to all other peoples.

From this standpoint, Egypt also objected to Jordanian schemes to extend sovereignty over the West Bank. A violent controversy erupted at that time between the Arab states on the future of the West Bank. Jordan, supported by Iraq, favored the annexation of these Palestinian territories, while Egypt, supported by Saudi Arabia, rejected the Hashemite plan and did not recognize Jordan's domination of the West Bank. In 1950 Egypt demanded the expulsion of Jordan from the Arab League because of its measures to annex the West Bank and its disregard of the rights of the Palestinian people to determine their own future on their own territory.

The Council of the Arab League adopted a resolution warning Jordan against the consequences of such action and reiterating a common Arab attitude. The resolution laid down that the Council:

reaffirms the unanimous resolution of April 12, 1948, that the entry into Palestine of the Arab Armies was to save it from the conspiracies and atrocities it was subjected to and that it should be considered as a provisional measure void of any intention or power to bring about the occupation or partition of Palestine; and that the Palestinian territories should be restored to their rightful owners. In case of violation of this Resolution by any Arab State, that State should be considered as having violated the pact of the Arab League and will be dealt with accordingly.

On the other hand, Egypt preserved the Palestinian identity and character of the Gaza Strip. Egypt refused to annex it and never claimed sovereignty over it. Egypt considered the Gaza Strip, placed under her administration after the armistice agreement, as a Palestinian territory entrusted to Egypt provisionally, to be ultimately restored to the Palestinian people.

Not only did Egypt defend Palestinian rights, and oppose and resist the annexation of Palestinian territories by any power, Arab and non-Arab alike, but she also insisted that Palestine should be represented in the Arab League as well as in other international forums. Thus Egypt's struggle in favor of Palestinian rights led— from the beginning—to several inter-Arab disputes in addition to the Arab-Israeli confrontation. Egypt strongly believed that the Palestinians were entitled to freedom, self-determination and their own state if they so chose.

After four wars and 34 years of bloodshed and untold suffering, the unprecedented and courageous visit of President Sadat to Israel in November 1977, and the conclusion of the peace treaty with Israel and the exchange of diplomatic relations with the Jewish state, Egypt in 1982 remains as solid in her commitment to the realization of the rights of the Palestinian people as she was in 1948.

There is continuity and consistency in that position which can be explained by the fact that the goal to be achieved supersedes the ways and means to reach it. Egypt did not at any stage deviate from the goal of restoring Palestinian rights. The Egyptian peace initiative of November 1977 was in its essence a new approach, a new methodology to attain peacefully a solution to the conflict that would be based on these rights as recognized by the Charter and resolutions of the United Nations.

The October War of 1973 ushered in a new era in the Middle East and opened the door for the first time to the possibility of reconciliation between Arabs and Israelis. It constituted a turning point on the whole geopolitical map of the Middle East conflict, thus paving the way for President Sadat's peace policy. After attempting to obtain recognition of Palestinian rights through military confrontation, Egypt is now trying to achieve the same aim through diplomatic efforts. Egypt is now trying to demonstrate that this can be done through peaceful means, through negotiation and a continuous dialogue.

This shift in the means, but not in the objective, was based on a rational analysis of regional power relations as well as on that of the attitudes of the two superpowers. The interests of the peoples of the area, without exception, and in fact the interests of world peace and stability, required that all responsible and lucid policymakers should eschew irrational reactions and misconceptions and reject from their thinking the possibility of war as an alternative.

On November 20, 1977, President Sadat pressed on the Israelis, in his address to the Knesset, the hard facts about the Palestinian cause and the right of the Palestinian people to their own state. He said:

> The problem is not that of Egypt and Israel. . . . Any separate peace between Egypt and Israel will not bring permanent peace. Rather, even if peace between all the confrontation States and Israel were achieved in the absence of a just solution to the Palestinian problem, there would never be the durable and just peace upon which the entire world today insists.
>   . . . As for the Palestinian cause, nobody can deny that it is the crux of the entire problem. Nobody in the world today can accept those slogans propagated in Israel ignoring the existence of the Palestinian people and questioning even their whereabouts. The cause of the Palestinian people and their legitimate rights are no longer ignored or denied today by anyone. . . . Even the United States, your prime ally, has opted to face up to reality and admit that the Palestinian people are entitled to their legitimate rights, as the Palestinian problem in the core and essence of the conflict. There can be no peace without the Palestinians. It is a grave error of unpredictable consequences to overlook or brush aside this cause.

President Sadat presented the elements of Egypt's peace plan before the Knesset, as follows:

—the termination of the Israeli occupation of all the Arab territories occupied since 1967, including East Jerusalem;

—the realization of the inalienable right of the Palestinian people and their rights of self-determination including the right to establish their own state;

—the right of all states in the area to live in peace within secure boundaries, based on the recognition that the security of international borders can be established through agreed upon arrangements and international guarantees;

—the commitment by all states in the region to conduct relations among themselves according to the purposes and principles of the U.N. Charter, in particular the peaceful settlement of disputes and the abstention from the threat or use of force; and

—the termination of the state of belligerency in the area.

Thus it was abundantly clear that Egypt viewed the Palestinian problem as being at the very heart of the Middle East conflict and that an unjust peace that would not guarantee the rights of the Palestinian people would have no future. Indeed, Egypt is seeking a comprehensive peace and not a separate or bilateral agreement with Israel. And during long hours of negotiations with the Israelis, Egyptians have sought to link the withdrawal of Israeli forces from Egyptian territory to the withdrawal of Israeli forces from Palestinian territory. Every effort was exerted by Egypt to associate the solution of the Egyptian question with that of the Palestinian question, in order to lay special emphasis on her comprehensive approach to the peace process.

This view was rejected by the Israelis, who opposed the linkage in the timing of the two courses. But in substance as well as in fact, the linkage does exist: on March 26, 1979, Egypt and Israel signed what amounts to two complementary treaties. The first one envisages a phased withdrawal of Israeli forces from Sinai, while the second one envisages the partial withdrawal of these forces from Gaza and the West Bank and the establishment of an autonomous Palestinian Authority in these territories during a transitional period. It also draws the outline for negotiations between all parties concerned on an agreement about the final status of these Palestinian territories.

Thus, the role of Egypt in the current autonomy talks is not to reach an agreement on this final status, but rather to agree on a number of transitional arrangements under which a Palestinian Authority would be established with a dual role: it would assume the powers and responsibilities now held by the Israeli military occupation regime, and it would also be able to participate in the negotiations on the final status of the Palestinian territories now under occupation.

Egypt does not pretend to speak for the Palestinians or to have a mandate to decide on their behalf. It is the Palestinian Authority which will be able to voice their wishes and concerns in the negotiations and pave the way for the process of self-determination. This, by itself, rationalizes the firm intention of Egyptian diplomacy to continue, after the Israeli withdrawal from Sinai due in April 1982, to pursue the negotiations with the Israelis and the

Americans with the aim of achieving full autonomy for the Palestinian people on their own territory according to the Camp David framework.

What Egypt has in mind is that the Palestinians and other Arab parties concerned join these negotiations. It is obvious, however, that only tangible and positive results would induce them to do so. Hence the emphasis laid by Egypt on the necessity for the Israelis to adopt a number of confidence-building measures, to discard the policies of economic sabotage, psychological warfare and cultural frustration being conducted against the Palestinians in the occupied lands.

In an official aide-mémoire dated October 13, 1980, Egypt specified her demands for such confidence-building measures and demanded a commitment by Israel to:

—freeze the establishment of settlements in the West Bank and Gaza during the five-year transitional period;

—affirm her readiness to engage in negotiations with any Palestinian group that would accept U.N. Security Council Resolution 242;

—give assurances that Israeli settlers in the West Bank and Gaza would have no right to participate in the vote concerning the establishment of the Palestinian Authority;

—recognize the fact that the Arabs of East Jerusalem constitute an integral part of the Palestinian people and will participate in the vote establishing the Palestinian Authority;

—restore the expropriated lands and properties in the West Bank and Gaza to the Palestinian Authority;

—permit the resumption of the activities and commercial operations of the Arab banks in the West Bank and return expropriated or frozen deposits;

—lift the ban on political meetings and allow freedom of expression in the West Bank and Gaza;

—suspend any policies or practices that would create tension or render difficult the implementation of the Camp David framework's provisions concerning the establishment of the Palestinian Authority;

—abolish all restrictions on the freedom of movement of the inhabitants in the occupied territories;

—grant an amnesty to Palestinian political prisoners;

—cease military maneuvers in the West Bank and Gaza;

—reunite Palestinian families by allowing the return of those members who were forced to flee their houses and villages in 1967;

—allow a number of displaced persons to return to the West Bank and Gaza;

—put an end to the restrictions on the use of water for irrigation purposes in the Gaza farms; and

—refrain from imposing any restrictions on the Arab producers of citrus fruits, etc.

If the Israelis do want a comprehensive peace, if they do want other Arabs to join the peace process, then it is up to them to respond to these Egyptian proposals and to desist from practices that can only deepen mistrust and hatred. Mass arrests, deportation of mayors and notables, destruction of homes, building of illegal settlements, violation of property rights, collective punishments, and the denial of freedom are not only contrary to the Fourth Geneva Convention but more importantly indicate a lack of will to reach a just settlement as defined in the Camp David accords. Only the achievement of positive results in the autonomy talks and a significant improvement in the quality of life of the Palestinians who for the last 15 years have been living under military occupation can give credibility to the peace process, and hope to the Palestinians. The alleviation of the sufferings of the Palestinians in the occupied territories and the creation of a positive atmosphere are vital to the success of the peace process. This would not in any way make military occupation more acceptable to the people, because an alien occupation is unacceptable as a matter of principle, lenient or harsh as it may be. However, it would help to initiate a dynamic motion and a strong momentum toward transitional arrangements leading to a comprehensive peace.

Occupation by Israel of the West Bank and Gaza will have to end, for three million Israelis cannot go on forever governing one and-a-half million Palestinians and ignoring their national rights and aspirations.

Needless to say, Egypt feels as strongly about ending the occupation of the Golan Heights as she does about ending the occupation of Gaza and the West Bank, including East Jerusalem. Egypt rejects totally both the annexation of East Jerusalem and that of the Golan, as illegal, unacceptable and obnoxious measures that are not conducive to the atmosphere that is necessary to reach a peaceful comprehensive solution. Such unilateral measures contradict the letter and the spirit of the Camp David accords. Egypt in an official statement on December 15, 1981, strongly condemned the Israeli decision to extend Israeli law, jurisdiction and administration to the occupied Syrian territory of the Golan Heights and termed it an illegal measure and a violation of international law and the Charter of the United Nations. In U.N. Security Council Resolution 242, which is the basis of the Camp David accords, it is stipulated that the acquisition of territory by war is inadmissible and that it is essential to respect the sovereignty and territorial integrity of every state in the area, including Syria.

Negotiations may have been rendered more difficult by the Israeli measure concerning the Golan, but they must, and will, go on. Through negotiation and dialogue, Egypt seeks to convey, both to the Israelis and to the Americans, her strong opposition to this unilateral Israeli action. She also seeks to exert every effort to have these measures rescinded. After all, what the Israeli Knesset has done, the Israeli Knesset can undo.

In spite of this Israeli attitude, Egypt continues to work for a positive and successful outcome for the autonomy talks. But in these talks Egypt does not for one moment claim to have a monopoly on the ways and means to solve the intricacies of the Middle East problem, or that hers is the only source of wisdom. On the contrary, Egypt has welcomed any attempt to contribute to the peace process, and has even invited new initiatives and suggestions.

The "European initiative" on the Middle East was to a great extent prompted by Egyptian diplomatic efforts to convince Europe that it could not remain unconcerned about the future of peace in the Middle East. With President Sékou Touré of Guinea and with former President Leopold Senghor of Senegal when he was in office, Egypt discussed the shape and timing of a possible African initiatives that would open new avenue to the peace process. Contacts between Cairo and several Latin American capitals also encouraged a genuine desire to contribute to the Middle East peace efforts by what might become a Latin peace initiative. In the meantime, when President Nicolae Ceauşescu of Romania and Soviet President Leonid Breshnev had new ideas and suggestions to make, Egypt welcomed them and indicated her willingness to discuss and study them thoroughly.

When Saudi Arabia took the bold step of putting forward what has become known as the "Fahd Peace Plan," Egypt could only welcome the fact that a major Arab state would opt for a constructive approach that could end the indecisiveness that has plagued the Arab scene. The Saudi proposals are a set of principles derived from Security Council Resolution 242 and other U.N. resolutions. But to translate these principles into practical realities, one would still need a framework and a negotiating process, which Camp David has provided. In other words, the Saudi proposals are not an alternative to Camp David, but they need a "Camp David" to be implemented satisfactorily.

Thus, Egypt does not consider that peace in the Middle East is her own exclusive concern. Any proposals are welcomed by Egypt provided that they build upon what has already been achieved through Camp David, take into account what has already been acquired through the present negotiations, and meet with the approval of all the parties concerned. Until such a formula is proposed and accepted by these parties, Egypt under President Mubarak is intent on pursuing the negotiations and efforts to reach a comprehensive, peaceful solution that would bring justice and security for all. Egypt is equally intent on continuing to play her historical role in the peace process and in the negotiations that may take place between the Arabs and Israel to achieve that goal.

The diplomatic relations established between Egypt and Israel will, needless to say, continue at the same level. As stipulated in the peace treaty, relations between the two countries are "normal" relations, the word normal meaning exactly what it says and not implying in any way a concept of special relations, alliance or strategic cooperation. This kind of cooperation might be envisaged the day a comprehensive and just peace is achieved, but nothing in the peace treaty commits Egypt to anything that goes further than normal relation governed by the factors and interests that govern normal relations between any two given countries.

The role of the United States in establishing a just, comprehensive peace cannot be overemphasized. The full partnership role played by the United States in the negotiations between Egypt and Israel has borne fruit in the form of the peace treaty. It is expected that the United States would continue to play the same positive role in order to achieve a just and lasting solution to the Palestinian problem, the crux of the Middle East problem.

Egypt's conviction is that American participation in the peace negotiations is an essential element. This participation has been instrumental in reaching the Camp David accords and the peace treaty. But there is an even more vital role for U.S. diplomacy to play in helping to define the terms of full Palestinian autonomy and to convince the Israelis that only a self-governing Palestinian body with wide-ranging jurisdiction in all fields would have a chance to be accepted by the Palestinians. The United States can also play a part in convincing the Palestinians and the Palestine Liberation Organization (PLO) that their legitimate rights can be obtained by negotiation and that they can find their place in the family of nations through a peaceful and legitimate process. But to be able to do that, the United States would have to start talking to the Palestinians, to the organization that is accepted by the majority of them as representative of their aspirations, to the organization that is recognized by the majority of nations—namely the PLO. Contacts have to be established between the U.S. government and the PLO and not only through impromptu meetings in the corridors of the United Nations or at diplomatic parties. This was the gist of the message carried by President Sadat on his last trip to Washington in August 1981. This remains a strong belief of Egyptian diplomacy.

Furthermore, attempts to work out a strategic consensus against foreign hegemony and intervention in the Middle East cannot be based on solid ground until significant progress is made on the Palestinian issue. Egypt, in the past, was drawn into armed conflict with Israel. We were sustained in our effort by Soviet help. We were compelled for long years to live in a "no war-no peace" stalemate. Now Egypt is attempting, with the help of the

United States, to make peace, a comprehensive, just and permanent peace. The Camp David process is the only negotiating process in existence which provides hope for the future. Its ultimate goal is a just, comprehensive and permanent peace, based on U.N. Security Council Resolutions 242 and 338. [See Appendix in this book.]

Egypt's relations with the United States transcend the confines of the Middle East problem, although, as stated above, the U.S. contribution to a stable and just, comprehensive peace is imperative. Egypt and the United States share the common goals of a stable and peaceful Middle East that would significantly contribute to international peace and security.

Egypt's Leading Role

Certain Arab governments criticize the peace process but have been unable to unite not only behind an alternative process but even behind the goals to be attained by such a process. This failure on the part of the Arab governments emphasizes the importance of Egypt's leadership. In playing a leading role in the search for a peaceful and just solution to the Arab-Israeli conflict, Egypt maintains a balance between her own national interests and the wider interests of the Arab nations.

This leading role is nothing new, for in 1949 Egypt was the first Arab state to sign, on February 24, an armistice agreement with Israel, and was followed a few weeks later by Lebanon (March 23), then Jordan (April 3) and Syria (July 20). Again, in 1974, Egypt concluded the first disengagement agreement with Israel on January 18, and was followed a few months later by Syria, which concluded a similar agreement with Israel on May 31, 1974. So it is in conformity with historical precedent that Egypt should take the first step toward a peaceful comprehensive settlement and that it would take some time for the other Arab states to be able to follow that lead.

The anxieties and pressures, internal as well as external, which have prevented Arab states from joining the peace process until now, are well understood by Egypt. Also understood are the factors that have induced them to voice, at least in public state-

ments, violent and strong objections to the peace process and
Egypt's peace policy.

Egypt, however, as early as December 1977 extended official
invitations to Jordan, Lebanon, Syria and the PLO to attend the
Mena House Conference together with the United States, Israel
and the United Nations. Egypt was and still is discouraged by the
Arab attitude and the emotional outbursts against the Camp David accords. Egypt intends to do her utmost to make Arab countries realize that her line of action is in the interest of the Arab
peoples in general and of the Palestinians in particular. Egypt's
diplomacy tends to convince the Arab states that the negotiations
on full Palestinian autonomy can and will bring substantial and
meaningful results and benefits for the Palestinians.

Sooner or later, Egypt's actions will make the other Arab governments grasp that the withdrawal of Israeli forces and the return of Sinai to full Egyptian sovereignty constitute a valuable
precedent, in accordance with the text of the Egyptian-Israeli
Treaty of Peace, which states in its preamble that: "The (Camp
David) Framework is intended to constitute a basis for peace not
only between Egypt and Israel, but also between Israel and each
of its Arab neighbours. . . . " The success of the Camp David accords is bound to have a "snowball" effect and give the peace process more strength, more dynamism and more credibility in Arab
eyes. Sooner or later, Arab governments are bound to join the
peace process and Egypt's efforts to induce them to do so will be
successful.

This is because the present disageeement between Egypt and
a number of Arab countries is not in any way the first inter-Arab
dispute and will not be the last. In the last three decades alone,
more than 30 conflicts between Arab states have erupted, in the
Maghreb as well as in the Mashrek, between revolutionary regimes as well as between conservative governments. Some of these
conflicts have turned into full-scale local wars and others have
caused tensions and diplomatic confrontations. To name only a
few, one can refer to the crisis between Syria and Lebanon in May
1949, between the Sudan and Egypt in February 1958, between
Lebanon and the United Arab Republic in May 1958, between
Kuwait and Iraq in June 1961, between Algeria and Morocco in

October 1963, and, last but not least, the Yemen war in 1962 in which Egypt and Saudi Arabia were deeply involved.

Neither is this the first conflict of opinion among Arabs concerning the future of Palestine. And it is not the first attempt by a number of Arab regimes to isolate Egypt from the rest of the Arab world. From the Chtaura Conference in 1962 to the Baghdad Conference in November 1978 or the ill-fated Fez Conference in November 1981, Arab states have tried but failed to take collective action against Egypt, to find an alternative to Egyptian leadership or to solve their differences and quarrels without Egypt.

Meeting in Tripoli in December 1977, after President Sadat's visit to Jerusalem, five Arab states (Iraq, Syria, South Yemen, Libya and Algeria) and the PLO vehemently condemned Egypt and the Jerusalem visit. Diplomatic relations between Egypt and those states were severed thereafter. The summit meeting which was held in Baghdad on November 2, 1978 denounced the Camp David accords and decided to suspend Egypt from the Arab League, to transfer the seat of the League from Cairo and to boycott Egyptian products in the event of Egypt's signing a peace treaty with Israel.

After the signing of the peace treaty on March 26, 1979, Jordan severed diplomatic relations with Egypt on April 1, Kuwait and Saudi Arabia on April 23, followed by other Gulf states, Morocco, Tunisia, Mauritania, Djibouti, and North Yemen. In all, official relations between Egypt and 17 Arab countries were severed. The notable exceptions were Oman, Somalia and Sudan. The PLO is still maintaining a diplomatic mission in Cairo. Several Arab meetings convened afterward (Baghdad, March 1979; Kuwait, April 1979; Tunis, November 1979) to take measures against Egypt and to isolate her. But all these moves proved futile. In fact the proposition that Egypt is or can be isolated from the rest of the Arab world is absurd: and the total failure of these attempts is due to the fact that the Egyptian population constitutes almost half of the Arabs. (The populations of Sudan and Egypt together constitute more than half.) Needless to say, the influence of Egypt in culture, science, the arts, technology and economics overshadows by far the rest of the Arab world. . . .

EGYPT AFTER SADAT[5]

The year 1981 marked the end of the rule of Muhammad Anwar Sadat, born December 25, 1918, in the Nile Delta village of
Mit Abul Kom. Assuming the presidency after the death in 1970
of Gamal Abdul Nasser, Sadat fell fatally wounded on October
6, 1981. For some, the highlight of his career was his November,
1977, trip to Jerusalem, capped with an address to the Israeli
Knesset. Although it was regarded as his greatest contribution by
the West, the memorable Jerusalem visit isolated Sadat from virtually all his Arab neighbors. Yet his opening to Israel led to the
Camp David Summit of September, 1978; and from the accords
hammered out there between Sadat and Israeli Prime Minister
Menachem Begin came the Egyptian-Israeli peace treaty signed
March 26, 1979—some five months after the two leaders were
joint recipients of the Nobel Peace Prize. For others, an earlier
turning point was the 1972 expulsion of the Soviet military presence.

History will have to decide why it was that the Egyptian President who was determined to do so much for his people as he led
them down a democratic path felt compelled finally to take an au-
thoritarian turn. His bold moves to reorient his country to the
West and to make peace with Israel were initially received with
high hopes by the Egyptian people, exhausted by 30 years of war
and a stalemate with Israel; but with the passage of time and little
result came growing disillusionment. Then too, economic and social problems arose during this period of rapprochement with Israel and the West, precipitated ironically by Sadat's new economic
policy—the 1974-launched Open Door, designed to rehabilitate
the Egyptian economy by encouraging private sector and foreign
investment. The results so far include insufficient long-term investment from either foreign or domestic sources, inflation, and a
surge of materialism among the newly rich, made possible by in-

[5] Magazine article by John G. Merriam, associate professor of political science, Bowling Green State
University. *Current History.* 81:5-8+. Ja. '82. Copyright, 1982, by Current History, Inc. Reprinted by permission.

come from oil exports, migrant worker remittances, Suez Canal tolls and tourist spending. Conspicuous consumption by the few with little benefit for the majority fostered the disruption of social and cultural traditions. Scant prospect of an Israeli grant of Palestinian Arab self-determination or even meaningful autonomy caused additional Egyptian anxiety.

The interrelationship of these disruptive forces contributed to the frustration suffered by Sadat and the Egyptian public. While professing to adhere to the democratic path, the President resorted to massive arrests of Muslim and Christian extremists and prominent members of the secular opposition in September, 1981. One month later, Muslim fundamentalists avenged their anger by assassination.

Who were the attackers? Defense Minister Lieutenant General Abdul-Halim Abu-Ghazzala, who stood to the left of the President but survived the attack, assured reporters that the assassins numbered only four and were not related to any foreign country. They were led by a Muslim fanatic, army Lieutenant Khaled Shawki al-Istanbuli. The Defense Minister insisted that despite their uniforms the army was not involved and remains loyal. Al-Istanbuli and his brother, who was arrested in a purge of 1,536 Muslim fundamentalists and other opponents the previous month, are members of *Takfir wal Hijra* (Repentance and Holy Flight). How widespread is the organization? According to American University in Cairo sociology professor Saad Ibrahim, Takfir wal Hijra is "a sizable movement of between 3,000 and 5,000 active members, highly organized and . . . spread horizontally and vertically throughout Egyptian society."

The members, far from being society's dropouts as some might imagine, possess "high achievement, motivation [and are] upwardly mobile, with science or engineering education, and are from normally cohesive families." Usually young (the median age of a group previously interviewed was 24) and frustrated members of the middle and lower middle classes, they tend to be newly arrived in the city from rural areas or small towns.

The ultimate goal of the movement, says Ibrahim, is to "topple Egypt's present social order and to establish an Islamic social order." President Sadat's murderers did not carry off a coup, but did achieve their first goal, killing the President himself. For them, Sadat deserved to be put to death because he made concessions to Islam's three main external enemies: atheistic communism (though he expelled the Russian advisers), the West (i.e., the United States) and, particularly, Zionism.

Intent on establishing a smooth, rapid transition at a critical moment, Egypt's ruling National Democratic party quickly nominated Vice President Hosni Mubarak as Sadat's successor the very night of the assassination, a decision confirmed by Parliament the next day in an emergency session, thus setting the stage for a national referendum.

Even before the election of Hosni Mubarak as President, the major foreign policy question was Egypt's ongoing commitment to the peace process in which Anwar Sadat had deeply believed. Israeli leaders stressed their hope, albeit with a cautious note, that the process would not be deterred by the death of the Egyptian President. In seeking to honor all international commitments, Mubarak specifically pledged pursuit of the peace mission. And Prime Minister Begin reaffirmed Israel's commitment to the peace process. . . . Other unresolved issues include autonomy for the 1.2 million Palestinians living under Israeli occupation.

Approval from the country's 12 million eligible voters was readily won October 13, one week after the assassination, although a shoot-out between five heavily armed Muslim extremists near the Giza pyramids the day of the referendum and other incidents indicated continued unrest. Police linked the group led by Lieutenant Colonel Abu Abdul Latif al-Zamor with the outbreak of violence October 7-8 in Asyut. (Police subsequently identified him as the mastermind behind the plot to kill Sadat and to establish an Islamic republic.)

Early reports on the September, 1981, crackdown described President Sadat as denouncing sectarian factionalism between the Muslim majority and the six million or more Coptic Christian minority. Moves purportedly to reduce this religious strife included the arrest at the outset of 1,536 whose only common characteristic was their opposition to the regime: university professors, journalists, television and radio producers allegedly engaging in activities "detrimental to public opinion," some of whom were assured of losing their posts. (Few foreign observers paid attention at the time to the thousand arrested Muslim fundamentalists in this group.)

Prominent among those arrested was Muhammad Hassanein Heykal (allegedly because he had "received money" from Pope Shenouda III of the Coptic church to start an anti-Sadat newspaper), a figure well-known in the West as an editor and a confidant of the late President Nasser. Those incarcerated were listed in *Mayo,* the publication of the National Democratic party, the ruling organization, though without identifying titles. Singled out for special presidential criticism was Pope Shenouda III. Towards the end of a three-hour speech to a special joint session of the 532-member People's Assembly and the Consultative Council September 5, Sadat announced cancellation of the 1971 decree installing the Pope as the 117th patriarch of the Coptic church of Egypt (in a line reaching back to St. Mark's founding of the church in 42 A.D.) and stressed the principle of "no religion in politics and no politics in religion."

Antagonism had long existed between President and Pope, despite certain conciliatory gestures to the Coptic community, sometimes estimated at 12 to 20 percent of the predominantly Muslim population, approximately double the official figure. While Sadat complained that the Coptic leader "wanted to become a political leader," the patriarch for his part was opposed to a yet-to-be implemented amendment of an article in the Egyptian constitution making the *Shariah* (Muslim law) the source of legislation, notwithstanding government assurances that personal status and inheritance laws for non-Muslims would remain intact.

Perhaps most significant was Shenouda's stand on the Camp David accords. Originally somewhat receptive to Sadat's call for acceptance of the idea of a peace settlement with Israel, Shenouda reportedly later assumed a more hostile stand. Earlier in 1981, he refused to lead a pilgrimage to Jerusalem despite government pleas because the visit would imply acceptance of a settlement. In July, it was reported that he had attended a meeting of political leaders seeking to unify their stand against the Egyptian President.

Also a target of presidential criticism was the banned Muslim Brotherhood, whose chief spokesman, 76-year-old Omar Telmessani, was returned to prison in March. (He had spent 17 years in jail during the Nasser era and had been released by Sadat.) A Muslim fundamentalist leader, 25-year-old Helmi al-Gazzar, was another target.

Sadat tried to legitimize his sweeping measures in a referendum where 99.45 percent of those voting approved his crackdown on religious extremists and political opposition. However, the administration campaign against destabilizing religious fundamentalism later shifted in emphasis to a Soviet plot allegedly designed to topple the regime. The Soviet Ambassador, Vladimir Polyakov, six diplomats, two journalists and in excess of 1,000 Soviet technical advisers for Egypt's heavy industry, who were said to be stirring up Muslim-Copt religious fundamentalism, were ordered to leave. The press reported that Egyptian military intelligence had uncovered three plots implicating Soviet and Hungarian diplomats.

Then the focus shifted to reform of the society, which would end religious unrest. In a televised speech September 14 Sadat promised reforms effective October 1 to deal with the "slackness" and "indiscipline" that "the people complain of." The government outlined an ambitious program to overcome virtually overnight the seemingly interminable problems of the poor, in a generally overburdened country, with a frustrating telephone service, traffic jams, street noise, inadequate public cleanliness, and housing shortages. Also cited were inefficiencies in public and private sector companies, the universities and the press.

Many of Egypt's problems seem to defy resolution even in industrialized countries. Yet the government had still further plans. The ministries would attempt to retrain superfluous workers hired in line with a Nasserist policy whereby the government acted for graduates as an employer of last resort. Beyond that, the government set aside $690,000 for additional security on university campuses, often strongholds of Islamic groups critical of the regime.

Domestic Problems

As the Arab country with the largest population (43 million), Egypt must be taken into account in regional affairs. Yet the size of the population, while a source of strength, creates challenges for any administration. Over 98 percent of the people are compressed into the four percent of the total territory that comprises the arable land, mostly along the banks of the Nile River and in the Delta. Few people realize the population density per unit of farmable land is higher in Egypt than in Bangladesh.

To feed the growing population, Sadat (as well as his predecessor, Gamal Abdul Nasser) relied on subsidies for basic foodstuffs and sought to improve agricultural productivity, but with scant success, through higher yields per acre and a vigorous land reclamation policy. Critics nevertheless questioned a land use policy focusing on the development of costly marginal lands while sacrificing prime agricultural land to urban development.

To make the industrial and agricultural sectors more productive, Sadat encouraged foreign investments under the much heralded *Infitah* or open door policy, which may be seen as a victim of its own success. If the idea was to attract foreign investment and to reenergize the private sector, it succeeded. But is Egypt better off with the 1974 decision to abandon Nasser policies and return to a free market economy? A climate of confidence, it was thought, would encourage local business and foreign investment. Indeed, a year ago the economy looked uncommonly bright, with record earnings in hard currency from oil exports, workers' remittances, Suez Canal dues and tourist spending. Foreign exchange earnings rapidly rose from $370 million (1970) to $1.8 billion just two years later, thanks to unflagging demand for oil and major world price increases that year. In 1980, earnings reached $2.9 billion, with hopes of $900 million more for 1981, only to run into reduced demand and a softening of world market prices.

Egypt has been producing 675,000 barrels of oil per day (September figures) but the price which reached $40.50 in early 1981 was down to $33 for Suez Blend toward the end of 1981. Year-end earnings were expected to be considerably below earlier expectations of $3.8 billion. The 1,000,000 b/d goal which would increase revenues may be difficult to attain.

Payments sent back to Egypt from two million workers in overseas (mostly Arab) jobs followed a similar pattern, a dramatic rise followed by a slump. Figures for 1978 were $1 billion, and 1980 figures were a record $2.8 billion, with the hope of topping $3 billion in 1981. But remittances are slowing down, not withstanding the continued presence of Egyptian workers in Libya next door and elsewhere in an Arab world generally hostile to the country that signed a peace treaty with Israel.

Although the Arab boycott in the wake of Camp David had only a temporary effect on tourism from neighboring Arab countries, and although the flow of Western, Japanese, European, and now American Jewish and Israeli tourists continues, revenues are sticking at about the $700-million level as sophisticated tourists learn to change money on the streets in the so-called "alternative market."

Suez Canal dues, raised in 1980, promised to bring in $1.2 billion in 1981, but the doubling of the 1979 figure must be weighed against paying off substantial improvement costs.

Egypt's not insignificant foreign exchange earnings coupled with foreign capital inflows and a real growth rate of 8 percent seemed to provide ground for optimism. Yet, genuine growth for which the open door policy must take substantial credit has been accompanied by mounting indebtedness and inflation. Medium- and long-term debt, only $1.6 billion the year Sadat came to power, soared to $12.5 billion in a decade.

Western aid, about $3 billion annually, must be increasingly devoted to the mounting food import bill. Egyptian food production has been marked by what John Waterbury earlier called "a stagnation of yields." United States agricultural trade with Egypt is expected to run at the $1-billion level by 1983. Wheat is Egypt's most important agricultural import from the United States and is crucial to supplying Cairo and the other urban centers. In 1980-1981, Egypt ranked as the sixth largest United States wheat customer, with purchases of some 1.5 million tons of wheat and slightly more than 500,000 tons of wheat flour. United States farm exports to Egypt, according to the United States Department of Agriculture, totaled $770 million.

Hard currency purchases are supplemented by food aid, which also must be paid for by the Egyptian government (and on which Americans also make a profit). The terms are, however, concessional, or below prevailing market rates. Egypt ranked as the largest recipient of United States Public Law 480 food aid program funds in the 1980-1981 marketing year. Again, these were mostly wheat and wheat flour purchases. President Mubarak's confident assumption of leadership will ensure continued food sales and aid. Nevertheless, loans must eventually be repaid. Payments on principal and interest have reached $1 billion a year; and the projects are slow to pay a return. Problems have been compounded by the 30-35 percent inflation rate.

The 1980 appointment of Planning Minister Abdul-Razzaq Abdul Maguid as economic czar was viewed as an effort to put Egypt's economic house in order—to rationalize trade, supply problems, and the economy itself. While many individuals in the city and the countryside have more material goods than before and although the shops are full, inflation, unemployment and the less detectable underemployment have led to resentment over the materialistic surge and the destruction of the religious-cultural heritage that some critics blame on the Infitah. Egypt's development, like development everywhere, is uneven. Yet Islamic fundamentalists may have a point when they stress that true development in Egypt cannot take place without incorporating traditional Muslim values. The open door policy has in many instances encouraged sheer growth, following the idea that "more must be better," rather than life-enriching development.

Absorbing the bulk of each year's crop of 300,000-400,000 new entrants into the workplace would tax any economic system. The government hopes to strengthen the industrial sector in an effort to improve the employment picture. In addition, much of the foreign currency coming into the country flows outside official channels. In an attempt to eradicate the problem, in August, 1981, the government effectively devalued the currency 20 percent in order to bring the country's artificially pegged currency more closely into line with the free market value.

More investment needs to find its way into the countryside; migration to the city and abroad may be partly explained by urban-oriented investment. Disinvestment of the rural areas can only contribute to Egypt's long-term problems of urban congestion and stagnant agricultural production.

Egypt Under Mubarak

Confirmed by a national referendum in which he won 98.46 percent of the vote, Hosni Mubarak officially took office on October 14, 1981. Depicted as modest, honest, cool-headed, and steady, not a risk taker, with an eye to precision, planning and essential detail, Mubarak is capable of firmness once he has made a decision. What lies ahead? He will ensure that nothing will preclude Israel's fulfillment of its obligation under the Camp David accord to withdraw from the remaining occupied Egyptian territory in the Sinai by April 25, 1982.

Even if American help is forthcoming, it will be more difficult to obtain a more substantial commitment to full autonomy for the Palestinians on the West Bank than Sadat received from Prime Minister Begin. Saudi Arabian leaders and Mubarak may agree that the moment is ripe to end Egypt's isolation from the rest of the Arab world. A "strategic consensus" in the Middle East, involving Egypt, Israel and Saudi Arabia, may meet American area interests, but it may cause problems for Mubarak regionally and with the Islamic fundamentalists whose influence, even in the 367,000-strong Egyptian army, may be more pervasive than the new administration would like to admit.

At this writing, truckloads of men from Egypt's paramilitary Central Security Forces (CSF) are watching key Cairo locations. Meanwhile, on October 17, 1981, the government banned urban use of firearms and conducted a nationwide round-up of some 1,500 more Muslim militants and political opponents. President Mubarak may need such forces if, like his predecessor, he tries to accomplish too much during a period of destabilizing transition. Much has been written about the excesses of Egypt's upper classes. As I see it, the rampant materialism that the Muslim fundamentalists find objectionable would be less offensive if the wealth that finds its way into the hands of the newly rich were channeled into productive, job-generating investments to foster rural development and to reduce urban poverty.

JORDAN AND ARAB POLARIZATION[6]

Against all odds, the Hashemite Kingdom of Jordan is still a going concern, some 60 years after Britain's Winston Churchill and his associates carved Transjordan from the Palestine Mandate and set the Emir Abdallah, the homeless son of Sherif Hussein, to reign over it with British protection and subsidy. By any measure, Jordan has not enjoyed a smooth or painless journey these past six decades. Jordan has no oil and little water. Although its population today, even counting the West Bank, is only around three million, it still exceeds the natural carrying capacity of the land. Jordan has never been able to support itself without substantial foreign aid and still cannot do so despite a vibrant economy.

Nevertheless, the kingdom has survived the turbulence of the interwar period, the continuous struggle with radical Palestinian nationalism and the Zionist movement, and the fact that it is "stuck on the wrong side" of the postwar polarization of the Arab world, a circumstance that undid the other family domain, in Iraq, in 1958. Jordan has experienced the trauma of two wars with two waves of refugees (1948 and 1967) and has nervously witnessed two others (1956 and 1973). Finally, the civil war of 1970 and the accompanying invasion by Syrian forces nearly put an end to the kingdom.

Against this history, the country today, particularly in its regional context, is surprising. Iran and Iraq are at war. Syria occupies Lebanon and is ruled by terror; Beirut is in ruins, yet the fighting there goes on. Israel suffers from unprecedented political division and economic distress. Saudi Arabia faces domestic instability, uneven economic development, and more foreign workers than it knows how to control. Egypt, despite great efforts, is desperately poor and politically isolated. Jordan, by contrast, is at

[6] Magazine article by Adam Garfinkle, research associate, Foreign Policy Research Institute. *Current History.* 81:22-5+. Ja. '82. Copyright, 1982, by Current History, Inc. Reprinted by permission.

peace (by Middle Eastern standards, at least). The country is experiencing an economic boom, indirectly benefiting from both the new power of oil and the devastation of Beirut, as well as from its own efforts. Its leader, King Hussein, is the longest genuinely reigning head of state in the world. Jordan maintains close, if periodically strained, relations with the United States and good relations with West European states, and the King is also welcome in Moscow. Domestic political violence has all but vanished. And, finally, Jordan is the subject of extraordinary diplomatic interest: by virtue of its pivotal geography, Palestinian demography and recent history, the country may hold the key to a settlement of the core issues in the Arab-Israeli conflict.

The improvement of Jordan's economic and regional political position over the past half dozen years or so has been the consequence of shifting cleavages within the Arab world and a patient and agile diplomacy designed to make the best of them. But Jordan has not always been so fortunate. Between King Hussein's accession to the throne in 1953 and the June, 1967, war, Jordan was plagued constantly by unstable or aggressive neighbors and the problem of controlling vast numbers of Palestinians—refugees and others—whose sympathies toward the Hashemite dynasty were either weak or absent altogether. These troubles proved especially volatile when mixed; Hussein's rule was frequently threatened by violent expressions of Palestinian nationalism precipitated by the emergence of Arab radicalism in Egypt and, later, in neighboring Iraq and Syria. But by judiciously combining physical repression and skillful co-option, Hussein survived his internal difficulties while managing, simultaneously, a stable but tense modus vivendi with Israel.

These fragile balances were disrupted by the 1967 war. After the loss of Jordan's West Bank and East Jerusalem and the humiliation of military defeat, the Palestinian nationalist antagonism toward the Hashemites reached new levels. The Palestinian fedayeen, the only Arab force not besmirched by ignominy, soon won the admiration of most Palestinians, who still comprise more than half of the Jordanian population on the East Bank. By mid-1970, Palestinian guerrilla organizations had established a loose state-within-a-state in Jordan, forcing Hashemite authority into retreat. The struggle exploded into civil war when Hussein scored his first significant diplomatic triumph after the 1967 war: Jordan's inclusion in the United States diplomatic initiative terminating the war of attrition, the ceasefire of August, 1970. Splinter factions within the Palestine Liberation Organization (PLO) conspired to plunge the country into civil war. But despite some assistance from allies in Syria, the fedayeen were defeated by the Jordanian army and, one year later, were finally expelled from the country.

Damaged by defeat in 1967 and the expulsion of the fedayeen, Jordan's standing in the Arab world was reduced still further by its very marginal participation in the October war of 1973. Between 1967 and 1973, Jordan's domestic cohesion and international position had reached a nadir. The country was economically bereft, diplomatically isolated, and vulnerable to political intrigue from any number of directions. This left the King in a weak position to fend off the PLO's political assault on Jordan's trusteeship for Palestinian interests—a claim that had carried weight not because of Arab enthusiasm for it but only because of the reality established by a quarter century of physical control. Especially after the October war, King Hussein had struggled against the deepening recognition of the PLO's claim to speak for the Palestinians. Recognizing that the status quo ante was out of the question but still seeking to maximize Jordanian influence over the West Bank, in March, 1972, Hussein proposed a federation plan that suggested two regions, two capitals, two Arab national cultures, but one army, one foreign policy and, most important, one King. The federation plan would not be forced upon the Palestinians, but the King expressed confidence that they would choose it if given the opportunity after liberation. Instead, at the Rabat summit meeting of 1974, the Arab countries gave the PLO the exclusive right to represent the Palestinian cause.

Under the circumstances, Jordan publicly accepted the verdict of the Rabat summit meeting, but the King strove to minimize its impact, particularly in the West Bank, where he deployed Jordan's remaining influence through the manipulation of money, legal favors, and family connections. Although Jordan's position suffered, as evidenced by the anti-Hashemite results of the West

Bank's 1976 municipal elections, Rabat alone could not overturn the overall relationship between Palestinian nationals and the Hashemite dynasty.

The Palestinian Arab Movement

The Palestinian Arab national movement arose during the 1920s and the 1930s in response to the British occupation of Palestine and the growing strength of the Jewish community motivated by Zionist ideology. The movement was unified by the simple and straightforward proposition that Palestine was Arab and should be ruled by Arabs, but it was divided over personalities and strategies. During the late 1930s and early 1940s, the Palestinians, led by Haj Amin al-Hussaini, the Grand Mufti of Jerusalem, courted Nazi patronage. This enraged the Emir Abdallah, who remained faithful to Britain; his abiding contempt for Palestinian politicians grew stronger. He opposed a Zionist state, but he also opposed a sovereign Arab entity in Palestine that blocked his aspirations for a "greater Syria." For their part, the Palestinian nationalists resented Abdallah for his connivance with the British and his tacit acceptance of the Balfour Declaration that provided for the establishment of Israel. The Palestinian movement failed to prevent the birth of the state of Israel in 1948. Even worse, those parts of Palestine not occupied by the new Jewish state fell into the hands of Abdallah, whose ambitions were forwarded by local Palestinian notables, who resented the al-Hussaini clan.

It is remarkable how little basic patterns have changed. The Palestinians are still engaged in a prolonged blood feud, some allied with the Hashemites and some standing against them. PLO leader Yasir Arafat has inherited the position of the Mufti and, in fact, descends from that very clan. But, as was the case 30 years ago, many Palestinian families have allied themselves with the Hashemites, a connection whose closeness has grown throughout the years as Jordanian society has developed. Today, Palestinians in Jordan are the loyal backbone of the state and are indispensable to the functioning of the monarchy.

King Hussein has inherited both the problems and the advantages of his grandfather, Abdallah. One of the problems is that the

PLO is the incarnation of the old Palestinian nationalist axiom that Palestine is all Arab and that there is no room for a Jewish state there. Like his grandfather before him, Hussein rejects this absolutism and is willing to live in peace with the Jewish state in part of post-1922 mandatory Palestine. Thus, the PLO political program is only marginally less hostile to Hashemite Jordan than it is to Israel.

Also, Hussein is no fonder of the PLO's close relations with the Soviet Union than his grandfather was pleased by the alliance between Palestinian nationalists and Nazi Germany. One of Jordan's advantages is that, despite Rabat, Hussein knows that Arafat's PLO is no more the sole representative of the Palestinians than the Mufti was 40 years ago. The PLO has never ruled any Palestinians; Hussein has and still does.

Between the Rabat summit meeting and the spring of 1976, Jordan hoped to break out of its isolation through a cautious alliance with Syria, by means of which Hussein sought to engage Egyptian interests in keeping Jordan from aligning itself too closely with Egypt's archrival in Syria. In doing so, he did not wish to encourage the American "step-by-step" approach supported by Israel and Egypt, nor to sever Jordan completely from useful future developments in which Egypt might play an important role. Inter-Arab quarrels rendered this a relatively ineffective stratagem, however, until Syria and the PLO came to blows over their respective conflicting interests in Lebanon. Since Jordan's own civil war had isolated Hussein, the Lebanese civil war offered him a way out.

Jordan was the only Arab state to support Syria's actions against the PLO in Lebanon in the late summer and early fall of 1976. At first, this support threatened to lead Jordan further away from Egypt. But, with its military in control of most of Lebanon, Syria soon found a shared interest with Egypt and Saudi Arabia in settling the Lebanese crisis: Syria wanting Arab support for the new *Pax Syrianica* and Egypt and Saudi Arabia hoping to extinguish the crisis in anticipation of new American peace initiatives. A spate of Arab summitry toward the end of 1976 resulted in (limited) collusion between Jordan, Syria and Egypt that exploited the PLO's weakness and that, in effect, undermined the Rabat resolutions.

By the time Jimmy Carter assumed the American presidency, Jordan had staged an impressive diplomatic comeback. Its economy, too, had revived with the increased flow of Arab financial subsidies (made possible by the oil price hikes of the previous few years) and the transfer of Western business from the rubble of Beirut to the new boom-town of Amman. Jordan's flexibility abroad and prosperity at home put the country in a receptive mood for the new United States administration's expected initiatives.

But as these initiatives developed, Jordan was displeased. The Carter administration seemed more eager to achieve a comprehensive solution to the Arab-Israeli dispute than its predecessor. And since it refused to support either an independent Palestinian state or the indefinite Israeli occupation of the West Bank, this pointed logically to United States support for an enhanced Jordanian role. Instead, through 1977, the Carter administration seemed more intent on encouraging the moderation of the PLO, enhancing its stature despite its adventure in Lebanon.

Moreover, as Soviet influence in the region reached a low ebb, Washington sought to reintroduce Soviet participation in regional diplomacy in pursuit of a comprehensive settlement via the Soviet-American communiqué of October, 1977. The decision to turn first to the most recalcitrant parties and the most intractable issues placed the entire effort at the mercy of those whose interest in peace was least pressing. Unwilling to tolerate stalemate, Egyptian President Anwar Sadat recast the hardening diplomatic mold by traveling to Jerusalem in November, 1977.

Jordan's initial reaction to Sadat's bold ploy was more cautious and less condemnatory than that of the rest of the Arab world. This demonstrated both the limits of Jordan's recent political emergence and its basic moderation. Although Egypt was the party most likely to advance a Jordanian role in the West Bank in the context of peace, the opposition of Saudi Arabia, Syria, Iraq and other Arabs made a Jordanian alignment with Egypt far too risky. This was particularly true because, in May, 1977, the Israeli elections had brought to power a political coalition, the Likud, whose attitude toward Jordan was vastly different from that of its Labor party predecessor. Instead of stressing Jordan's role as a potential negotiating partner, the Likud claimed Jewish rights in the West Bank based on religious and ideological rather than security grounds. The new Prime Minister, Menachem Begin, had never recognized the 1947 United Nations partition; some members of his Cabinet suggested that there already was a Palestinian state—Jordan—only its ruler was not a Palestinian.

Given the unlikelihood that negotiation with Israel could satisfy even minimum Jordanian interests and the dangers of antagonizing stronger and wealthier neighbors, Hussein resisted the persistent attempts of the Carter administration to draw him into the peace process as it strove to magnify the multilateral implications of Israeli-Egyptian negotiations. At the same time, Hussein never closed the door on joining the talks and, when the opportunity presented itself, negotiated by proxy to maximize United States pressure on Israel in a way that might serve Jordanian interests. This tactic worked to a limited degree, but in the aftermath of Camp David and the Israeli-Egyptian peace treaty, the balance of risks and benefits involved in joining the Untited States-brokered negotiations apparently precluded Husscin's participation.

Arab Polarization

Within months of Sadat's visit to Jerusalem, the Arab world exhibited signs of further division and polarization. For Jordan, a united Arab world is a convenient Arab world, where choices that will invariably antagonize a stronger country are not forced on it. As the Arab world fractured between the "Rejectionist" front led by Iraq, Saudi Arabia and the Gulf sheikdoms and the "Steadfastness" front led by Lybia, Syria and South Yemen, Jordan was forced to choose. Given Jordan's political affinities with the more anti-Soviet, conservative regimes in the area, Hussein sought protective refuge from the Rejectionists, whose association was solidified at the Baghdad summit meeting of November, 1978. In order to assure Jordan's separation from Egyptian policy, the Baghdad Summit offered Jordan $1.25 billion per year, with most of the funds coming from Iraq. But Jordan was not only a compliant recipient. Fearing a retrogressive spasm of radicalism as a response to Egyptian policy, Jordan worked hard to moderate the

resolutions of the Baghdad Summit. Although they established
very demanding conditions for peace, the Baghdad resolutions did
commit Iraq, for the first time, to the principle of a negotiated
peace with Israel, implying tacit recognition of Israel's existence.

The fracturing of the Arab world after the Sadat initiative was
also uncomfortable for the PLO which, like Jordan, is not well
served by choices that cannot fail to make enemies. In the case of
the PLO, whose various groups are beholden in differing degrees
to many sources of funding and support, cleavages in the Arab
world are especially aggravating. While it behooves Jordan to
minimize divisions among the Arab countries and to blunt extremism on the central issues where possible, it suits Jordan to maximize divisions within the PLO and to exploit those divisions
wherever possible. To this end, since mid-1979, Jordan had managed to erect a new détente with parts of the PLO based on grudg-
ingly shared interests. The rapprochement allows prominent
Palestinians simultaneously to associate with the PLO to defend
cooperation with Jordan, to talk with Israelis, and even to call
publicly for moderating changes in the PLO's political platform.
That such a combination is even possible explains why the smaller, more radical PLO groups vehemently oppose any cooperation
with Jordan, fearing Hussein's attempt to eviscerate the PLO politically and to co-opt it into submission.

Indeed, it appears to be Hashemite policy to seek out and ally
with those Palestinians willing to cooperate with the monarchy
and to weaken and isolate those who are not. Today, this struggle
not only pits PLO Palestinians against non-PLO Palestinians but
also parts of the PLO against other parts. Hussein's intent is to
join those elements willing to accept a more moderate approach
to peace with Israel with like-minded Palestinians on the West
and East Banks who are already at peace with Jordan, either out
of economic interests accumulated over some 35 years or out of the
realization that a Jordanian solution represents the best Arab
hope of recovering the occupied territories. This Palestinian coalition, cooperating with Jordan, will call itself the PLO only if the
King and his allies seize the label for the sake of legitimacy.

While Jordan's policy of co-optive moderation may seem narrowly cynical, it is not so simple as that. By all accounts, King

Hussein is a sincere Pan-Arabist and a devout Muslim whose concern for the plight of the Palestinians is genuine and deep. But Hussein, like his grandfather before him, has never been convinced that Palestinian interests are well served by hostility to the Hashemite family or by an absolutist rejection of Israel. In Hussein's view, it is the extremists among the Palestinians who bring ruin and suffering on their people.

Jordan's public avowal of support for an independent Palestinian state and for the PLO seems a part of Hussein's plan. Such a declaratory posture helps Palestinian moderates inside and outside the PLO to defend cooperation with Jordan and helps Jordan to defend itself against accusations of betrayal. Although Jordan's posture may enhance the PLO's international stature, the risks are manageable. Because of the local balance of political forces, Hussein does not greatly fear the possibility of a PLO-led, Soviet-supported independent ministate in the West Bank and Gaza.

Even if Israel were not determined to prevent such an irredentist-prone entity, Hussein apparently believes that if serious negotiations about returning the West Bank to Arab sovereignty begin, the Palestinian poeple will be represented not by Marxist intellectuals from Beirut but rather by the middle-class, family notables of the West Bank; the middle- and upper middle-class Palestinians of the East Bank; and the Hashemite and East Bank aristocracy itself.

King Hussein's enthusiastic encouragement of the Middle East diplomacy of the European Community (EC) also fits this strategy. No matter how much EC statements enrage the Israelis, the Community has never eschewed explicit recognition of Israel's right to exist and is not likely to do so. The Community has refused to recognize the PLO as the "sole" Palestinian representative and has not, as a group, called for a separate Palestinian national state. The EC's insistence on the mutual recognition of Israeli and Palestinian rights is a demand that no group within the PLO can now meet and one that most PLO groups will never accept. It is in Jordan's interest to push this choice on the PLO, for it either encourages the would-be moderates to associate with Jordan or forces the PLO to move itself out of the diplomatic mainstream, to Jordan's benefit. Jordan's attitude toward the

PLO and the EC initiative was voiced by Crown Prince Hassan in January, 1981. Asked about the need for the PLO fully to recognize the right of Israel to exist as a sovereign state, Hassan answered:

Yes, we are having trouble in promoting moderation within the ranks of the PLO. They must be brought to accept the credibility of the Venice declaration as a whole; they must evolve. . . .

Current and Future Problems

Although Jordan seems to have developed a sensible diplomatic strategy to advance its interests, many problems persist. With respect to its basic design to moderate and co-opt the PLO, the verdict is not yet in. The cycle of radicalization that has hit the region since Camp David and the Iranian revolution has made its goal more difficult. Moreover, Jordan's association with the Iraqi-led coalition of the Baghdad Summit has led predictably to a worsening of relations with Syria. Since the summer of 1980, tension between the two countries has threatened periodically to erupt in large-scale violence. This was especially evident in December, 1980, and again in August, 1981, following the cease-fire in Lebanon. This worries Jordan very much, for while the Syrian military is thinly spread, a marked disparity in military force, especially air power, favors the Soviet-supplied Syrians.

Even Jordan's apparent wealth and economic health carry with them many problems. The flood of foreign money into a country with so little inherent wealth has spurred inflation and made it difficult for the government to keep up with the private sector in attracting quality personnel for the army and the civil service. Even more ominous, Iraq, Jordan's main benefactor, is involved in a protracted war with Iran that has greatly slowed Iraqi oil exports and revenue collection. As Iraq's own financial situation deteriorates, Baghdad can less easily afford its generosity to Jordan.

This is a far cry from Jordan's expectation when it assertively supported Iraq in its war against Iran's Ayatollah Ruhollah Khomeini regime in September, 1980. Hussein apparently hoped that Iraq could quickly overthrow Khomeini, thus stemming the tide of the Islamic fundamentalist revival and the advance of Soviet interests in the Persian Gulf. In any case, with so much of Jordan's budget at stake and with logic dictating that, without a port on the Gulf, Jordan would either have to help or, in effect, betray Iraq, Hussein had little choice. But if the destabilizing effects of the Gulf war seep into Jordan, it could prove dangerous. Aside from the financial stress, with predictable effects on the level of foreign investment, Hussein could lose control over the Muslim Brotherhood (Ikhwa), with whom he has a cautious and limited working rela tionship.

Last, but certainly not least, Jordan faces problems with Israel. The results of the June, 1981, Israeli elections, which resulted in the reelection of Menachem Begin at the head of an even harder-line coalition, bode ill for the prospects of a peace that could satisfy Jordanian interests. The King and other members of the Jordanian political establishment also fear an attempt by Israel either to force another wave of refugees on Jordan or, in a general war, to seize the East Bank temporarily with the objective of replacing the Hashemites with compliant Palestinians, thus "solving" the Palestinian issue at Jordan's expense. More generally, the current Israeli government creates problems for Jordan because its actions and its attitudes make Jordan's efforts to moderate Arab political tendencies more difficult. This includes Israeli administrative practices in the occupied territories that have (inadvertently) aided the PLO and reduced Jordanian influence. True moderates, willing to accept Israel, must face the question from the radicals: given Israel's attitude, what is there to gain from moderation and political solutions that cannot be gained from armed struggle?

What of Jordan's relations with the United States? Ideally Hussein wants Washington to help him fob off Arab radicalism and to co-opt and control the PLO. To do this, Washington must lean harder on Israel so that Arab moderates will have something to show for their moderation. In Jordan's view, Washington must also encourage PLO moderation directly by engaging in old-fashioned, hardheaded carrot-and-stick diplomacy. Quiet coordination with Jordan would not hurt.

This may be what Hussein wants, but he is not optimistic about the chances of getting it. Despite an initial improvement with the Ronald Reagan administration, United States-Jordanian relations have again fallen into disrepair over the American response—totally inadequate in Amman's view—to the Israeli attack on Iraqi nuclear installations and its raids into Lebanon, and over the new Israeli-United States "strategic realtionship." The Israeli mission against Iraq maximally violated Jordanian airspace—Israeli aircraft traversed the entire width of the country—thus depicting the King as an accomplice or inept. The very mild handslap administered by Washington to Israel, coupled with Jordan's continued inability to purchase a modern air defense system from the United States, occasioned much frustration. The American "strategic relationship" with Israel runs directly counter to Jordan's hopes for its relationship with the United States. Only specific United States-Jordanian "institutional" arrangements, like the biannual Joint Military Commission, and Hussein's even greater suspicion of Moscow and its local clients keep United States-Jordanian ties alive. Still, despite state visits and laudatory speeches, Hussein is unlikely to switch sides and befriend the Soviet Union, even if Jordan accepts limited military purchases from the U.S.S.R. Nor is full and genuine neutrality an option for a weak state in a polarized Middle East.

Jordanians hope that Washington will acknowledge the logic of the moderate Arab argument and recognize that United States interests in the region cannot survive everlasting support for Israeli occupation of the West Bank. In the meantime, Jordan will continue to take a keen interest in Palestinian political evolution and in the fissures of the Arab and Islamic worlds, as well as the Mideast diplomacy of the superpowers.

JORDAN'S QUEST FOR PEACE[7]

After more than a third of a century of conflict, the Middle East remains the greatest threat to international peace and security. In a fitting close to 1981, and as if to signal its own recognition of the fact, and further ensure that the so-called Camp David accords can never lead to a general settlement, the Israeli government enacted legislation that for all intents and purposes annexes the Syrian Golan Heights to Israel. And a new chapter in the conflict begins.

Despite what is often said in moments of frustration, most of us here in the Middle East believe it is in America's interest, as it is in the whole world's interest, to settle the Arab-Israeli conflict. Most of us continue to believe that U.S. policy has such a settlement as one of its principal objectives for regional and global and even domestic American reasons. What we see, however, is a tendency on the part of U.S. policymakers to fall into the same traps that we, who have suffered so long with this tragic problem, also allowed to impede us earlier. These traps include the "peace by pieces" fallacy, the related "squeaky wheel" tendency, and the "peace-on-the-cheap" syndrome.

Americans are not alone in their attraction to the concept of the realization of peace gradually. Whether expressed in traditional functionalist theory or neo-functionalism, whether in terms of concrete proposals such as the Johnson plan or Secretary Kissinger's step-by-step diplomacy, "peace by pieces" is a fascinating and useful concept. But no theory, no concept, should be considered universally applicable. We in Jordan supported Secretary Kissinger's attempt to use "step-by-step" diplomacy *as a confidence-building measure* to effect a necessary disengagement of forces on the Golan and Sinai after the 1973 War. It was the extension of this piecemeal approach to the peace process as a whole that we felt was misplaced.

[7] Magazine article by El Hassan Bin Talal, Crown Prince of Jordan. *Foreign Affairs*. 68:802-13. Spring '82. Reprinted by permission of *Foreign Affairs*. Copyright, 1982, Council on Foreign Relations, Inc.

The Middle East problem is a complex of issues. To disaggregate the whole into its parts may help reduce one or two of those issues, but as we have seen time and time again, inevitably eliminates the possibility of addressing the core issues. It must be recalled that the several parties will have to effect numerous compromises to arrive at a general regional settlement. On highly charged and complex questions such as the Palestinian problem, compromises will undoubtedly have to be made on an interdependent basis. The Arab-Israeli conflict cannot be disaggregated, because the solutions will necessarily be as interdependent as the problems are. Even a cursory glance at the positions of all the parties demonstrates this interdependence.

The tendency to grease the squeaky wheel has also been characteristic of American diplomacy. If we can put peace together in pieces, then let us deal with the most threatening piece immediately. The Camp David accords, designed to remove Egypt from the Arab coalition and thereby eliminate at one time both the largest Arab army and a second front that forces Israel to divide its forces and efforts, illustrates this approach too. Without Egypt, there is no credible military threat to Israeli security—so goes the argument. After Camp David, problems in Lebanon both demonstrated the fallacy of the squeaky wheel tendency and became the next "squeaky wheel." Once again, though, the integral nature of the Middle East conflict made of Ambassador Philip Habib's laudable efforts and considerable achievements only a brief respite from the underlying tensions.

Finally, but no less futile, we have "peace on the cheap." This has been our biggest problem in the Arab world, and it now has become a significant consideration for the United States. By "peace on the cheap" we mean the attempt to bring about a settlement at no cost to oneself. No problem that has endured as long, has cost as many lives, and has engendered as much distrust, hatred, and discord as the Arab-Israeli conflict can have a cost-free solution. We in the Arab world know that now, for we have paid an inordinate price already, by anybody's accounting.

Nor will a peace be cost-free for the United States, however. The U.S. government has been afraid to face certain political realities, both domestic and Middle Eastern, because of the special nature of America's relationship with Israel and, to a lesser extent, with some Arab countries. But there is no escaping it: "biting the bullet" is the price Americans will pay, will have to pay, if we are to realize an end to this enduring tragedy.

We believe it *is* in America's interest, as we *know* it is in ours, to move toward a settlement. We hope, as Americans do, that such a resolution will eventuate, but it cannot come about without fullest consideration to the requirements and perspectives of each of the principal parties to the conflict. One of those parties—and we in Jordan wish it were otherwise, wish it could be otherwise—is the Hashemite Kingdom of Jordan. Over the last few years, the United States, Israel and, frankly, many Arab countries, have tended to overlook or take for granted our country. Yet, Jordan is critical to a settlement, to any settlement, of the Middle East problem.

Jordan's Palestinian Connection

Because Jordan is a small country, we were often discounted as a major factor in what is clearly the greatest threat to international security. We do not have a large population like Egypt or Syria. We do not have a position of military superiority like Israel. We do not have oil like Saudi Arabia or Iraq. So, then, why is Jordan important? Do we assert its centrality because we are Jordanian?

No, Jordan's views are important. Apart from the Sinai, which is in the process of being returned to Egypt, most of the territory Israel occupied in 1967, and therefore which is referred to in U.N. Security Council Resolution 242, was Jordanian. East Jerusalem was Jordanian. There are more Palestinians in Jordan than in any other state, most of them refugees from the wars of 1948 and 1967. Jordan and Israel have outstanding territorial conflicts dating from 1948. Although it is our position and belief that the Palestine Liberation Organization is and can only be the sole representative of the Palestinian people, still it is incontestable that large numbers of Arabs in the West Bank continue to attend closely to Jordan's actions and policies.

It is clear today that the sine qua non of any general and effective settlement of the Arab-Israeli conflict must address and resolve the Palestinian issue. It is not our purpose here to posit the requirements for such a resolution; indeed, the requirements are part of the dispute. What is clear, however, is that all parties today recognize that, to use the words of former U.S. Assistant Secretary of State Harold Saunders, "The Palestinians collectively are a political factor which must be dealt with if there is to be a peace between Israel and its neighbors." Even a cursory review of Israeli statements demonstrates conclusively that there too is a recognition of the crucial nature of the Palestinian problem. Whether in terms of "autonomy" proposals or hints that the Palestinians already have their state in Jordan, it is evident that Israeli leaders, too, have come to accept, implicitly or explicitly, the unavoidable fact that no settlement is possible without dealing with the Palestinian problem.

We Jordanians must add that, practically speaking, a settlement must also take into account our perceptions. Small as Jordan is, our country is politically, socially, economically, militarily and historically inseparable from the Palestinian issue. Not that we can speak in place of the Palestinians; we cannot. As His Majesty King Hussein has said recently, "Palestinians alone have the right to determine their future. There are no other options acceptable to Jordan nor is there any substitute for the Palestine Liberation Organization, the sole legitimate representative of the people of Palestine. . . . " We cannot speak in place of the Palestinians. At the same time, however, as a leading Jordanian social scientist has written, "The Jordanians and Palestinians are now one people, and no political loyalty, however strong, will separate them permanently."

Consider for a moment the following:

—Half Jordan's population is Palestinian.

—The West Bank and East Jerusalem, both captured by Israel in 1967, were part of Jordan.

—If there is large-scale Palestinian migration as a result of any regional settlement, Jordan will necessarily be greatly affected.

—Virtually all Palestinians currently resident in Jordan are Jordanian nationals.

—Israel and Jordan have vital interests in development of regional water resources in the Jordan River. Israel has already illegally diverted much of the Jordan River, but the importance of cooperation in the future cannot be overestimated. In other areas such as tourism, there is also substantial need for cooperation.

—After any settlement as before it, Jordan will share a long border with Israel. For us, development is not just an abstract goal, but a pressing need. We do not wish to continue to divert so much of Jordan's small resource base to a costly armaments program to defend our overexposed position or in order to reduce the risks along this extended border.

—Pending the creation of a Palestinian state, it is still Jordan which pays the salaries and pensions of West Bank officials; it is Jordan that bears some development costs of the territory and whose approval is necessary for such projects; it is in the Jordanian parliament that the inhabitants of the West Bank are represented; it is Jordanian law that has effect in the West Bank. This is not to deny that Israel is also involved in these activities, for that is true, albeit a clear violation of international law. Rather, we intend only to show how concrete and contemporary are Jordan's interests.

In point of fact and history, independent analysts and national governments alike have at least implicitly recognized Jordan's importance to a settlement. Most peace proposals provide for a central role for the kingdom, even if they misconstrue our attitudes, perceptions, and policies. The more specific the proposals, i.e., the more modalities are delineated, the clearer generally is the role allocated to Jordan. For example, both the initiative of Saudi Arabia's Crown Prince Fahd on August 8, 1981, and the Camp David agreements between Egypt and Israel—the former a set of general proposals designed to stimulate movement toward a settlement, the latter a complex and much more specific set of bilateral agreements—assume that Jordan will play a key role. Without such a role, neither approach is feasible.

Similarly, for their part, Israelis have consistently recognized the central role of Jordan in any viable settlement arrangement. Some propose to "bury the Palestinian problem in Jordan," others to transform our country into a Palestinian state, and still others to confer upon us what amounts to a policeman's role in a West Bank virtually incorporated into Israel. Mind you, these options scarcely scratch the surface of the catalog of Israeli ideas. But all see in Jordan an important actor.

The Palestinians too recognize our critical role, and the range of Palestinian ideas and proposals is perhaps broader even than that of the Israelis. Yet even those Palestinians who find our Hashemite tradition, our form of government, and our abiding faith in God distasteful, those blinded by ideology who see us as reactionaries or lackeys or worse, even they understand today how deep and indissoluble have grown the relationships between Palestinian and Jordanian.

Settling the Conflict

We have seen that Jordan is central to any Arab-Israeli settlement, that Jordanian views must be very seriously considered if any initiative is to have a chance at success. Yet lately we in Jordan have begun to hear and read that "Jordan opposes an Arab-Israeli settlement." Let us be clear on this point: no one, no country, no people wants a settlement more than we do. Certainly, no one pays a heavier price for the continuation of the conflict than do we here in Jordan.

No, we do not oppose the resolution of this merciless dispute. To the contrary, his Majesty King Hussein has seen most of his life consumed by the search for an end to the unending violence, a remission from the unremitting hatred, a break in the yet-unbroken cycle of hostility and fear and distrust. Moreover, our grandfather, King Abdullah, also beloved of the Jordanian people, gave his life to this tragic conflict even as his grandsons' lives have often been threatened by it. Some in the West, thousands of miles from this sanguinary battlefield, may reach a facile conclusion that we oppose a resolution; but God knows, and we know, that this is not and could not be so.

Since the earliest days of the Arab-Israeli conflict our government, frequently opposed by our Arab brothers who were not asked to bear such a heavy burden, pursued many paths toward a settlement. In retrospect, had the other Arab countries and peoples seen the situation as clearly as we did, had they been so situated as to recognize irreversible political realities, it might have been possible to arrive at an agreement that provided the minimum needs of all parties and national self-determination for the Palestinian people. But we were all, Jordanians too, overwhelmed at the unprecedented injustice done to the Palestinians in 1948, determined to reverse this, and it was not possible to pursue more constructive paths for some years.

After the 1967 War, other Arab governments learned—and what a costly lesson—what we had known for almost two decades: Israel was to be an enduring reality of the Middle East, and the issue was not to undo the 1947 injustice to Palestinians and all Arabs but rather to constrain an Israel hungry for territorial expansion and powerful enough to obtain it. In the late 1960s and early 1970s the United Nations and the United States both made serious efforts to attain a settlement, or even to attain a workable framework for settlement. One need only read the documents concerning the Jarring mission or the exchanges associated with the Rogers plan to see how forthcoming Jordan has been. We have supported these initiatives not because we agree with each point or idea or tendency, but because we knew that somehow a break was necessary in the stalemate.

Perhaps it is germane to say at this point that we Jordanians do not have a precise blueprint of a settlement in mind. Indeed, I believe I can speak for all the Arab countries, and probably for Israel too, in saying that the range of ideas or alternatives or minimums or maximums that is advanced in any of our countries is appallingly varied. For us, Jordanians, there are a few clear-cut requirements. Certainly, the same can be said for Egyptians, Israelis, Iraqis, Palestinians, Saudis and Syrians. We have learned through successive tragedies to keep our requirements few, to question them, to be sure they are truly vital. This is true also of other Arab parties. Sadly, it is not true for Israel, whose list of requirements has grown with each passing year.

—Today, Israel claims districts she never claimed before. The Golan is annexed, even though no Israeli government before today has ever even suggested the Golan was other than Syrian.

—Today, Israel claims resources she never claimed before. She uses the waters of the Litani and unlawfully takes our waters from the Yarmuk River-Jordan River confluence. She prevents us from developing these hydrological resources in our own countries by threat or use of force when necessary, all so that Israel may use all the region's water as she pleases.

—Today, Israel claims private lands she never claimed before. In the West Bank occupied by Israel since 1967, over one-third of the land (and 90 percent of the waters) has been confiscated for Jewish settlements in contravention of all international law.

—Today, Israel claims rights she never claimed before. When Iraq purchased a nuclear reactor for energy purposes, Israel, which does not even border Iraq, launched an air attack on the reactor. No government in the world except Israel arrogates such rights unto itself.

—Today, Israel claims duties she never claimed before. "Hot pursuit" has been claimed by many countries at many times to permit retaliatory or punitive excursions. Israel alone claims the right of "preemptive retaliation," which is as violative of the law as it is of logic. And these novelties are *in addition* to earlier Israeli demands.

In spite of Israel's intransigence, which is growing apace with her appetite, the Arab governments including Jordan still seek a settlement. We have to, for let us be candid: Israel has designs on the West Bank, East Jerusalem, the Golan Heights, and southern Lebanon—whose territories are these? Arab territories. We do not want to provide a pretext for further Israeli expansion. So, yes, Jordan, and, yes, the other Arab states near Israel favor a settlement.

Yet it is true that we do not favor *any* settlement. Neither Jordan, nor Syria nor Lebanon nor Saudi Arabia nor Egypt nor Israel—none of the Middle East countries—is prepared to accept, or should be prepared to accept, "peace at any price." Again, let us all be honest. A "settlement" that did not resolve the Palestinian problem, or the question of the Golan, or Israel's or Jordan's or Lebanon's or Syria's rights to exist with reasonable security within a recognized territory—such an outcome would be no settlement at all, for natural forces would be at work to overturn it before it was signed. We understand Israel's needs, and believe Israel's truly vital requirements can be met, but we too have a few vital requirements. Each nation must enjoy some security as a result of a settlement, and none of us can have perfect security, for as has often been shown, one nation's perfect security is another's perfect insecurity.

It is true that agreement on what a settlement should look like is lacking both within and among Arab states, as it is lacking in fact within Israel and between Israel and other states. But a resolution to the conflict is much less likely to be found

—if Israel continues to expand what are clearly illegal settlements in the occupied territories;

—if Israel continues to decide unilaterally to annex Arab land;

—if private land is confiscated to be handed out to Israeli settlers;

—if peace agreements are made in the name of rather than with other parties;

—if Israel continues to play with internal vulnerabilities of Arab states, increasing instability and distrust;

—if Israel continues to intervene militarily in Arab states, seeing her role as a regional policeman.

Let there be no mistake. I am not holding the Arabs blameless for the depth and duration of the Arab-Israeli conflict. For too long Arab states thought the monumental injustice perpetrated against the Palestinian people in 1948 was the only reality. For too long many Arabs held that justice would be served in the end, that justice would triumph, and could see only a return to their lands by the refugees as just. After all, we knew the Palestinian Arabs, native to the land, as our Arab brothers. We did not know the Jews who had suddenly seized it. What was to happen to them? Arabs didn't care; they cared deeply, though, about the Palestinians. This was unrealistic. Today, we understand that the Palestinian problems must be dealt with *in the context* of the existence of Israel. Nevertheless, that problem *must* be resolved. We Arabs too have some requirements, but there is no question that we seek, favor, and deeply desire a resolution to this disastrous conflict.

Prerequisites for Peace

As we in Jordan see the Arab-Israeli conflict today, prospects for a settlement in the near term have dimmed substantially. At one time, after 1975, we were very hopeful. All the conflict states wanted a settlement, and their minimum positions were not as far apart as they are today. It looked for several years as if a peace might be possible within a decade. Moreover, there seemed to have developed a near-consensus about the general shape of a settlement. This consensus was perhaps best exemplified in *Toward Peace in the Middle East,* an influential report of a study group that met in 1975 under the auspices of The Brookings Institution in Washington, D.C.

Not one of the parties to the Arab-Israeli conflict ever issued a statement about the Brookings report, and certainly we in Jordan and other Arabs had views and preferences that departed from those voiced in the report. It is clear that the same may be said of Israel. Still, the report seemed at least accurately to portray the trends of thinking *and* the hope that a settlement was possible.

Today, some five years later, another pamphlet has recently been issued, this one by the Seven Springs Center, Mt. Kisco, New York. Its conclusions accurately reflect the renascence of pessimism:

1. "Hopes for a negotiated peace . . . are fading. Many Arabs and Israelis are beginning to resign themselves to prolonged confrontation and violence because they see no alternative that promises a just comprehensive peace."

2. These hopes are fading "just at a moment when acceptance of Palestinian national identity in the Arab world and beyond and growing Arab willingness to accept the Israeli state have created the best possiblity of an Arab-Palestinian-Israeli negotiation since Israel was established."

3. "Palestinian nationalism and the Palestinian desire for a state must be fairly faced and dealt with in negotiation in ways consistent with the rights and security of their neighbors. . . . "

4. "A basis for negotiation between Israel and its eastern neighbors . . . [must] acknowledge but transcend what was achieved under the Camp David accords and go on to define practical steps. . . .

5. "There is widespread conviction in the Middle East that only the United States can effectively help to achieve peace, but there is deep doubt that the U.S. is prepared to play a role as a just mediator and to work actively for a negotiated peace."

In 1977 the late Egyptian President, Anwar Sadat, made a decision to go to Israel. His objective, as he recounted in his autobiography and speeches, was to break though the psychological barrier to peace. We in Jordan understand that this was no mean task, but a very important one, and we were concerned that President Sadat undertook his approach without consulting other Arab governments no less concerned about the "psychological barrier" and no less threatened by its impediment to peace. Nevertheless, although we reserved judgment on the historic trip, we became more concerned as Sadat's initiative began to take on a momentum of its own leading inexorably toward a separate peace between Israel and Egypt. Such an approach only encourages Israeli hawks, whetting their expansionist appetites.

It must be noted that the Israeli annexation of Arab Jerusalem and the Golan have both taken place in the aftermath of the Egyptian-Israeli peace treaty. Even Israelis never claimed historic rights to the Golan. Now that they have purported to annex the Golan Heights, can anyone doubt that the next step will be the West Bank? Never mind the concept of autonomy. Never mind the ideas of Palestinian self-rule. It is clear that Israel is intent upon adding this Arab territory to Greater Israel.

It was the inevitability of this result to the Camp David separate peace that led us to remain outside the discussions. We ask for a process of peace, not a process of annexation. Jordan and other Arab governments want a true peace, a peace of compromise, a peace that will allow Arab and Jew and Christian to live side by side in this region so important to all three faiths and the many peoples who embrace them. We seek a peace that will not force us to divert our meager resources to a constant cycle of arming to deter others and defend ourselves, a peace that will allow us to develop our land, our people, and our society both economically and spiritually, not bury the people in the land with continuing bitterness and hatred.

And what are the essentials of such a peace? Clearly, the modalities must be negotiated, but several prerequisites are manifestly central to bring about a peace that can endure. Happily, the prerequisites are few. Sadly, they are more elusive today than they were when Presiedent Sadat traveled to Jerusalem.

First, it is clear that the Palestinians must be allowed to freely exercise their national right of self-determination. The whole world, including the United States, and implicitly even Israel, has recognized that the Palestinian problem is at the core of the continuing Middle East tragedy. Put another way, there will never be a true peace in the region until the first requirement is met.

The second requirement is Israeli withdrawal from territories occupied in the 1967 War. Indeed, these two requirements may be viewed as related. We understand that timing can be important, that security measures (such as arms or forces limitations, observers, and the like) may be an integral part of any agreement. Issues such as security measures, juridical status, corridors of transit and communication, representation, foreign nationals, and so forth are important and are proper subjects of negotiation. Moreover, it is clear that in some cases security requirements may dictate minor modifications to specific lines previously disputed. Yet, such exchanges must result from negotiations aimed at *mutual* security and based on the two principles we have identified, not as a result of force or threat. Certainly, the Arab governments and Israel alike will be seeking means to provide for their security, including recognized borders and perhaps guarantees. Yet no one can question that the two requirements we have noted here are clearly prerequisites to *any* viable settlement.

Jordan and the other Arab countries have made clear their willingness to discuss and accept various forms of security arrangements to underwrite the peace—demilitarized zones, peacekeeping forces, and so forth. It is Israel that refuses such measures, even though Israel attacked the Arab countries in 1956 and 1967 and has occupied our land since.

The United States has important—some would say, vital—interests in the Middle East. It is also true that we have critical interests in the West, not least with the United States. Much in our tradition is shared, from our great monotheistic traditions to our prolonged and close association with Western Europe. We have resources of faith as well as of minerals; America has resources of science and technology as well as capital. The world is interdependent, and those Arabs who ignore or castigate our interdependence with the West, like their counterparts here, are out of step with more than their compatriots—they are out of step with reality itself.

Thus, when some Arabs say that American or Western interests are at risk in the continued failure to achieve a settlement, what they are really saying is that world interests, our interests as well as yours, are at stake. A future that condemns us to pervert the nature and value of our relationship into that of a gunrunner's, that forces America's friends to confront and even do violence to other friends, that perpetuates poverty and ignorance and narrowly limits the resources to overcome these common enemies—this is not a hopeful destiny, this is not a humane destiny, this is not an acceptable destiny.

Yes, the Middle East problem is complex, but perhaps not more so than the mysteries of human life itself, the physics of space travel, or the conquest of poliomyelitis. A United States that has shown it can meet such challenges need not, and, we hope, will not be intimidated by the problems of the Middle East. A similar commitment is what is required. After all, Arabs do not and cannot console ourselves with the thought that the problem is thousands of miles away. Of *our* commitment to attain a settlement I can give complete and categorical assurance.

IRAQ: PRAGMATIC RADICALISM IN THE FERTILE CRESCENT[8]

Since the heavy decline in Iranian oil production, Iraq ranks as the second largest oil producer in the Middle East, outranked

[8] Magazine article by Arthur C. Turner, professor of political science, University of California at Riverside. *Current History.* 81:14-7. Ja. '82. Copyright, 1982, by Current History, Inc. Reprinted by permission.

only by Saudi Arabia. It may be the Middle East state that has most successfully used abundant oil revenues to bring about industrialization and development and to achieve a workable accommodation with new wealth and Western technology. This process received a rude shock on June 7, 1981, when the centerpiece of the new technology, the nearly completed nuclear reactor in the Baghdad area, was destroyed by Israeli planes. But that raid did not alter the general trend.

In a region of the world not noted for stability, Iraq has been reasonably stable for well over a decade. Its current governing group established itself in 1968, and for 13 years there has been no serious threat to its rule. Only two men have held supreme power in that period, and the transition from one to the other was peaceful. Nor is Iraq's stability accounted for solely by repression. Any expression of discontent, far less rebellion, is severely punished, but it is not at all certain that there is much discontent.

Iraqi policies reflect many paradoxes. In one sense a hotbed of nationalism (Iraq has been one of the states most adamantly hostile to any accommodation with Israel and since 1958 has always been vocally anti-Western); in another sense it is questionable whether Iraq is a nation at all. Iraqi nationalism has usually been subsumed in a larger pan-Arab nationalism. Yet this standard bearer of pan-Arab nationalism, this inveterate opponent of Israel, was the only major Arab oil-exporting country that did not participate in the oil boycott of 1973-1974. Pragmatism and profit took precedence.

Nor has its enthusiasm for pan-Arabism led Iraq to work with other Arab states. On the contrary, in the past 20 years, Iraq has disagreed with every one of its neighbors, Arab and non-Arab alike; but disagreements with Arab states have tended to be more serious.

Again, Iraq's theoretical hostility to the West has pulled in double harness with actual cooperation, especially with the United States and France. And although since 1967 Iraq and the United States have not had normal diplomatic relations, American diplomats live and work in Baghdad and Iraqi diplomats live in Washington, D.C., and American economic activity in Iraq is lively.

Geographically as well as culturally, Iraq is the very core of the Middle East—wherever one sets the limits of that hard-to-define entity. Placed at the northwest corner of the Persian (Arabs prefer "Arabian") Gulf, to which it has somewhat limited access, Iraq's neighbors are Kuwait, Saudi Arabia, Jordan, Syria, Turkey and Iran. With its area of 168,000 square miles and a population of about 12.5 million, Iraq combines a moderately large size and population with a central location and, for the past several decades, enormous oil revenues—over $10 billion in 1978.

It has frequently been pointed out that the model of the nation as invented in Europe is singularly ill-adapted to the realities of Africa and Asia. Of this generalization there is no better example than Iraq, a "made" nation, the outcome of British policy. This is precisely the basic difficulty, the exercise in nation-building, with which the present regime in Iraq—like regimes over the past 60 years—has been wrestling in its 13 years of power. In this case, the struggle has met some success.

What are these different groups? Iraq has over millenia suffered waves of conquest and immigration, but a strong tendency towards arabization (voluntary or involuntary) has limited what might otherwise have been indescribable diversity. Three-fourths, or a little less, of the populaion may be described as Arabs. The well-populated center and south are almost entirely Arab. Arabic, the official language, is the language of the great majority of the population. The most important minority is Kurdish; the two million Kurds who live in the mountainous north constitute the most serious of all Iraq's internal problems. The distinction between Kurd and Arab is the only distinction in Iraq that is perceived in terms of nationality or race.

Although about 93 percent of the Iraqis are Muslim, the fundamental divisive factor in Iraqi society is not race but religion, or more precisely the division between two branches of one religion, the mutually intolerant Shia and Sunni sects of Islam. The Kurds, who are Muslim though not Arab, are Sunni; but even so, the Shias are thought to outnumber the Sunnis nationally in the ratio of seven or eight to five. Within the Arab community, they are almost certainly a clear majority. The Sunni Arabs comprise only about one-fourth of the population. Yet almost continuously

since the creation of the Iraqi state political power has largely
been in the hands of the Sunni Arabs. This was true under the
pre-1958, prerevolutionary monarchical government. It is true
now.

The politically predominant Sunni community is a majority
only in the area roughly west of the line Baghdad-Mosul. It is beyond question the most articulate and politically sophisticated part
of the population as well as the most prosperous (Sunni Arabs being on the average more affluent than the Arab Shia population
of the south). But it is distinctly a minority, whose political concepts, loyalties and aims have been formulated more in terms of
the "Arab nation" as a whole than in terms of an Iraqi nation comprising at least three diverse elements—Sunni Arabs, Shia Arabs
and Kurds. It also has to be remembered that Sunni Islam is the
mainstream or orthodox version in Islam. Only in Iran are Shiites
a ruling majority. Thus the identification of the ruling Sunni Arabs in Iraq with the "Arab nation" necessarily sets them apart
from their fellow Iraqi Arabs of the Shia persuasion. Religion is
a divisive, not a unifying, force.

In Iraq there are other minorities, among them Turkomans,
Persians and Jews, but they are not politically significant. The
Jewish population nearly all left after the founding of Israel. A
Persian minority of some 200,000 resident near the Iranian border
was reduced to half or less by forcible deportations to Iran in the
early 1970s. The most diverse areas of Iraq, ethnically, are the
northern provinces of Mosul and Erbil.

Modern Iraq was invented by a small band of British colonial
administrators, notably Sir Arnold Wilson, and the incredible
Gertrude Bell. They proceeded, with the dauntless self-confidence
possessed by the British overseas in that era, to create a modern
state out of some remnants of the Ottoman Empire, after Turkey
had disintegrated. Britain secured the League of Nations Mandate for Iraq, Palestine, and Transjordan. It thus controlled almost all the territory between Egypt and India, except for Persia.

Faisal, a member of the noble Hashemite family from the He-
jaz, was placed on the Iraqi throne in 1921; a well-managed referendum subsequently confirmed his place on the throne. (Another
member of the Hashemite family was placed on the throne of the

adjacent mandated territory of Transjordan, where Hashemites remain.) A treaty between Britain and the new Iraq defined the relationship in 1922: Iraq was to be semi-autonomous, with the British exercising a large measure of control through advisory rights in military and financial matters and foreign relations.

At first not even the boundaries of Iraq were certain. The Arab riverine and delta lands comprising the vilayets of Basra and Baghdad were not in question, but Kemal Ataturk's Turkey claimed the vilayet of Mosul; it was not assigned to Iraq until the Treaty of Ankara in 1926. The name of the new state reflected the dominance of the Arab element—the Arab geographical term *Al Iraq* means the "cliff" or "shore" and refers to the delta lands.

A new treaty in 1930 looked to Iraq's imminent independence but gave Britain inter alia the right to maintain air bases. The mandate terminated in 1932 when Iraq became independent and was admitted to the League of Nations under British sponsorship. British and Western influence remained strong during World War II (a British force intervened in 1941 to oust the pro-German Rashid Ali regime in Baghdad) and afterward, until the 1958 revolution. During much of the monarchical period, Iraq was run by the veteran pro-British Premier Nuri es-Said, who embarked on an extensive program of building roads, hospitals and schools, and who encouraged economic development as soon as oil revenues made this possible. Oil began to flow from the Kirkuk field in the late 1920s; additional discoveries were made later at Mosuand at the Rumaila field, near Basra, but the Kirkuk field remains the chief source of Iraqi crude.

The 1958 Revolution

The domestic policies pursued by Iraqi governments before 1958 were similar to the policies being pursued in neighboring Iran by the Pahlavi dynasty, father and son; there is a strong resemblance between events in Iran in 1978-1979 and events in Iraq 20 years earlier. In each country, a dynasty perished. In each, an openly pro-Western regime and military ally gave way to a revolutionary government hostile to the West and rabidly nationalist.

Iraq seemed solidly ensconced in the Western camp when, in 1955, it became the only Arab state to sign the Baghdad Pact. But nationalist, socialist and Communist forces were growing in strength, especially in the cities; and in the coup of July 14, 1958, Nuri and the royal family were murdered and a republican regime of nationalist officers, led by Brigadier Abdul Karim Kassim, took over. This inaugurated a period of violent upheaval alternating with praetorian governments that lasted 10 years until a new stability was achieved.

The government that emerged in July, 1968, led by President Ahmed Hassan al-Bakr, was made up of Baath party members. The Baath, or Arab Socialist Renaissance party, had emerged in Syria in the 1940s, but became important only in the 1950s. The party's aims combine pan-Arab nationalism with socialism. In Syria, the Baath has been the ruling party since 1963; in Iraq, it has ruled since 1958. But the two Baath regimes are bitterly hostile toward each other, each claiming to be the sole repository of ideological purity. Within Iraq, the party has borrowed from the Communists the idea of organizing into cells all over the country; and informing on any symptoms of disloyalty is encouraged under the watchful eyes of a vigilant and ruthless security police (whose use of torture has recently been condemned by Amnesty International).

In July, 1979, Sadam Hussein Takriti took over peaceably from the ailing al-Bakr. While he was Vice President, Sadam Hussein's power had long rivaled and may have surpassed that of the President. It is typical of the tightly knit core of power-holders in Iraq that both Hussein and al-Bakr come from the same town, Takrit, as do many other members of the Revolutionary Command Council. It is also symptomatic that the head of the security police is President Hussein's brother.

Domestic Policies

The regime faced attempted coups against its authority in 1970 and 1973, but by the mid-1970s stability and general acceptance had been achieved. Today Iraq faces what most observers feel is the most promising economic and social future in the Arab world. For the first time since the fall of the monarchy, elections were held for a national Parliament on July 20, 1980. It was an impressive, albeit well-managed, demonstration. Six million Iraqis voted, women for the first time.

The central paradox of contemporary Iraqi politics is the fact that a regime so committed in theory to an extreme ideology can pursue in practice such flexible and expedient policies. In the domestic sphere, police-state methods consort oddly with social, economic and educational policies that can only be described as enlightened. Iraq has rich resources in minerals, in agriculture, and in its hard-working population. The money, flowing since 1973 in an increasing abundance from an oil industry that was nationalized in 1972, makes good use of the country's resources. An excellent system of free education has been introduced. Women enjoy full economic rights. Comprehensive social welfare programs and central economic planning are well established. The latifundia of the largest landowners have been broken up, and land has been redistributed to peasants. Unlike the Shah's Iran, Iraq has assigned a high priority to agriculture, although many new industries have also been established. The percentage of success in government ventures has been surprisingly high. No doubt that the ruling Baath party elite and the military profited most from the new wealth, but there was also a general rise in the standard of living.

The greatest domestic problem for many years has been ethnic, not economic. The Kurds, an ancient people who have not achieved their own state, live partly in Iraq and partly in adjacent areas of Iran and Turkey; the areas they live in are collectively known as Kurdistan. Since 1958, every government in Baghdad has acknowledged that Iraq consists of two people, Arab and Kurd, but the reluctance to grant the Kurds any genuine autonomy has been great. An autonomous Kurdish region was promised in 1970, but the promise was implemented only in 1974, and that in so half-hearted a fashion that a fierce rebellion, the last of many, broke out in Iraqi Kurdistan and raged until 1975. That year the Shah (who had hitherto supported the Kurds) negotiated a treaty (the Algiers pact) with Iraq, in which he withdrew Iran's support from the Kurds in return for Iraqi concessions in the matter of the Shatt al-Arab waterway.

Kurdish resistance inevitably collapsed, and the veteran Kurdish national leader, Mustafa Barzani, died in March, 1979, in Washington, D.C. Many Kurds were forcibly relocated in the south of Iraq, far from their native mountains. At the same time, language and cultural rights were conceded to Kurdistan, and a measure of autonomy was granted. In September, 1980, Hussein's government held the first elections in Kurdistan for the regional legislative assembly. Before the Iranian revolution, the Kurds of Iran were better treated than their national brethren in Iraq or Turkey; but now, realistically speaking, the Iraqi group are the most fortunate, because the Iranian Kurds are in a state of chronic rebellion against the fanatical Shiite government in Teheran.

Contemporary Iraq has in general been a bad neighbor. Its bitter feud with the Syrian Baathists, interrupted only for a moment by military cooperation in the 1973 war against Israel, is the most obvious example of this. In July, 1980, more than 200 people were arrested in Baghdad and, on August 8, 21 former officials and ministers were executed by firing squad. Their supposed offense was plotting against the government with the aid of an unnamed foreign Arab power—obviously Syria. Yet chimerical plans for an Iraqi-Syrian union continue to be bruited from time to time. Iraqi oil is—somewhat intermittently—pumped across Syria to Mediterranean ports, but this route is so vulnerable that a new pipeline that swings north instead, across Turkey, has recently been built.

Iraq regards its small but rich neighbor Kuwait as properly Iraqi, a sort of *Iraq irredenta*. When the British gave Kuwait independence in 1961, Iraq threatened to take it over. British forces subsequently returned as a safeguard and the Iraqi threat receded in the face of united Arab pressure. There was almost a replay in 1973, when Iraq attacked Kuwaiti border posts and demanded concessions Kuwait found intolerable; again, the joint pressure of Arab states induced Iraq to desist. In the war with Iran, however, Kuwait is cooperating with Iraq to the extent of providing the main supply route by which supplies from the Gulf pass into Iraq, Iraqi Gulf ports being unusable.

On September 22, 1980, Iraq initiated an attack on Iran and occupied a considerable strip of territory along the border, launching a war that continues after more than a year. The scale of fighting has, in fact, been small for many months, and casualties are light. The Iranian city of Abadan was freed in September, 1981, but the war continues.

Iraq's motivation is obscure, but certain lines of speculation suggest themselves. The immediate cause was claimed to be the international boundary on the Shatt al-Arab. There was also the matter of the three small (non-Iraqi) islands in the Gulf that had been annexed by the Shah in 1971, an act protested at that time by Iraq. The Shatt al-Arab boundary question is a complicated legal issue going back to the days of the Ottoman Empire. It is of much more significance to Iraq than to Iran, for the Shatt al-Arab is Iraq's sole access to the Persian Gulf, whereas the Iranian coastline extends along its whole north shore, and Iran has several alternative oil terminals. In 1937, the international boundary was set on the Iranian bank: Iraq controlled the waterway, but there were guarantees for Iranian use of the channel. Iran disputed this settlement several times, notably in 1969. The 1975 Algiers agreement declared that the boundary was on the *talweg,* the center of the deep channel. In 1980, during a moment of Iranian weakness and disunity, Sadam Hussein attempted to reestablish Iraqi sovereignty over the whole waterway.

A quick victory seemed to offer several possibilities: Iraq could become the champion of the Arab world against non-Arab Iran; Iraq might detach oil-rich Khorramshar province, largely Arab in population, from Iran; Iraq might stand for the principle of modernization and development against the reactionary zealots who had taken over Iran. Again, Hussein and his ruling group nurtured a deep (but, as it turned out, exaggerated) fear of Iran's Ayatollah Ruhollah Khomeini's appeal to Shiites in Iraq. Iran seemed, in general terms, a threat to the status quo everywhere, and by attacking Iran Hussein certainly earned the silent thanks of every conservative regime in the Middle East.

Nevertheless, the war in all probability reflected a total miscalculation. The opportunity for an easy and quick victory was illusory; Iraq was soon bogged down in a long war against an enemy with vastly superior manpower resources. Yet all reports indicate that the war has increased President Hussein's populari-

ty. Food and other supplies have remained ample. Casualties have
been light; propaganda is incessant; and Hussein has shown himself adept in the arts of courting popularity by appearing unex-
pectedly in remote villages and towns to charm the inhabitants.

Relations With the United States and the Soviet Union

Since 1968, Iraq has followed a delicate middle path in its relations with the Soviet Union and the United States, bending first
one way and then the other. In 1972, an alliance was signed with
the U.S.S.R., but although the treaty was never abrogated, relations have progressively cooled. In the late 1970s, Communists
were ousted unmercifully from the army, the government and all
positions of influence in Iraq. While Iraqi communism, once an
important force, was being reduced to virtual impotence, Iraq was
cooperating more closely with the West, especially with France
and the United States.

The atomic reactor destroyed by the Israelis in June, 1981,
was French-built. The theoretical breach in Iraqi-American relations that has prevailed since the 1967 war has been circumvented
by the ingenious device of "interest sections" in each other's capitals in place of embassies. American economic activity in Iraq is
large and growing. American technicians are currently assisting
in the hunt for oil in areas west of Baghdad, where prospects look
promising. This is only one of the innumerable plans for economic
development in Iraq that assume American participation. Iraqi
Airways operates with American planes. All this is combined with
continuing rhetorical denunciations of Israel and of the United
States as Israel's chief supporter.

The historian Michael Hudson sees the basic goal of Arab
governments, especially revolutionary governments, as "the quest
for legitimacy." In Iraq, thanks to a curious combination of seemingly incompatible policies, the quest seems to be making progress.
The keys to legitimacy for a revolutionary government are time
and success. Success, in some measure, has already been achieved
in Iraq, and the years are passing. But all this could be endangered
by a long war with Iran.

THE POLITICS OF EXTREMISM IN IRAN[9]

As Iran approaches the third anniversary of the revolutionary overthrow of the regime of Muhammad Resa Shah Pahlavi, it is fighting to survive as a coherent nation-state. In 1981, the country had three different Presidents and four different Prime Ministers when the post-revolutionary fissures in the body politic deepened and an undeclared civil war broke out in the form of a contest between regime repression and opposition by terrorism. With the destruction of the government of President Abol Hassan Bani Sadr in June, much of the legitimacy was stripped from the political process in formation. Ayatollah Ruhollah Khomeini began to lose control and indeed contributed to the violence and bloodshed in the wake of Bani Sadr's downfall. The shocking bomb incident of June 28, 1981, represented the end of the first stage of the Iranian revolution and introduced a time of terror. In the bombing, 74 members of the political elite were assassinated, including the founder of the Islamic Republican party (IRP), Ayatollah Muhammad Hussein Beheshti, four Cabinet ministers, six deputy ministers, and 27 majlis (parliamentary) deputies.

In retaliation for the massacre, the IRP initiated a campaign of repression that resulted in over 2,000 executions and many thousands of arrests. This, in turn, provoked the opposition groups to a policy of terror that had as its targets the most powerful leaders of the IRP itself. The crippling campaign of violence resulted in the unprecedented assassination of both the Head of Government and the Head of State on August 30, when Prime Minister Muhammad Javad Bahonar and President Muhammad Ali Rajai died together in a bombing of the heavily guarded prime ministry. Many other extremist leaders died violent deaths in 1981, including influential majlis deputy Hassan Ayat (August 5), prosecutor-general Ayatollah Ali Qodusi (September 5), and Khomeini's personal representative in Tabriz, Ayatollah Asadollah Madani (September 11). The IRP, through its coercive arm,

[9] Magazine article by James A. Bill, professor of government, University of Texas at Austin. *Current History*, 81:9-13+. Ja. '82. Copyright, 1982, by Current History, Inc. Reprinted by permission.

the Revolutionary Guards (*Pasdaran*), reacted by intensifying its own campaign of repression and execution. The last half of 1981 found Iran trapped in a vicious and spiraling cycle of violence.

The social and political fabric of post-Pahlavi Iran has continued to unravel in the face of government factionalism, personal rivalry, ethnic cleavages, religious fanaticism, ideological confrontation, and economic malaise. Externally, Iran's debilitating war with Iraq moved into its second year, sapping Iran of badly needed human and economic resources. (This war helped deter the Iranian military from intervening directly in the chaotic domestic political situation.) The release of the American diplomatic hostages on January 20 did little to temper internal hostilities as new debates developed about the terms of the agreement. The United States was continually held responsible for failures and upheaval in Iran while the Soviet Union was also deeply distrusted and often condemned. In both its internal and external policies, the Iranian political elite pursued programs that can best be described as incoherent and counterproductive.

To students of the history of revolution and to analysts of social forces and class conflict, the contemporary situation in Iran is not unexpected. The failure of the Pahlavi system to build political institutions and its promotion of social cynicism and factionalism provided a legacy that ensured chaos and violence. The character and ethnicity of the Iranian people, the mind-set of certain leaders of Shi'i Islam, the violence of the revolution itself and the untimely actions of the superpowers contributed their share to today's morass in Iran. The revolution itself was a multiclass movement that has inexorably come under the control of the lower and lower middle classes. In the process, it has devoured many of its own supporters; the upper middle and middle classes have been attacked and peeled away from the post-Pahlavi power structure. While 1979 and 1980 saw the demise of the old aristocracy and the upper middle classes, 1981 was the year in which the professional middle class and liberal intelligentsia became political casualties. At the same time, the merchants and the bourgeois middle class of the bazaar found themselves increasingly under attack and began to organize quietly against the revolution that they helped to finance.

The competing political forces in Iran can be placed along a continuum from the radical left to the extremist right. It is useful to attempt to freeze the alignments temporarily in order to compare and contrast the forces involved. There are four major groupings of the radical left, two centrist coalitions, and one major extremist force on the far right.

The Fedayan-e Khalq is a nationalist, Marxist group on the far left whose support is drawn from young students and the radical wing of the intelligentsia. Although the theoreticians of the Fedayan differ sharply over tactics, they all condemn what they consider capitalist and imperialist exploitation and seek to build a radical socialist state in Iran. The members of the Fedayan are intensely ideological and have a 15-year history of guerrilla resistance. In 1980, the Fedayan splintered into three main factions including the Fedayan Guerrillas (*Cherikha*), the Minority (*Aqaliyyat*), and the Majority (*Aksariyyat*). While the Guerrilla and Minority splinters have sought to pursue their radical goals independently, the Majority group has revealed a willingness to compromise and to form a front with the powerful extremist rightwing IRP in order to protect their existence and to promote their interests. The Paykar group is a small radical Marxist force with organizational strength among both students and workers. Its position approximates that of the minority wing of the Fedayan.

The Mujahedin-e Khalq is an impressive constellation of Islamic radicals who profess many of the same goals as those of the Fedayan and Paykar groupings. The major principle of the Mujahedin is the concept of *towhid* which refers to "a divinely integrated classless society, a society with total equity." In this ideal society, there will purportedly be an end to the exploitation of man by man. The Mujahedin's campaign against capitalism, imperialism and ethnic exploitation is carefully articulated within an Islamic context and as such represents a major challenge and potential alternative to rule by the extremist right.

Unlike the Fedayan, whose credibility has been severely damaged by its policy of compromise, the Mujahedin forces have refused to waver from their professed goals. Although they intitially expressed support for Ayatollah Khomeini, they consistently attacked the rule of the religious leaders on the right, whom they regard as repressive, reactionary and revolutionary dilettantes. In the last months of 1981, the Mujahedin became the major armed force fighting the extremist regime of IRP clerics. Well over 60 percent of those arrested or executed by the government were Mujahedin members or sympathizers.

The other group of the left is the old Tudeh party, which has from the beginning of the revolution sought to protect itself by entering into an accommodation with Khomeini and the IRP. Unlike the Mujahedin who have stood by their ideological commitments, the Tudeh party has pursued a policy of political pragmatism. This has worked as a double-edged sword, protecting the existence of the party in the violent early years of the revolution while damaging its long-term credibility and recruitment potential. The Tudeh party has one further weakness: it has always maintained very close associations with the Soviet Union, an external great power considered a dangerous imperialist threat by the other nationalist groups on the left.

In the center of the political spectrum of Iran today stand two important but amorphous groupings: the secular professional-intelligentsia and the bourgeois middle class. Unlike the more radical and disciplined parties of the left, the moderate groups of the center are large, loose aggregations of individuals who more closely approximate objective social classes than political parties or movements. As such, they have been highly ineffective in the political conflict that has dominated Iran since the overthrow of the Shah. This has been especially true of the professional-intelligentsia, which proclaimed liberal goals and preached progressive reform. Trapped between the ideological radicalism of the left and the religious extremism of the right, the members of the professional middle class have watched their influence destroyed and their revolutionary role disparaged. From Shapur Bakhtiar to Mehdi Bazargan to Bani Sadr, the demise of the center has been complete.

Unlike the secular professionals, the bazaar middle class is somewhat more difficult to write out of the Iranian revolution. It was the merchant class that formed a tight alliance with the Shi'i religious leaders who were central to the success of the victory over the Shah. The bazaaris provide the economic backbone of Iran, and the period of radical-extremist politics has slowly but steadily alienated them. In late 1980, Ayatollah Khomeini himself publicly and frontally attacked the bazaaris, accusing them of preferring profits to the revolution. The forced resignation of President Bani Sadr in June convinced many merchants that the revolution as interpreted by the extremist right had gone astray. Bani Sadr had become popular in merchant circles and his downfall increased their doubts. In mid-July, two prominent bazaar merchants were executed by the regime for allegedly engaging in anti-state activities. Throughout, the bazaaris had become more and more disturbed by the deteriorating economic status of Iran. During 1981, the bazaar began to detach itself from the hardline IRP programs and policies.

The final bloc of players in the contemporary political drama of Iran is the huge and influential religious right, which stresses fundamentalist Islam and which is dominated by the Islamic Republican party. Supported by the masses of Shi'i believers who compose the lower and lower middle class of society, the extremists of the religious right have come to control Iran. This control, won at the expense of both radicals and moderates, is backed by organized Revolutionary Guards and street mobs known as the Partisans of God (*Hezbollahis*). Although many of the most eminent religious leaders of Iran are moderate progressives, not hardline extremists, the role of these clerics has become submerged by the torrential influence of the Hashemi-Rafsanjanis, Mahdavi-Kanis, and Khamene'is. These are individuals who, like their leader Ayatollah Khomeini, were aptly described by Crane Brinton when he wrote that " . . . only a sincere extremist in a revolution can kill men because he loves man, [can] attain peace through violence, and free men by enslaving them." History teaches that extremism inevitably comes to prevail as revolutions run their violent courses.

The Dialectics of Disaster

By mid-1981, the turbulent revolutionary process in Iran had reached a crossover point. The struggle between the left and right for control of the revolution had been filtered and buffered by the existence of a moderate center consisting of technocrats, professionals, writers, intellectuals, social scientists, and a wide variety of other liberal thinkers. In the early months of the revolution, these professionals, represented by individuals like Mehdi Bazargan, Ibrahim Yazdi, Abbas Amir-Entezam, Sadeq Qotbzadeh, Ali Akbar Moinfar, Hassan Nazih, Ali Asghar Haj-Seyyed-Javadi, Ali Reza Nobari, and Abol Hassan Bani Sadr, were a critical and visible force in the revolutionary government. Although radical and immoderate in many of their ideas and actions, these leaders were neither Marxist believers nor religious zealots. One by one, they were defeated and their influence was destroyed by the inexorable attacks of the extremists; they found themselves caught in the withering crossfire between the true believers of left and right.

In 1981, the remnants of the moderate center felt increasing pressure from the religious right in general and the IRP in particular. The moderates' last hope resided in the person of Bani Sadr, the first popularly elected President in the history of Iran. Partly out of desperation and self-defense, Bani Sadr and his group of supporting technocrats began to move leftward on the political continuum and to form an alliance with the Mujahedin-e Khalq. At the same time, Bani Sadr worked hard to establish close relations with the military leaders and was in constant consultation with them at the Iranian-Iraqi war front. This alarmed the religious rulers, who stepped up their campaign against Bani Sadr whom they regarded as part and parcel of the radical Marxist left.

As the IRP accelerated its attacks on moderate and radical groupings, the middle classes were driven further left as they sought refuge from the repression of the right. This convinced the religious extremists that their own predictions concerning the liberals had been correct and that the moderates were little more than Westernized Marxists who sought to turn the revolution away from Shi'ism and toward a form of atheistic imperialism. Thus they intensified their campaign against the moderate intelligentsia in general and against Bani Sadr in particular. Bani Sadr managed to stave off defeat by utilizing his special relationship with Ayatollah Khomeini who at first stood somewhat above the conflicting factions while acting as supreme political arbiter.

In late May, 1981, the leaders of the IRP convinced Khomeini that Bani Sadr was plotting a coup against them and provided the Imam with enough evidence to convince him that Bani Sadr was a threat to the revolution. Khomeini was particularly upset about Bani Sadr's growing relationship with the Mujahedin and asked the President to sever that relationship immediately. Bani Sadr's refusal to do so convinced Khomeini that the President had become a serious liability to the Islamic revolution. On June 10, Khomeini dismissed Bani Sadr from his important post as commander-in-chief of the armed forces. The Majlis voted to declare the President politically incompetent on June 21; a few hours later, the prosecutor-general ordered his arrest and on the following day he was dismissed as President. His term of office had lasted less than 17 months.

On July 29, 1981, Abol Hassan Bani Sadr, accompanied by Mujahedin leader Massoud Rajavi, fled from Iran and was granted political asylum in Paris. The extremist victory over the moderate center was completed on July 24 when Muhammad Ali Raja'i, with substantial IRP backing, won an overwhelming electoral victory for the presidency.

With the fall and flight of Bani Sadr, Khomeini turned his attention to the organized threat from the radical groups on the left. His scorn for liberal elements in exile was summarized in an address he gave on August 10, 1981.

Hypocrites and infidels can never form a united front. All they do is interview and talk and curse each other, talk and curse us and curse themselves. A group of bankrupt politicians who escaped the country disguised in women's clothes are now claiming that they are going to lead the country! They claim that the whole of Iran supports them. Well, if the whole of Iran supports you, why have you gone? You were in Iran and you had all your supporters with you.

During the vicious struggle for power between the President and the IRP, the other major political groupings were also undergoing significant shifts in policy and popularity. The major loser during this period was the Fedayan-e Khalq, which splintered into three pieces, with the largest section forming an alliance of convenience with the extremist right. In the process, the Fedayan lost much of its appeal, and its supporters became visibly fewer in number. The Mujahedin-e Khalq, on the other hand, increased its strength enormously and found itself drawing large numbers of supporters both from the ranks of the Fedayan to its left and from the moderate intelligentsia to its right. In the first few months after the overthrow of the Shah, the Fedayan's supporters outnumbered those of the Mujahedin by an approximate ratio of five to one. By April, 1981, this ratio remained essentially the same except that the positions of the two parties were reversed: now the Mujahedin clearly outnumbered the Fedayan. With its commitment to Islam, its unwillingness to compromise with the repressive right, its history of opposition to Pahlavi despotism and Western intervention, its appeal to the growing numbers of Iranians disaffected with the state of the revolution, the Mujahedin will undoubtedly be a critical force in the political future of Iran. It is important to note that as the Mujahedin have increasingly challenged the ruling religious extremists, they have slowly but clearly moderated their own social and political positions.

After Bani Sadr

The fall of Bani Sadr has four major consequences. First, the middle classes are without genuine political representation for the first time in revolutionary Iran. This can only result in their continued flight from the country, their cynical withdrawal from serious technical and professional responsibility, and their increased radicalization born of desperation. Second, with the fall of Bani Sadr and his skilled team of administrators, subsequent governments have lacked the professional talents necessary to run a country in today's world. Already, the revolution's cannibalistic tendencies have stripped Iran of its top three or four layers of technocrats. Piety and ideological purity seem poor substitutes for the skills of talented professionals, administrators, technicians, doctors and scientists. Third, Bani Sadr's fall cracked the legitimacy of the post-Pahlavi revolutionary government of Iran. Elected in a popular election in which he received over 70 percent of the vote, the President was a primary creature of the new constitution. His ignominious collapse helped undercut the entire edifice of legitimacy erected so painstakingly after the Pahlavi overthrow. If the

Republic's first President is subject to such dismissal, where does political legitimacy reside?

The major consequence of the disappearance of President Bani Sadr was the direct conflict between radical left and extremist right. Positions immediately hardened and confrontation could no longer be filtered through intermediary forces. Khomeini himself lost important leverage. The result was a war for political survival. Very shortly after Bani Sadr's disappearance, an assassination attempt on President-to-be Seyyed Ali Hussein Khamene'i nearly succeeded and seriously injured the powerful mullah. It is especially significant that it was exactly one week after Bani Sadr was impeached that the bombing at IRP headquarters brutally and instantly eliminated much of the leadership of that party. This incident only strengthened the resolve and determination of the extremists in power, who counterattacked the left through a massive wave of arrests, imprisonments and executions. The killing of Ayatollah Muhammad Beheshti transformed an increasingly unpopular political figure into an instant martyr. Despite the deaths of Beheshti and six dozen other members of the IRP political elite in June and the subsequent assassinations of leaders like Raja'i and Bahonar, several important extremists have survived. These included mullahs like Seyyed Ali Hussein Khamene'i and his brother Muhammad Hassan Khamene'i, Ali Akbar Hashemi-Rafsanjani, Muhammad Reza Mahdavi-Kani, Hadi Ghaffuri, and Muhammad Yazdi.

The cleavages that divided yet balanced the contending forces in the two years after the fall of the Shah were sharply reduced in the third year. The balanced tension exploited by Ayatollah Khomeini gave way to direct confrontation between two dedicated forces of fanatical commitment. By the latter half of 1981, the clash had become so intense that the hardened but outnumbered groups on the left reverted to their old tactics of urban guerrilla warfare and terrorism. Both the extremist mullahs of the IRP and the fighting brothers of the Mujahedin have repeatedly demonstrated their willingness to die for their beliefs. This mind-set of martyrdom has seasoned the internal conflict in Iran with a flavor of fanaticism, the effects of which will remain in the society for many years.

Ayatollah Khomeini and the Future of Iran

The major hero of the Iranian revolution, 81-year-old Ayatollah Ruhollah Khomeini, found the revolution's third year to be difficult. On several occasions, the wily old leader expressed his exasperation at the continuing conflict and political turmoil that dominated Iranian politics in 1981. His manipulative tactics proved to be increasingly inadequate to the tasks at hand. For example, his policy of playing the two extreme forces off against one another backfired when the Bani Sadr balancing wheel disintegrated and when, by mid-1981, Khomeini threw all his support to the side of the religious extremists. This compromised his leverage and brought him for the first time directly into the political melee.

During 1981, the Shi'i religious leaders played an unprecedented direct role in the day-to-day business of government. The clerics penetrated the Cabinet, where Muhammad Reza Mahdavi-Kani and Muhammad Javad Bahonar held the influential posts of Minister of Interior and Minister of Education respectively. With the bombings of June and August, the places of fallen mullahs like Beheshti and Bahonar were taken by other clerics, and an even higher percentage of extremist religious figures found themselves in government positions. Bahonar had moved from the ministry of education to the prime ministership and head of the Islamic Republican party. In the new government established on September 1, Muhammad Reza Mahdavi-Kani was the provisional Prime Minister and Ali Hussein Khamenei was the new head of the IRP. Another mullah, Abol Majid Mo'adikhah, remained on as Minister of National Guidance. On October 2, the militant cleric, Hojjat ol-Islam Ali Hussein Khamene'i, was elected President of the Islamic Republic of Iran.

An examination of the mullahs in key political positions indicates that the most extremist among them were precisely those who wielded the most political influence. Moderates like Ali Golzadeh-Ghaffuri, Muhammad Javad Hojjati-Kermani, and Ayatollah Hassan Lahuti were noticeably and abruptly silenced. The triumph of the extremist clerics was clearly seen in a revealing Majlis incident in June, when the parliamentary body was debating the fate of President Bani Sadr. One of the few individuals who courageously stood to speak in defense of Bani Sadr was a mullah, Muhammad Javad Hojjati-Kermani. Hojjati-Kermani's comments were suddenly smothered when the Majlis Speaker, Ali Akbar Hashemi-Rafsanjani, simply cut off the power to Hojjati's microphone. In the heyday of extremism, the moderate mullahs found themselves in a position of suffocating impotence.

Subsequently, Ayatollah Khomeini threw his support to the religious extremists. Early in 1981, he had attempted to curb the expanding and arbitrary power of the religious right. On March 16, for example, he made an effort to contain the influence of the extremists who were already threatening to destroy Bani Sadr. On this occasion, he called a private conference of eight feuding political leaders and told them to terminate their quarrels. Khomeini's grandson also worked to keep the extremist right under control. In an April interview, the grandson, Seyyed Hussein Khomeini, made the following statement:

I think generally it is not necessary to have a religious government. The people should decide and they themselves should run the country. It is not impossible for religious leaders to rule or reign, but it is not necessary. In our country, religious leaders have neither the merit nor the ability to run the country, therefore we need statesmen.

Despite these incidents, by mid-1981 events had begun moving too quickly, and Khomeini abandoned his balancing policy. Doubtless, the Ayatollah's sympathies had rested primarily with the religious extremists all along, but he joined them openly and decisively for two reasons. First, he was worried about Bani Sadr's flirtation with the military and especially with the Mujahedin-e Khalq. Most important, Khomeini maintained a special antipathy against the radical left. He carefully noted the huge demonstration of April 27 in Teheran, where the Mujahedin rallied over 100,000 supporters to protest regime repression. The more the Mujahedin gained in popularity and strength, the more concerned and involved Khomeini became. By June, he decided that it was time to strike a crippling blow against them.

Once Ayatollah Khomeini had cast his lot with the extremists, Iran became the scene of a bitter if undeclared civil war between radicals and extremists. During the last six months of 1981, violence and bloodshed became the order of the day, and the Ayatollah found himself losing both popularity and influence.

By the end of 1981, the internecine political conflict in Iran had hardened into internal war in which true believers faced off against one another. In this setting, the future of the country seemed to rest more and more in the hands of some kind of military rule. The disappearance of the moderate center, the increasing anarchy and violence, the worsening economic situation, and the inexperience of the latest round of government leaders brought closer the time when a new authoritarianism would appear in order to prevent the disastrous disintegration of a critically important and venerable member of the community of nations.

SYRIA: RETREAT INTO ISOLATION[10]

President Hafez Assad's regime is under periodic pressure from Muslim fundamentalists at home. His country could be at war with Israel at any moment. Relations with Jordan and Iraq, Syria's two closest Arab neighbors, are venomous; a diplomatic quarrel has broken out with France. The oil-rich Persian Gulf sheikdoms, angered by Syria's open support for Iran in the war with Iraq, threaten to cut off the financial aid that helps keep Syria's economy afloat. As these troubles have mounted, however, Syria has retreated into increasingly defiant isolation. "A very dangerous fortress-Syria mentality had developed," says one senior Western analyst in the country's capital. "Damascus is in the mood to tell everyone to go to hell."

At the moment, Damascus is girding for another round of war with Israel. Syria believes that Israel will follow up its withdrawal from the Sinai with a major assault on the Palestine Liberation Organization in Lebanon—a challenge that Syria cannot ignore. Recently, Syria moved elements of two armored brigades to forward positions in Lebanon's Bekaa Valley, presumably to take the

[10] Magazine article by Angus Deming and Ray Wilkinson, correspondents in Damascus. *Newsweek.* 99:61. My. 10, '82. Copyright, 1982, Newsweek, Inc. Reprinted by permission.

brunt of any initial Israeli thrust directed toward Damascus itself. Syria's strategy, apparently, would be to pin down the Israelis in Lebanon until Washington and Moscow imposed a cease-fire and a political settlement—or until Syria's Soviet patrons came to the rescue. Syria, which is equipped with advanced Soviet arms, appears to be moving toward even closer military ties with Moscow. Soviet VIP's, including the chief of the Soviet Air Force, have been in Damascus recently and Syrian President Hafez Assad has announced plans to visit Moscow soon. "Moscow seems to have made it clear," says one diplomat, "that it will not tolerate another defeat of Soviet equipment in the Middle East."

Syria is adamantly opposed to reconciliation with Egypt in the post-Sinai era. "The attempt to bring the regime of President [Hosni] Mubarak closer to the Arab ranks only serves the interests of American imperialism and Zionism," warns the government-controlled daily *Al Thawrah*. The Syrians, probably in alliance with the PLO, would not hesitate to block any future move to welcome Egypt back to the fold. Syrian officials talk as though everyone else were out of step. "Syria is the heart of the Arab world," says a senior government official in Damascus. "In war or peace, other nations cannot do without us."

Rivalry

Typically, Syria is the only nation in the Arab world to side openly with Iran in the Iran-Iraq war. It does so largely because of a blood feud with Iraq, the result of a bitter rivalry between the Syrian and Iraqi branches of the Baath Socialist Party. Syria vilifies Iraq's President Saddam Hussein as "the butcher of Baghdad" and openly plots his overthrow. Last month Syria closed the trans-Syrian pipeline through which Iraq had moved crude oil to Mediterranean refineries; the move cut Iraq's oil exports by 40 percent and reduced Iraq's foreign-exchange earnings by 15 percent. At the same time, Syria contracted to buy 8.7 million tons of Iranian crude over the next ten years at rock-bottom prices. Syria will re-export much of the Iranian oil, presumably at a markup. "Syria's alignment with Iran has turned Arab politics upside down," says one Western diplomat. "But from the Syrian point of view, in the short term it is a very attractive deal."

Syria's tendency to view the rest of the world with "colossal contempt," as one analyst puts it, could prove costly in the long run. Syria's relations with Jordan are so bad that Jordan has openly allied itself with Iraq. France has come close to severing diplomatic relations because of allegedly Syrian-inspired terrorist acts. Last month, after a car-bomb exploded outside a pro-Iraqi newspaper in Paris, killing two persons and injuring 45, France expelled two Syrian Embassy officials and recalled its own ambassador from Damascus. More damaging, Saudi Arabia and other Gulf states are reassessing the subsidy they pay Syria—said to total $1.5 billion a year—which enables Syria to maintain 22,000 "peace-keeping" troops in Lebanon.

Bodies

Thus far, Assad has outwitted his opponents—or has crushed them. Last February, when Islamic fundamentalists rose in rebellion in Hama, government troops sealed off the city and pounded it with artillery. In a month of savage fighting nearly 40 percent of the picturesque old city was reduced to rubble. The number of casualties may never be known, but trucks were used to dump bodies into mass graves, and as many as 15,000 men, women, and children may have died. Bulldozers carved roads where houses once stood, and the government appeared determined to make Hama an example to would-be plotters. "Hama," said one Syrian Cabinet minister, "provides us with a golden opportunity to practice urban renewal." If Assad is a ruthless leader, he also knows when to back off. "We'd all be in deep trouble if Assad left the scene," maintains one diplomat in Damascus. "We would probably get a bunch of very wild boys in power here then." The Mideast doesn't need any more of that particular sort than it has right now.

EDITOR'S INTRODUCTION

In his book *Living With the Bible*, former Israeli Defense Minister Moshe Dayan reveals both the mystical and rational roots binding Israelis to the land of Palestine, claiming that "love of homeland springs from the timeless verses of the Book of Books . . . " This link, combined with endurance and Zionist convictions, impelled the creation of the nation of Israel amid chaos and supported its survival in an exceedingly hostile environment. Dayan's prologue to his book is the first selection in this section. It is followed by an excerpt from the Foreign Policy Association's *Israel and the U.S,* which provides a history of Israel from the Balfour Declaration in 1917 to the Camp David accords in 1979.

Having the support of U.S. arms and money, Israel has sometimes been referred to as the "strongman" of the Middle East. In the third article, reprinted from *Current History,* Harold Waller discusses the development and evolution of Israeli foreign policy in the light of its vital security interests and describes the operation of the country's multi-party political system. The next article, from *Foreign Affairs,* is written by Yitzhak Shamir, Israel's Foreign Minister, who tells of his country's four wars in search of secure boundaries, concentrating on the conflict over Israeli claims to the West Bank. Denying that resolution of the Palestinian problem will lead to peace and aware of Israel's rejection by the Arab world, he maintains that Jordan *is* Palestine and that what Israel wants is recognition of its existence by the Arabs.

Israel's military occupation of the West Bank and acceleration of Jewish settlements on Arab land have exacerbated the Palestinian problem. In the fifth article, taken from the *Nation,* Boas Evron, an Israeli journalist, investigates the Zionist *paradox* between religion and nationalism. He casts doubt on the "idea of a dispersed nation with an age-old yearning for a homeland," suggesting instead that for many Diaspora Jews "Israel is one of their last choices for a destination." On the other hand, in line with Zionist expansionism, he thinks that granting full political and civil rights to the vanquished Palestinians on the West Bank would be in Israel's own national interest. Walter Goodman visited the Israeli occupied territories in the spring of 1982 and, in his firsthand report in the *New Leader,* he observed the harsh military occupation and the Palestinians as outsiders in their own land, but he was also impressed with West Bank "deserts turned into gardens."

Concerning Israel's authority over the West Bank, Michael Reisman, in his article in the *Nation,* sees what is called "belligerent occupation" of the Arab land. He measures government deportation, censorship, appropriation of land, and violation of human rights against international law and speculates on the question of just occupation of the West Bank or its annexation by Israel. In this connection, a *Commonweal* editorial, which is the final article in this section, probes the true reasons for Israel's June 1982 invasion of Lebanon ostensibly to destroy the Palestine Liberation Organization. Citing the vacillation and the labyrinthine character of Middle Eastern politics, the editorial suggests that Israel's real objective is annexation of the West Bank.

PROLOGUE[1]

The people of Israel were exiled from their land, but their land was never exiled from their hearts. In whatever country they dwelt throughout the nineteen Diaspora centuries, they yearned for their homeland, Israel. The Jordan and the Kishon were their rivers, Sharon and Jezreel their valleys, Tabor and Carmel their mountains, and the cities of their fathers were Jerusalem, Hebron, Bethel, and Samaria.

[1] From book entitled *Living With the Bible,* by Moshe Dayan. Prologue. Copyright © 1978, by Moshe Dayan. By permission of William Morrow & Company.

In 1937 the British government, which was then the mandatory power in Palestine, recommended the partition of the land of Israel into two states, Jewish and Arab. Under this proposal, the Jewish State was to include Galilee, the valleys and the coastal plain, but not the remaining territory which had been part of biblical Israel. Jerusalem and Mount Hebron were to be excluded.

This British partition proposal was hotly debated by the Jewish community, and I followed the discussion between our leaders with keen interest. David Ben-Gurion favored its acceptance. His friend Berl Katznelson, the leading Zionist theoretician in the country, urged its rejection. He argued that the nation of Israel cherished not only the parts of its land which it had settled by then, but also its age-old yearnings, not only 'its today but also its tomorrow,' and it should never agree to its division and abandon the hope of returning to its ancient homeland.

My own feelings were with Berl Katznelson. My heart responded particularly to his words on love of homeland:

What is its source? [he asked]. Is it the physical link with the soil our feet have trodden since childhood? It is the flowers which have delighted our eyes, the purity of the air we breathed, the dramatic landscape, the sunsets we have known? No, no. Our love of homeland springs from the timeless verses of the Book of Books, from the very sound of the biblical names. We loved an abstract homeland, and we planted this love in our soul and carried it with us wherever we went throughout the generations.

To one who was born in Israel, love of homeland was not an abstraction. The Rose of Sharon and Mount Carmel were very real to me, as were the sweet-scented blossom and the hills whose paths I climbed. Yet this was not enough. I was not content only with the Israel I could see and touch. I also longed for the Israel of antiquity, the Israel of the 'timeless verses' and the 'biblical names,' and I wanted to give tangibility to that too. I wished to see not only the River Kishon marking off the fields of Nahalal from those of neighboring Kfar Yehoshua; I wished also to visualize the biblical Kishon sweeping away the Canaanite chariot forces of Sisera.

My parents who came from another country sought to make the Israel of their imagination, drawn from descriptions in the Bible, their physical homeland. In somewhat the reverse way, I sought to give my real and tangible homeland the added dimension of historical depth, to bring to life the strata of the past which now lay beneath the desolated ruins and archaeological mounds—the Israel of our patriarchs, our judges, our kings, our prophets.

ISRAEL'S BACKGROUND[2]

The state of Israel was born out of conflict in the British mandate of Palestine. In the Balfour Declaration of 1917, the British viewed with favor the creation of a Jewish national home. But by the end of World War II, a financially pressed Britain was no longer willing to pay the cost of suppressing both Arab and Jewish nationalist revolt, and in 1947 it placed the question of Palestine before the United Nations. President Harry S. Truman, moved by the plight of the survivors of the Holocaust, which cost the lives of 6 million Jews, felt deeply that the Jewish people should have a nation to call their own. He therefore lobbied heavily, against the advice of many in his own State Department, for the approval in November 1947 of the UN's recommendation to partition Palestine into Arab and Jewish states. The Jewish Agency, which represented the Jewish community in Palestine, accepted the UN partition plan; the Arabs rejected it. Fighting in Palestine rapidly escalated. Israel declared its statehood on May 14, 1948, the eve of Britain's withdrawal from Palestine. The United States extended Israel recognition within minutes, followed two days later by the Soviet Union, which was happy to take a slap at British imperialism.

The new Jewish state was invaded the following day by armies from the neighboring Arab states of Syria, Egypt, Jordan and Iraq. In the struggle for its very existence, Israel had to rely on World War II surplus weapons and arms shipments from Czechoslovakia and France. The United States embargoed the sale of weapons to all combatants. Nonetheless, the U.S. public

[2] Excerpt from *Israel and the U.S.: Friendship and Discord.* a booklet by the Editors of the Foreign Policy Association.   p 3. Copyright, 1982. Foreign Policy Association, Inc. Reprinted by permission.

sympathized with Israel's uphill fight for survival. American Jewish groups donated $200 million to Israel in 1948 alone, and their aid contributed in no small measure to Israel's survival and triumph. The armistice lines of January 1949 left Israel in control of 78 percent of the former mandate of Palestine and divided the city of Jerusalem. The West Bank of the Jordan, including the walled Old City of Jerusalem with its holy sites sacred to three faiths, was annexed by Jordan in 1950. Egypt controlled the Gaza Strip—a 5-mile wide, 25-mile-long territory separating Israel's Negev desert from the Mediterranean.

After the war President Truman inaugurated a program of official U.S. aid to Israel with a $100 million loan from the U.S. Export-Import Bank. The United States, Britain and France rationed arms sales to the region, as they hoped to maintain the military balance and the fragile armistice between Israel and the Arab states.

Under the guidance of Secretary of State John Foster Dulles, the United States attempted to organize a Middle East defense organization. But the Arabs would not join if Israel were a member, and Dulles then tried to organize one without Israel. This step, coupled with Britain's agreement in 1954 to evacuate the Suez Canal, which links the Mediterranean and the Red Sea, distressed Israel. Egypt's 1955 arms deal with the Soviet bloc, and Dulles' refusal to sell arms to Israel, further increased Israel's sense of danger and isolation. After Egyptian President Gamal Abdel Nasser nationalized the Suez Canal Company in July 1956, the Israelis met in secret with the British and the French. The following October they launched a surprise strike against Egypt to topple Nasser. Israel seized the Sinai Peninsula, a sparsely populated desert.

The Suez adventure infuriated President Dwight D. Eisenhower. He had not been consulted beforehand, he disapproved of it, and the expedition's timing—in the midst of the Soviet suppression of Hungary—could not have been worse. Even as the United States condemned the Russian invasion of Hungary, its own allies' Suez expedition was undermining its credibility. Through a series of UN resolutions and blunt warnings, the United States engineered a cessation of hostilities and forced the French and the British, and finally the Israelis, to withdraw. In return, the Eisenhower Administration pledged to protect Israel's right of "innocent passage" through the Strait of Tiran and to insure that the Gaza Strip would not be used as a base for future raids against Israel.

Border tensions between Israel and the Arab states increased again in the spring of 1967. From Israel's point of view, the most serious step was Nasser's demand that the neutral UN Emergency Force, in place since 1957, leave its observation posts in the Sinai. UN Secretary General U Thant complied. Nasser also closed the Strait of Tiran, blocking Israeli ships' passage through the Gulf of Aqaba. Israel called on Washington to honor its 1956 pledge. But President Lyndon B. Johnson, burdened with the war in Vietnam, felt he could not act alone, and tried to organize an international flotilla to demonstrate free passage through the strait. The international plan collapsed.

Israel thereupon took its fate into its own hands and launched a preemptive attack. In the Six-Day War of June 1967 it quickly defeated the combined forces of Egypt, Jordan and Syria, and seized territories three times greater than its pre-1967 size, including the whole of the Sinai, the Gaza Strip, the West Bank of the Jordan River, the Arab section of Jerusalem, and Syria's Golan Heights. In the first flush of victory, Israel was prepared to return virtually all the territories, except Jerusalem and certain security points on the West Bank, to the Arab states in exchange for peace. Israeli Defense Minister Moshe Dayan spoke of waiting for a "phone call" from the Arabs to make peace. But the call never came.

The American public applauded Israel's triumph. The United States soon after became Israel's foremost military supplier, in part because France was no longer willing to sell it weapons. In 1968 President Johnson approved the first shipment to Israel of advanced F-4 fighter planes.

The United States at the same time had serious misgivings about Israeli policy. President Johnson declared that the United States could not accept the forcible and unilateral unification of Jerusalem by the Israelis. At the UN the United States voted in November 1967 for Security Council Resolution 242. This resolution, approved unanimously, called for Israel to withdraw "from territories occupied in the recent conflict" and called in turn for the Arab states to make peace with Israel and respect its "right to live in peace within secure and recognized boundaries free from threats or acts of force." The resolution was endorsed by Egypt, Jordan and Israel. But 242 was a deliberately ambiguous document: it did not specifically call for Israeli withdrawal from all occupied territories, and Israel maintains that withdrawal to its pre-1967 borders would contradict the resolution's provision for secure boundaries.

U.S. peacemaking efforts after the 1967 war, including the broad peace plan of U.S. Secretary of State William P. Rogers, were substantially based on Resolution 242. But the 1969 Rogers plan failed to win either Egyptian or Israeli support. The United States had little leverage with the Arabs, and it also saw little point in pressuring Israel, particularly when Israeli assistance seemed so valuable in deterring Syria from invading Jordan during the crisis of September 1970, when Jordanian troops expelled the PLO. U.S. strategy was to keep Israel militarily strong to deter future Arab attacks against it. Peacemaking efforts drifted.

The October War and Its Aftermath

The stalemate of no war and no peace ended abruptly on October 6—Yom Kippur—1973. Syria and Egypt achieved astonishing initial success in a coordinated surprise attack on Israel. Israel, after grave fears of impending defeat in the first days of the war gained the offensive and eventually defeated both Arab states. The war, however, pointed up Israel's vulnerability and extreme dependence on U.S. ammunition and weapons, some of which were airlifted to Israel after the war began. Israelis were deeply suspicious that the U.S. military airlift was intentionally delayed for several days in order to force Israel to accept U.S. terms for peace. Secretary of State Henry A. Kissinger bitterly denied this accusation.

The 1973 war also focused the world's attention anew on the Middle East because of the oil embargo which the Arab oil producers imposed on the United States and the Netherlands for supporting Israel. The embargo prompted panic buying, drove up prices, and resulted in the historic fourfold increase in the price of petroleum by the organization of Petroleum Exporting Countries (OPEC) between October 1973 and January 1974. The 1973 war also brought the superpowers to the brink of confrontation. When a UN cease-fire failed to stop the fighting, the Soviet Union informed Washington on October 24 that unless it agreed to the dispatch of a joint U.S.-Soviet peacekeeping force, Moscow would send its own airborne troops to enforce a cease-fire and prevent Israel's destruction of Egypt's Third Army. The White House in turn, ordered a worldwide U.S. military alert to signal the Russians that the United States would not tolerate Soviet intervention. Fortunately, the superpower crisis passed. But the war amply demonstrated that the West's economic health and the avoidance of general war depended on defusing the Arab-Israeli keg.

In his famous "shuttle diplomacy," Secretary of State Kissinger played the "honest broker" and negotiated troop disengagements in the Sinai (January 1974) and on the Golan Heights (May 1974). Negotiations on a second disengagement accord in the Sinai foundered in March 1975, and President Gerald R. Ford ordered a "total reassessment" of U.S.-Israeli relations in the light of what Kissinger viewed as Israel's lack of cooperation. A further Israeli withdrawal in the Sinai was finally achieved in September 1975, but only after the United States promised Israel future supplies of arms, economic aid, and oil—and pledged not to negotiate with the PLO until it recognized Israel's existence.

On entering office in 1977, President Jimmy Carter tried to reconvene a Middle East peace conference (adjourned since 1973) of all interested parties—including the Soviet Union—in Geneva. This effort was sidetracked in November 1977, however, by Egyptian President Sadat's historic visit to Jerusalem. Carter offered the good offices of the United States to Begin's and Sadat's bilateral peace effort, which the other Arab states boycotted. Through Carter's direct personal intervention at a 13-day summit of the three leaders at Camp David, Md. in September 1978, the United States achieved a breakthrough that pointed the way to the Egyptian-Israeli peace treaty of 1979. Israel agreed to return the whole of the Sinai, the last third of it in April 1982, in exchange for a peace treaty with Egypt. Israel and Egypt also agreed on negotiations aimed at achieving a self-governing authority to provide "full autonomy" for the Palestinians of the West Bank and Gaza. After five years of full autonomy, the parties, including the Palestinians, would agree on the final disposition of the West Bank and Gaza's territorial status.

Since the 1979 peace treaty, Egypt and Israel have strictly observed their agreement on the return of the Sinai, but the negotiations on the creation of a Palestinian self-governing authority have proven inconclusive. Egypt wants a large body of about 120 members with wide legislative and administrative authority. The Egyptians hope that this body will evolve someday into a Palestinian national government. Israel, on the other hand, wants to limit strictly the size and scope of any Palestinian council precisely because of fears that it will become the kernel of a Palestinian government and state. Israel would prefer a small, primarily advisory group of 15 members or so with its authority limited to municipal functions. Egypt and Israel remain far apart as well on the issues of Israeli settlements in the occupied territories, the control of land and water resources, and whose forces will maintain security during the five-year transition period. Also in dispute is whether the Arabs of East Jerusalem should be included in the autonomy plan. The original target date of May 1980 for Palestinian autonomy came and went; the negotiations broke off at the end of the Carter Administration.

ISRAEL'S FOREIGN POLICY CHALLENGE[3]

For years, Israel has been a focal point of United States interest in the Middle East, especially during the years since 1967. Although one can argue that the prominence accorded to that small state by the media and the government exaggerates its importance

[3] Magazine article by Harold M. Waller, associate professor of political science, McGill University. *Current History.* 81:18-21+. Ja. '82. Copyright 1982 by Current History, Inc. Reprinted by permission.

in the regional context, there is little doubt that it will continue to be a vital factor in future political developments. Now that it is possible to place the 1981 election in some perspective, it is appropriate to assess Israel's political condition, and specifically its foreign policy.

There are two key considerations involved in an understanding of the development and evolution of Israel's foreign policy. The first is the ideological factor, which is particularly important because of the intense ideological character of Israeli party politics. A more prosaic but no less important factor is the nature of the political system itself, wherein a Cabinet representing an intricately constructed coalition of often divergent parties assumes collective responsibility for decisions.

The ideological underpinnings of Israeli foreign policy are closely tied to the principles of political Zionism, with its nineteenth century European origins. All the important political parties in Israeli politics accept the notion that the Jewish people have a right to reestablish a polity in the biblical land of Israel, although there are wide variations in details.

The historical experience and Jewish consciousness that helped to influence Israeli foreign policymakers over the years since 1948 include the connection between ancient Israel's land and people and the contemporary Jewish people, the idea that all Jews belong to the Jewish people and are entitled to return to their land, and the centrality of Israel, especially in the aftermath of the Holocaust. Furthermore, skepticism about dependable outside support and the concern for simple survival have always been paramount in Israeli foreign policy because Israelis are convinced that the loss of a war might well signal the end of statehood and jeopardize the survival of the Jewish people.

Most of these basic principles have not changed much over the years, with the notable exception of the peace negotiations with Egypt. If anything, the Yom Kippur War of 1973 only reinforced an already existing Israeli unsecurity, which was further accentuated by the subsequent diplomatic isolation, the never ending condemnations from the United Nations and other international forums, and Israeli doubts about great power motivations. Ironically, even when Israel was seen as a very strong power, perhaps the strongest in the region, Israelis saw themselves as being in a far weaker position. The peace treaty with Egypt, however, brought about some major changes, because the possibility of coming to reasonable terms with an Arab enemy became plausible for the first time.

The treaty with Egypt marked a significant departure for Israel in other ways as well. Most of the early political leadership had not thought through the question of relations with the Arabs. They came to assume that they could expect only hostility from that quarter, and preferred to concentrate on strengthening the Jewish presence. Although there were various attempts to find a modus vivendi, developments under the British Mandate precluded amicable relations. By the time the Arabs invaded Israel in 1948, the assumption of Arab hostility had become a dominant strain in Israeli perceptions of the outside world. Even now that the peace treaty with Egypt is a reality, Israel's assumption of continued hostility in other Arab countries influences its foreign policy stance.

The second key consideration for an understanding of Israeli foreign policy is the way in which the political system operates. Because the members of the Knesset are elected in a pure proportional representation system with national lists, the parties and their announced principles become very important in determining policy outcomes. An individual voter cannot call an individual member of the Knesset to account, but as a voter he can take the party to task for not holding true to its promised intentions. The ideological nature of most parties may act as a constraint, because fundamental party positions often deal with matters central to foreign policy decisions. Such positions can easily become hardened over the years because they acquire a status similar to an article of faith.

Another relevant feature of the Israeli political system is its reliance on coalition governments, because no party has ever achieved an absolute majority in the Knesset. Coalition partners are represented in the Cabinet, which has the major responsibility for foreign policy and security decisions. The existence of a coalition that accepts the idea of collective responsibility implies voting in the Cabinet. Depending on the political and personal strength of the Prime Minister, unexpected outcomes may follow. Usually there is genuine debate and finally a vote in the Cabinet. But the Prime Minister and the Foreign Minister (and perhaps the Defense Minister) do not have a free hand on important issues and, in fact, are often bound by explicit Cabinet guidelines. When the governing coalition is formed, usually after protracted and complex bargaining and negotiation, a formal agreement spells out in some detail what policies the government will follow, including foreign policy.

In general, then, the structure and practices of the government tend to limit the flexibility of those formally charged with responsibility for foreign affairs. Insofar as they are strong leaders within their own parties they can usually obtain approval, but the diverse nature of the coalitions requires considerable deference to various partners; witness the designation of Interior Minister Yosef Burg, head of the National Religious party (NRP), as the chief negotiator for the autonomy talks.

At present, Begin has considerable latitude in foreign affairs, although he does not operate without restraints. Since his Likud is the major rightist party, he does not have to worry very much about attacks from further right, even though the small Tehiya party criticizes him from that perspective. From the left, the Labor Alignment has been sharply critical of several aspects of his policies toward the territories, most notably the relinquishing of the Sinai settlements near the international border and the basic concept of the autonomy plan. Presumably, Labor would prefer a new partition of western Palestine between Israel and Jordan to an autonomy plan for the West Bank and the Gaza Strip. But these criticisms are not enough to prevent Begin from proceeding with any chosen course of action. Labor also challenged aspects of two controversial actions in the summer of 1981, the destruction of the Iraqi nuclear reactor and the bombing of Palestine Liberation Organization (PLO) installations in Beirut, but with only marginal effect.

The Liberals within the Likud, which is itself an alignment of Begin's own Herut party and the Liberals, also constitute a potential check on Begin's flexibility, although their power is limited by the widely held perception that they could not succeed electorally without Begin. Hence, if they create too much difficulty in the Likud caucus they might face oblivion, forced to run under their own banner in the next election. On balance then, Begin has considerable flexibility with regard to foreign policy options. Were he to embark on a risky adventure or initiative, however, that situation would probably change.

In assessing Israel's current foreign relations, one must first turn to the domestic scene. Domestically, the salient event of 1981 was the surprising victory of the Likud in the June 30 parliamentary election. Actually Likud and Labor finished in a deadlock with 48 seats each in the 120-member Knesset, but Begin was the preferred choice for Prime Minister of the main smaller parties, so that a Labor-led coalition was simply not feasible.

Because of overconfidence and internal bickering, Labor failed to capitalize on an opportunity for a smashing victory, a prospect that seemed most likely through the winter and into the spring. Begin ran a clever campaign, utilized the powers of the government to great advantage in terms of both economics and foreign policy, and established a surprising rapport with the majority of Sephardic voters, particularly those of North African origin. Begin, who is certainly no less Polish in origin than Labor party leader Shimon Peres, was immensely popular among North African Jews, perhaps because of his deference to Jewish tradition, which contrasted sharply with the usual Labor insensitivity. As a result, Likud had a clear majority among Jewish voters, while the Labor totals were augmented by the votes of many Israeli Arabs. Thus the apparent closeness of the election is probably misleading. Most analysts believe that Labor is in a fundamentally weaker position politically than Likud, and events tend to bear this out.

Among the smaller parties, the National Religious Party (NRP) lost half its seats, causing a great deal of soul-searching among the party faithful, who perceive that their constituency may be drifting toward the Likud. The NRP also lost votes to an ethnic splinter group (Tami) led by Aharon Abuhatzeira but retained an influential role in government nonetheless because of the arithmetic of a coalition. The ultra-Orthodox Agudat Yisrael held its ground electorally and was rewarded handsomely when it joined the coalition under very favorable terms.

The most important observation about the election was the unusually high portion of the total vote garnered by the two leading parties (about 80 percent), which led some observers to believe that the country is moving toward a two-party system despite the limitation of proportional representation. If so, this is probably a healthy development, though the voters still seem reluctant to contemplate majority government.

After the election, Israel continued to be beset by internal conflict. Most of the issues are not new, including economic strategy and disparities between European and Oriental Jews. What the election did produce was a heightened concern over religious questions. Secular interests have accused Begin of making concessions to the religious elements in order to put his coalition together at the expense of the traditional status quo. The intense feelings on both sides, combined with the political reality of a government that can command only 61 seats out of 120, make it likely that religious differences will continue to plague the government. The specific issues are not terribly important (greater public Sabbath observance, more financial support for the religious sector), but the implications are taken very seriously. In essence, the religious groups want the state to be Jewish in a religious as well as in a national sense. Even though they recognize that the majority of Israelis will never practice Judaism as they do, they wish to maximize public observance. Secular Jews, in contrast, wish to maximize their individual liberty, which is often reduced by religious strictures.

Begin, who is beholden to the religious parties for political support, made a number of commitments to them in order to induce them to join the coalition, but does not seem disposed to accede fully to their demands. The threat of new elections has been most helpful to him. On the crucial question of determining the national and religious identification of Jewish converts from outside Israel who apply to immigrate, Begin has expressed support for the religious parties' legislative objectives but refuses to impose party discipline when the matter comes up for a vote. On a free vote, the measure is unlikely to pass.

Economically, Israel is still beset by the massive problems that emerged in the wake of the 1973 war. The country has so far managed to cope with the world's highest inflation rate, primarily by indexing all sorts of financial values. To North Americans who cringe as inflation rates climb into the low teens, it is impossible to understand how Israel can cope with rates 10 or 12 times higher. Yet until now the system has managed to function, and the economy seems reasonably prosperous, despite a continuing serious imbalance between exports and imports.

Although no Israeli can be untouched by economic problems, the great issues of war and peace and, more particularly, the ultimate disposition of the various territories now held by Israel continue to animate public and private discussions. The peace treaty with Egypt has enjoyed wide support, despite some misgivings regarding the complete return of Sinai. There . . . [was] some organized opposition to the final pullback in April, 1982, including people who are not personally involved in the Sinai settlements but are concerned about security questions. This movement has had relatively little impact. . . . Unless the Egyptian government changes course dramatically, it is unlikely that support for a reconsideration of the treaty obligations will become very strong. Nonetheless, Israelis will be giving careful thought to the implications of the treaty and the risks that are being undertaken for the sake of peace.

The West Bank presents an even more complex problem, because of the intensity and commitment of the settlers there and their supporters throughout Israel. They remain a small minority, but they cannot be overlooked or ignored politically. And they are often joined by a broader group of citizens who worry about a West Bank under hostile control. This broader group is a powerful check on policy. In fact, Begin or his successor could be faced with extremist opposition to his West Bank policies, operating outside the parliamentary framework. At present, the prospects for an agreement that would activate the extremist opposition appear slim, but as long as negotiations are in progress the situation is fluid.

Turning to foreign policy, Israel was badly shaken by Sadat's death, despite reassurances from the new leadership. The question, usually unposed, of what would happen to the peace with Egypt should Sadat die, had been in everyone's mind since Camp David. The question had to be answered sooner than had been anticipated. Sadat's blunt pronouncements, which were probably idiosyncratic, had reassured Israelis and contributed to a sense of well-being. The differences between Israel and Egypt over the autonomy plan were always substantial, but Sadat's attitudes and behavior encouraged optimism. Furthermore, Sadat's isolation from the rest of the Arab world, coupled with his American support, made the notion of an alliance, with Israel and Egypt as the cornerstone, a logical objective of United States policy. Egyptian President Hosni Mubarak's efforts to repair his country's severely diminished standing in the Arab world may invalidate much of this optimism. The changed situation is likely to make Israeli policymakers wary and less likely to take risks. That would mean a tough Israeli line at the autonomy talks and a reluctance to consider any initiatives.

Is is obvious that one of Israel's major foreign policy objectives in the post-Sadat period is to keep relations with Egypt on an even keel, to make sure that normalization proceeds apace, and to convince the Egyptians that, whatever their relationship with the rest of the Arab world, it is in their own interest to maintain peaceful relations with Israel. The months after the Israeli withdrawal from Sinai is completed will be particularly dangerous because of possible pressure on Egypt to nullify the effect of the treaty. If the autonomy negotiations have not been completed successfully by then, the continuing failure to agree could serve as a pretext for Egypt to retreat from its obligations. Thus both Begin and Mubarak have a great incentive to conclude the talks successfully before April, 1982, and thereby to eliminate the major points of disagreement between them. Unfortunately, each has a different interpretation of the critical points, which were deliberately left ambiguous in the Camp David accords. The difficulties in overcoming these differences cannot be minimized.

The pressure on both sides for accommodation on the autonomy plan is offset by the mutual desire not to offer new concessions during a time of great uncertainty. This places Begin in an extremely difficult situation: if he makes further concessions on the autonomy issue, even reciprocated concessions, he may have to accept defense and security risks that exceed the level he considers prudent. But if he holds firm and no autonomy agreement is concluded, he runs the risk that the peace with Egypt, at least in the sense of normalization, will be jeopardized. And the April 25, 1982, deadline poses a significant additional constraint on an already difficult situation.

Even while Sadat was alive, the normalization process had not been moving smothly. Many Begin-Sadat meetings dealt with Israeli grievances on this question, like the slow pace of tourism (which has primarily meant Israelis visiting Egypt), the negligible academic exchanges, and the disappointingly few intellectual and cultural interactions. Israel sees progress toward the normalization of relations as one test of Egyptian goodwill, the significance of which is all the greater now that a new government must be evaluated.

"Jordan Is Palestine"

On a matter that has bearing on the autonomy plan, Israel's government seems to be pursuing a new policy that is intended to complement it. The essence of the policy is the emphasis on the fact that "Jordan is Palestine." Of course, that country now known as Jordan was part of the original Palestine Mandate assumed by the British after World War I, although what was then called Trans-Jordan was severed from the rest of the Mandate in 1922 in order to establish a throne for the Hashemites. Moreover, most of Jordan's population is Palestinian. The Israeli objective is to identify Jordan with Palestine in order to reduce the pressure for a three-state solution. If it is agreed that a two-state solution (i.e., Israel and Jordan-Palestine, dividing the territory of the original Mandate and perhaps operating a joint condominium over some of that territory) is acceptable, negotiations become considerably easier, because both the Jewish and the Palestinian Arab peoples would have homelands. Demands for a third state sandwiched between Israel and Jordan have always been met with fierce opposition from Israel on the grounds of security and the threat to Israel's existence. Current speculation about the "Jordan is Palestine" gambit focuses on Defense Minister Ariel Sharon, who reportedly views the plan as a way to defuse PLO demands, with or without King Hussein.

Progress in gaining recognition that Jordan is Palestine would also take pressure off Begin with regard to the autonomy plan. There are indications that Begin had not thought through all the implications of the plan when he agreed to it at Camp David. Even if he were able to proceed with autonomy based on his own interpretation of what it would mean, the prospects of preventing the emergence of a new state in the autonomous area after the five-year transitional period would be dim. Therefore, Israel is looking beyond the five years as it negotiates the terms of transitional autonomy arrangements.

As for the PLO, the Begin government will resist recognition, probably even mutual recognition, on the grounds that this leopard at least cannot change its spots. The Palestine National Covenant clearly states objectives that are incompatible with the existence of the Israeli state, a point that all Israeli governments have taken most seriously. Consequently, Begin must try to negotiate an agreement on the West Bank and Gaza Strip with another group, an exceedingly difficult task.

When Saudi Arabia announced a "peace plan" during the summer of 1981, Israel did not find it very encouraging, both because of the content, which was unacceptable, and because of Israel's profound suspicion about Saudi motivation. Although Israel has recognized that Saudi Arabia is not radical as Arab regimes go, Israelis perceive the Saudis as extremely hostile and not constructive in terms of the peace process. In a speech last fall, Foreign Minister Shamir denounced Saudi Arabia as "one of the major obstacles to the Camp David process for peace" and described Prince Fahd's plan as "a perescription for the dismemberment of Israel, not for peace with Israel." Israelis would need to see concrete changes in Saudi attitudes before they could begin to take Saudi proposals seriously.

The other main concern of Israeli foreign policy is the relationship with the United States. Although the two countries have considerable affinity for each other, Israel has been concerned for the past several years that the courting of certain Arab countries by the United States will have a deleterious effect on Israel, especially were open warfare to recur, but even in the context of peace negotiations. Begin's response has been to stress Israel's value to

the United States as a reliable and valuable ally, as the only democratic country in the region, one which can guarantee stability and
policy continuity, and as a military force in the broadest sense, one
that could be a most helpful contributor to the realization of
American strategic objectives. The challenge to the United States
is to find Arab countries other than Egypt that are willing to participate in an informal alliance that includes Israel, despite the
hostility that accompanies the local Arab-Israeli conflict. A com-
plication for the United States is that the Egyptians were crucial
to the American conception of the strategic alliance; it is too soon
to predict whether Mubarak will be as solid a base for the enterprise as his predecessor was thought to be.

For its part, Israel must seek ways to gain the favor of the
United States in order to balance the occasions when it antago-
nizes the American government. The dispute over the United
States sale of Airborne Warning and Control System (Awacs)
planes to Saudi Arabia is a case in point. Begin felt that his nation's security interests did not allow him to stand idly by while
the package went through. Yet although much of the opposition
to the sale was inspired by concerns other than the security of Israel, the main responsibility for the opposition was assigned to Israel
in the American media and by many government officials, from
President Ronald Reagan on down. The heavy commitment of
presidential prestige meant that Israel was bound to lose politically, regardless of the outcome in the United States Congress.

In general, Israel under Begin seems committed to doing what
it considers necessary in foreign policy, regardless of the costs.
This results from an Israeli conviction that other nations do not
share the same problems, cannot see things from the same perspective, and may not care even if they understand the issues. Israel's
policy continues to be predicated on the belief that its vital security
interests are always at risk and that the basic responsibility for defense against those risks is in Israel's own hands.

ISRAEL'S ROLE IN A CHANGING MIDDLE EAST[4]

Traditionally, the twin goals of Israel's foreign policy have always been peace and security—two concepts that are closely interrelated: Where there is strength, there is peace—at least, shall we say, peace has a chance. Peace will be unattainable if Israel is weak or perceived to be so. This, indeed, is one of the most crucial lessons to be learned from the history of the Middle East since the end of the Second World War—in terms not only of the Arab-Israel conflict, but of the area as a whole.

The Middle East is a mosaic of peoples, religions, languages and cultures. Although the Muslim-Arab culture is predominant, it has not produced any homogeneity. A vast number of currents—religious and political—are vying with each other, cutting across political borders. The region is permanently in ferment, and frequently unrest flares up in violence, terror, insurrection, civil strife and open and sometimes prolonged warfare. The surprise invasion of a weakened Iran, still in the throes of the Khomeini upheaval, by neighboring Iraq, whose armed forces have been substantially beefed up by the Soviet Union, is perhaps the most dramatic and the most obvious example, but there are of course many others.

The most remarkable feature, in our context, of these chronic manifestations of unrest and belligerence is the fact that the great majority of them have nothing to do with Israel or with the Arab-Israel conflict. There were some outsiders, 20 and 30 years ago, who sincerely, but out of ignorance, believed that a solution of the Arab-Israel conflict would lead to regional stability and open a new era of progress. Nothing could be further from the truth. There have, it is true, been four major wars between Israel and its Arab neighbors. However, a full count of the instances of trouble and strife, both domestic and international, in North Africa and Western Asia, would show that the overwhelming majority have no connection whatsoever with the Arab relationship to Israel.

[4] Magazine article by Yitzhak Shamir, Israel's Foreign Minister. *Foreign Affairs.* 68:789-801. Spring '82. Reprinted by permission of *Foreign Affairs.* Copyright 1982, Council on Foreign Relations, Inc.

The Palestinian Problem

A more recent version of the old theory that the Arab-Israel conflict is the root of all the trouble in this region is the contention that the solution of the "Palestinian problem" is an absolute condition to any progress towards peace and stability.

The term, "the Palestinian problem" is deliberately flexible and lends itself to several simultaneous interpretations. One is humanitarian and focuses on the Palestinian Arabs displaced in 1948, whose plight should be alleviated, if not resolved, by economic means. Another interpretation is quasi-humanitarian, quasi-political. It maintains that there is a Palestinian people, not just refugees in the humanitarian sense, and since they have no home (after all, there is no country called Palestine), justice requires they should be provided a homeland in some portion of the land once called Palestine, alongside of Israel. The third interpretation is rejectionist and politicidal. According to this theory, the right to that land which was once called Palestine belongs exclusively to those who today call themselves Palestinians (by which they mean Palestinian Arabs). This right, the theory holds, should first be universally recognized, title to the land should be "restored" to them, and they should be allowed to decide whether and under what terms to coexist with a truncated Israel or insist on its dissolution as a distinct state.

These definitions are not precise, and there are variations and combinations. Arab spokesmen have taken to making obscure references to "the rights of the Palestinian people," using variations on the above themes, all as a means of masking their rejection of Israel and of its right to exist as a permanent, viable entity in the Middle East. The standard-bearer of the totality of Arab attitudes against Israel's existence is the Palestine Liberation Organization(PLO). Entrusted with the task of serving as a spearhead of the Arab action against Israel, its leaders have perfected the use of a wide range of themes to suit their tactical needs in their terrorist and propaganda war against Israel. Hence, outsiders who voice support of the solution of "the Palestinian problem" would do well to adopt much more precise language, lest they discover that they were unwittingly providing encouragement to the proponents of Israel's elimination.

On its part, Israel has addressed itself to the substance of the problem squarely and comprehensively with a sincere desire to contribute to a fair and just solution of the legitimate aspects of this problem.

On the subject of a political entity, a homeland for the Arabs of the former British-mandated territory of Palestine, the facts speak for themselves. The state known today as the Kingdom of Jordan is an integral part of what once was known as Palestine (77 percent of the territory); its inhabitants therefore are Palestinian—not different in their language, culture or religious and demographic composition from other Palestinians. No wonder, then, that Palestinian Arab leaders of all political persuasions have on numerous occasions declared that Jordan and Palestine are identical, and that Jordanians and Palestinians are one and the same. It is merely an accident of history that this state is called the Kingdom of Jordan and not the Kingdom of Palestine.

As a result of political decisions, military conflict and movements of population over a period of some 30 years (1920 to 1950), Palestine was effectively partitioned into two parts. Palestinian Arabs have exclusive domain over Trans-Jordan, or eastern Palestine, while Palestinian Jews form a majority of Cis-Jordan, or 23 percent of the original Palestine, comprising Israel within the pre-June 1967 armistice lines, Judea, Samaria and the Gaza district. The reintroduction of the term "Palestinian" and its exclusive application to Arabs of Cis-Jordan (the "West Bank") is, therefore, a semantic exercise and a calculated maneuver designed to back a new claim to the entire area of western Palestine and to undermine the legitimacy of Israel. As for the humanitarian aspect of the dislocation of population resulting from the Arab wars on Israel, it is time for the international community to address a call to the Arab governments, especially those with large financial resources at their disposal, to extend their help to their brethren, as Israel did for the close to a million Jews from Arab lands who fled to Israel as a result of the same conflict.

Reduced to its true proportions, the problem is clearly *not* the lack of a homeland for the Palestinian Arabs. That homeland is Trans-Jordan, or eastern Palestine. There are, however, 1.2 million Palestinian Arabs living in the territories which have been administered by Israel since 1967 in Judea, Samaria and Gaza. Their status and problems were discussed at great length at Camp David. The granting of sovereignty to those areas was ruled out by Israel. A second Palestinian Arab state to the west of the River Jordan is a prescription for anarchy, a threat to both Israel and Jordan, and a likely base for terrorist and Soviet penetration. Hence, it was finally resolved at Camp David to implement an Autonomy Plan for the inhabitants of those areas, on a five-year interim basis. The proposal was made by Israel and accepted by the other partners of the Camp David accords, Egypt and the United States. It is not intended as the ultimate solution of the problems represented by these areas and their inhabitants, but as an interim arrangement designed to achieve two objectives: (a) to allow the Arab inhabitants of these areas the fullest feasible freedom in running their own lives, and (b) to create optimal conditions of peaceful coexistence between Arab and Jew.

Israel has made it clear, at Camp David and since, that it has a claim to sovereignty over Judea, Samaria and Gaza. In order, however, to keep the door open to a solution that will be acceptable to the parties, as envisaged at Camp David, Israel has deliberately refrained from exercising its rights under this claim. The claim will undoubtedly be presented at the end of the five-year interim period, and, while it is realized that there will be a similar claim on the Arab side, by that time one would hope that the kind of atmosphere will have been created that will make it possible to reach an agreement involving a solution acceptable to both sides. It should be clearly understood, therefore, that just as Israel is refraining from pushing its own solution at this time, by the same token the Arab side must refrain from pushing now for measures or the adoption of principles (such as self-determination, an embryo parliament in the autonomous territories, and the like), that would clearly fall beyond the parameters of Camp David and that would tend to prejudge the ultimate outcome of the negotiations on the final status of these areas. Autonomy, in other words, must be allowed to perform the function it was intended to perform— namely, to serve as an interim arrangement, pending the ultimate solution that is to be addressed at a later stage.

Meanwhile, Israelis and Arabs are learning to coexist in Judea, Samaria and Gaza—ultimately the best way to reconciliation and peace. Israelis will continue to reside in those areas. As in the past, this will not be done, of course, at the expense of the Arab inhabitants and their property. But, as Judea and Samaria constitute the heartland of the Jewish people's birth and development as a nation, Israel will not be party to a design that would deny Jews residence in those areas.

No less important, the Israeli presence in these areas, both civilian and military, is vital to Israel's defense—as should be abundantly clear against the background of the recent history of the region and of Israel's patent inability to maintain a large standing army on its borders. The defunct pre-1967 armistice lines—which for nearly 20 years proved to be a prescription for chronic instability and warfare—have long since ceased to have any relevance in the context of the search for a viable Middle East peace. Certainly, Israel will not entertain any notion of a return to those lines or anything approximating them. On this point there is, in Israel, virtually universal agreement.

A final word on the Palestinian subject. There are some, no doubt well-intentioned but largely unaware of some very important facts, who have proposed that Israel negotiate with the PLO. They point to the absence of any organized voice, other than the PLO, representing "the Palestinians" and to the existence of ostensibly moderate elements in that organization that may be encouraged to seek a political solution that would include recognition of Israel.

The real problem is not whether to deal with the PLO or not, but whether it would serve any useful purpose whatsoever. Even if one were to overlook their bloodthirsty modus operandi, their subservience to Soviet aims and their key role in international terror, the PLO's very raison d'être is the denial of Israel's right to exist, thinly veiled behind the cover of an ostensibly legitimate call for Palestinian statehood. The very act of granting the PLO a status—any status—in the political negotiations would be self-defeating. It would elevate its standing from that of a terrorist organization to that of a recognized aspirant to a totally superfluous political entity. Hence, association of the PLO with any aspect whatsoever of the political process and the propects of peace are mutually exclusive.

Camp David Accomplishments

In the course of arduous negotiations at Camp David, the obstacles to peace with Israel were finally removed when Egypt broke away from the PLO-rejectionist platform on the Palestinian issue. The demand for a second Palestinian Arab state—one major obstacle—was set aside, in favor of an attempt at coexistence through the Autonomy Plan. Another hurdle was cleared with the unequivocal acceptance of Israel by Egypt and the undertaking of the steps necessary to normalize relations between the two states.

By the beginning of May 1982, implementation of the territorial aspects of the Egypt-Israel Treaty will have been completed and the former international border between the two countries reestablished. The normalization of relations between Egypt and Israel will enter a new phase.

On its part, Israel will do everything it can to ensure that the peace treaty with Egypt will serve as a solid base from which to expand the peace process toward a wider circle of participants. This can be achieved only by means of an Israel-Egypt partnership that is encouraged by active U.S. participation. It has a chance of success, provided that no alternative proposals and plans other than the Camp David accords are introduced into the process. No one is so naive as to believe that this is a goal which will be easily attained. But this combination of states, working together toward a worthy and vital objective, has already proved its capacity to overcome obstacles and make progress. Together, they are a formidable force for stability that cannot be bypassed by any factor in the Middle East. In order for this policy to bear fruit, much patience and persistent effort are required.

Israel perceives the Camp David accords as a process and a program of action that may take considerable time to reach full fruition. Steps taken in this process until now should be seen as deposits on a long-term installment plan. Both Israel and Egypt have made commitments at the bilateral level of relations and beyond. Hence it is mischievous and destructive to imply that Camp

David has run its course and other avenues should be explored. Such an attitude—particularly when displayed by governments that refused or hesitated to support the accords—is no less than cynical.

Those who have hesitated to voice their support and offer their contribution to buttressing the Egypt-Israel peace because of opposition to it by the rejectionist Arab governments have committed a serious blunder. If, God forbid, the first step toward Arab-Israel accommodation were to falter or fail, it would take the entire region back to a situation of sustained deadlock, if not belligerency. Moreover, it would serve as proof that the Arab world as a whole is not ready for peace. The chances, then, for a renewal of the peace effort would be drastically reduced. No one, least of all Israel, would be willing to take the slightest risk in order to re-energize the process. The rejectionists and the terrorists would applaud, but the interests of those who shortsightedly turned their backs on Camp David would, in all likelihood, be exposed to grave danger in a deteriorating situation. After three decades of hostility and strife, the process of peace and normalization must be given a chance to take hold and bear fruit. In time, it should have a beneficial impact on other issues, beyond the strictly bilateral Israel-Egypt level.

The magnitude of Israel's sacrifice for the achievement of the peace treaty has not been given proper recognition by the international community. From 1968 onward, Israel invested $17 billion in the Sinai Peninsula—in airfields, military installations, development of oilfields, infrastructure, towns and farm villages. The cost of the military redeployment to the Negev is estimated at $4.4 billion. Beyond the financial burden, and the strategic significance of the withdrawal from Sinai, the uprooting of several thousand Israelis who built their homes in the townships and villages along the eastern edge of Sinai is a traumatic event that has made a deep imprint on the entire nation.

With the transfer of the Sinai Peninsula to Egyptian sovereignty and the normalization of relations with Egypt under the peace treaty, Israel has gone a long way toward implementing the provisions of the 1967 U.N. Security Council Resolution 242. The Sinai Peninsula, it should be remembered, covers more than 90 percent of the territory that came into Israel's possession in the Six-Day War. Thus Israel has demonstrated, through concrete action and considerable risk and sacrifice, that it seeks peace and coexistence with its neighbors. It is now up to its neighbors to come forth with a similar demonstration of peaceful intent and readiness.

The Golan Heights

On December 14, 1981, Israel decided to abolish the military administration over the Golan Heights that was established after the 1967 Six-Day War and to apply Israeli law, jurisdiction and administration to that area.

Ever since 1948, the Syrian army had, from the Golan Heights, intermittently shelled and sniped at civilian targets in the valley in northeastern Israel. A 700-square-mile strip of the Heights was captured by Israel in the course of the Six-Day War of June 1967. The area was again the scene of heavy fighting during the 1973 Yom Kippur War, when the Syrians launched their surprise attack in an effort to drive Israel from the Heights and continue their push into the Galilee. Israel's possession of the Heights was a crucial factor that prevented the Syrian tanks from invading Israel, delaying them up on the plateau until reinforcements could be rushed to the Golan. In the course of the Israeli counterattack, the Israel Defense Forces captured a large additional area, coming to within some 25 miles of the Syrian capital of Damascus.

In May 1974, in an effort to achieve the beginning of an accommodation with the Syrian Government, Israel's then Prime Minister Golda Meir agreed to return to the Syrians, unilaterally, the entire area it had captured in the Yom Kippur War, plus the town of Kuneitra, which had been occupied in 1967. This gesture was undertaken, through the good offices of U.S. Secretary of State Henry Kissinger, in the context of a disengagement agreement. It was designed to facilitate progress towards a more stable political agreement and make possible the return of civilian life on both sides of the cease-fire lines.

The Syrian Government, however, chose to revert to its former hostile and belligerent posture. It rejected all negotiation with Israel and refused to accept U.N. Security Council Resolution 242. It did not permit the return of civilians to Kuneitra. It spearheaded the Arab Rejectionist Front against Israel and gave military and political support to various PLO terrorist groups, especially those that specialized in bomb outrages against Jewish targets in Europe. President Hafiz al-Assad left no doubt with regard to his intentions when he stated on December 13, 1981, that "even if the PLO were to recognize Israel, Syria would not be able to recognize it." In the face of this total denial of Israel and of accommodation with it, a broad national consensus developed in Israel that we should not return the Golan Heights to Syria under any circumstances. After 14 years, Israel decided to give formal expression to this position by an act of law.

Since Syrian leaders have repeatedly stated that they would refuse to make peace even if the Golan Heights were to be returned to their possession, it is simply erroneous to contend that Israel's Golan law has added an obstacle to peace with Syria. Now as before, Israel remains ready to negotiate a peace treaty with Syria without prior conditions.

Arab-Israeli Contacts

The circumstances surrounding Israel's rebirth in which the entire Arab world rejected what it chose to regard as an alien entity, have been undergoing a subtle change. The ostracizing of the Jewish State, coupled with periodic warfare, implanted in many minds a picture of total polarization between two hostile camps. The reality was different, especially since the 1967 Six-Day War, but the change was barely noticed. Hence, President Sadat's visit to Jerusalem in November 1977 came as a total surprise to the outside world.

Behind the scenes, however, many bridges had already been extended across the wide gulf separating Arab and Israeli. After June 1967, Israel administered areas inhabited by more than a million Arabs, many of whom had close connections with the neighboring states. The bridges remained, even expanded, and an unofficial human relationship developed. At the same time, clandestine contacts between Israel and leading personalities in several Arab states were maintained on a continuing basis. Without them, the late President Sadat's first visit to Jerusalem would not have been possible. Some prominent Arabs visited Israel incognito. Thousands of nationals of Arab states who were related to Arabs residing in Israel-controlled territories were permitted to visit their relatives, and most of them took advantage of the opportunity to tour Israel and meet with Israelis.

Beyond the expanding personal contacts, Israel, as a Middle Eastern country, was drawn into growing involvement in international relationships that had no direct bearing on the Arab-Israel level. Israeli governments have studiously refrained from intervening in the internal affairs of Israel's neighbors. But Israel could not maintain a disinterested stance when conflicts between its neighbors threatened its own security or increased the danger of upsetting a tenuous regional balance.

Thus, Israel, in coordination with the United States, acted in September 1970 to deter a Soviet-sponsored Syrian invasion of Jordan. In 1975, Israel was involved in an American-sponsored attempt at defining the limits of Syrian intervention in Lebanon. As a result of the Syrian invasion of Lebanon, the continuing threat of a total Syrian annexation of that hapless country and the terrorist attacks from southern Lebanon, Israel was drawn into the Lebanese situation.

The crowning event in a growing Israeli involvement in regional realities was, of course, the Egypt-Israel peace and the opening of the borders between the two countries. We are aware of strong voices, in some Arab countries, pressing Egypt to close its borders with Israel once the last Israeli has departed from Sinai. The message being beamed to Cairo runs along these lines: "We understand you had to conclude a treaty, establish embassies, and open the borders, because these were the only means of restoring Sinai to Arab sovereignty. From this point on, however, it would be treasonable to the Arab cause for Egypt to continue this relationship with the Zionist enemy. We will welcome you back to the Arab fold only if you reestablish the wall around Israel and resume the siege." Egypt has rejected this message and stated clearly that it will not resume relations with the other Arab states at the expense of peace with Israel. There are signs that some Arab governments are attuning themselves to this reality, in spite of their continued rejection of Israel on the ideological level. Elsewhere in the Arab world, the rejectionist spirit is as vibrantly negative as ever.

Of course, it will be up to Egypt's leadership to contend with the rejectionists and show them the way to breach the psychological barrier behind which they are entrenched. Whatever the outcome of this test, I am convinced that, sooner or later, Israel will establish relations with other Arab capitals. I will not rule out even Damascus among those capitals. Such developments are typical of paradoxical Middle Eastern realities, which outsiders find so difficult to digest. Accommodation with Israel by some will be accompanied by sustained total hostility to Israel by others. Those defined by the West as moderates are not necessarily so. Plans and proposals launched on occasion by these supposedly moderate countries—such as the Saudi eight-point plan of last summer—are often designed, in reality, to reduce Israel to a situation of defenselessness.

Thus, within the context of a powerful, basically unchanging ideological rejection of Israel, there are two conflicting currents coursing through the Arab world. One—which is, as of now, the prevailing current—rejects the Jewish State wholly and without reservation, in theory and in practice. The other—only just beginning to crack the surface of developments in the Middle East—accepts the fact of Israel's existence and is ready, in some sort of pragmatic fashion, to come to terms with that existence. Israel is learning to live with this reality, and to try to build on the hope that, in the course of time, this pragmatism can be developed into something more permanent and more meaningful.

International Involvement in the Conflict

A crucial role in determining the future direction of events in the region can be played by forces and influences outside the region.

The history of the involvement of foreign governments in Middle Eastern politics is not a happy one. Attracted by the strategic importance of the region and, more recently, by its immense natural resources and bank deposits, most governments have sought to apply a political gloss to their perceived economic interests by making political statements on the Arab-Israel issue in response to Arab pressures.

The internationalization of the conflict between Israel and its Arab neighbors has proved futile. For the Arab governments, for a long time, it served as a means of mobilizing international pressure on Israel, imposing a solution on it and evading the need for recognition and peace with Israel. Camp David has dealt a death blow to this course of action and, with it, to the notion that a viable Arab-Israel peace can be negotiated in a framework such as the defunct Geneva Conference. In particular, the late President Sadat demonstrated that Israel can be dealt with directly, with meaningful and far-reaching results.

Nevertheless, the Soviet Union has not given up on the "Geneva approach" to Middle East problems. Moscow in recent years has been steadily increasing its identification with the Arab Rejectionist Front and the PLO. Notwithstanding protestations to the contrary by its spokesmen, it has aided and abetted the Arab cause against Israel's existence. Soviet political and ideological support for Arab extremism against Israel has found expression in treaties of friendship it has concluded with Syria, Iraq and the People's Democratic Republic of Yemen, in which the U.S.S.R. joined in the obscene castigation of Zionism. Arab hopes of exercising the military option against Israel would not have been sustained as they are if not for the immense supplies of sophisticated offensive military supplies from Russia. The Soviet government has steadily increased its political and military support of the PLO in spite of, or perhaps because of, this organization's central role in international terror and its declared aim of destroying Israel and its population. This totally one-sided stand by the Soviet Union is compounded by its policy of boycotting Israel, and of persisting in its non-relations with Israel since 1967.

Soviet actions demonstrate clearly that the Soviet Union is opposed to peace in the Middle East, is bent on expanding its pres-

ence and influence in the region at the expense of regional
stability, and has no problem in the choice of means to achieve its
objective. Public opinion is far from being a factor in Soviet deci-
sionmaking.

The Soviets will persist in their negative, obstructive role so
long as local governments seek its support against Israel and continue to place their faith in the military option. Once those Arab
governments decide that peace is more important and will better
serve their own interests, the Soviet role will, of necessity, dimin-
ish, and the peace camp will expand and encompass a wider circle
of participants. It follows that the massive supply of arms by
the West to governments in the region, in competition with the
U.S.S.R., directly conflicts with the interests of stability and the
chances of peace in our region. The Soviets, in any case, have demonstrated again and again that they are capable of matching or
outdoing any Western arms supply, both in quantity and in sophistication.

Other powers have not resisted the temptation to exploit local
conflicts and domestic insecurity for the purpose of selling immense quantities of arms to Middle Eastern governments. The influx of so much military equipment has become a prime source
of danger and even greater instability in the region. Since 1980,
the Arab "confrontation states" have concluded arms deals worth
approximately $30 billion. It is a most unfortunately chosen
means of recycling petrodollars. It cannot, by any stretch of the
imagination, enhance moderation or contribute to a better and
more peaceful Middle East. It places an impossible burden on Israel's shoulders.

In contrast to the other superpower, the United States has a
paramount interest in peace and stability in the Middle East. The
congruence of interests between Israel and the United States has
forged an alliance that has proved to be a formidable factor in promoting these goals. The Camp David accords are an outstanding
product of this joint endeavor. America's continued and undeviat-
ing support of those accords represents the only way to assure
progress toward regional stability and peace.

Normalization of relations with Israel will undoubtedly contribute to the prospects of peace in our region. This applies equal-

ly to the African states that broke off diplomatic ties with Israel, at the behest of Egypt and other Arab countries, in the wake of the Yom Kippur War. The ostensible reason for the break was the occupation of African territory—the Sinai Peninsula—by Israel. The peace treaty with Egypt should have removed this obstacle to normalization, and indeed we have been informed that there is a desire on the part of African governments to restore those relations.

A number of Arab governments have been making efforts to thwart the resumption of relations with Israel, using threats and financial inducements. Our experience with African nations has shown that such attempts on African integrity and pride tend to backfire. We hope and expect that Black Africa will assert its independent course and reject such attempts at dictating its policies. For more than a decade, Israel maintained a close and warm relationship with most governments in sub-Saharan Africa. It was a fruitful, practical and mutually satisfying relationship, in spite of Israel's limited capacity to finance technical assistance and cooperation programs. It can be resumed at any time, at least insofar as Israel is concerned.

Steps to Insure Peace

Peace is fundamental to Israel's way of life, and Israel's determination to achieve it is permanent. Security is a vital guarantee of the viability and maintenance of peace. Together these two objectives provided the conceptual framework that produced the Camp David accords, and the march along this road must continue unabated.

A program for continued action to secure regional stability and peace must originate from the countries and governments that will have to implement the peace and live by it. Israel believes that it should include the following elements:

1. Negotiations between Israel and each of its neighbors, aimed at agreement on a just and lasting peace, laid out in formal peace treaties, that would provide for the establishment of normal diplomatic, economic and good-neighborly relations.

2. Recognition of the sovereignty and political independence of all existing states in the region, and of their right to live in peace within secure and recognized boundaries, free from threats or acts of force, including terrorist activity of any kind.

3. Autonomy for the Arab inhabitants of Judea, Samaria and the Gaza district for a five-year interim period, as set forth in the Camp David accords, and deferment of the final determination of the status of these areas until the end of this transitional period.

4. Restoration of the full independence of Lebanon, through the withdrawal of Syrian and PLO forces from Lebanese territory.

5. Negotiations, among all the states of the Middle East, aimed at declaring the region a nuclear-weapons-free zone, for the security and well-being of all its inhabitants.

ISRAEL AFTER ZIONISM[5]

Before he founded Zionism, Theodore Herzl, that quintessential assimilated Jew, had a wonderful idea for the solution of the "Jewish problem": all Jews should convert simultaneously to Christianity, and the problem would fade away. Zionism was essentially the same solution. If Jews had a country of their own, like other peoples, they would cease to be "Jews," and the problem would fade away.

There is, however, a basic difference between the two solutions. The first solution was based on the assumption that only the barrier of religion kept Jews from full participation in Christian European civilization. The second solution assumed that Jews were basically a nation, and that religion was only one aspect of their identity. Unlike other nations, the Jews lacked a land of their own, making them "abnormal" and causing the unpleasant traits that anti-Semites ascribed to them (there was a surprising corre-

[5] Magazine article by Boas Evron, Israeli writer and commentator for *Yediot Aharonot*, a leading daily in Israel. *Nation*. 233:597-600. D. 5, '81. Copyright, 1981, by The Nation Magazine. Reprinted by permission.

spondence between some anti-Semitic stereotypes and the traits that the early Zionists purported to find in Diaspora Jews). Religion was perceived as a "protective covering" assumed by the nation during the Exile for the purpose of self-preservation. Once the nation was reassembled in its homeland, Jews would achieve dignity and security, and be defended by their own army. No longer would they need the protective covering of religion; the real Jewish culture would blossom forth, revealing "the true Jewish essence."

But now, more than a century after the founding of Zionism in Czarist Russia, eighty-five years after Herzl wrote *Der Judenstaat,* thirty-three years after the establishment of the state of Israel, historical developments have called into question most of these articles of faith.

The opposition to their ideas that Herzl and other early Zionists encountered from the outset among nearly all orthodox Jews should have warned them that something was wrong. These religious Jews did not find their existence "a problem," as did Herzl and his freethinking colleagues, nor did they consider themselves "abnormal." They believed that they were in exile, in the sense of living in an unredeemed historical world awaiting the Messiah, much like fundamentalist Christians consider themselves to be living in a state of original sin awaiting the Second Coming. And when they went to Palestine, they went as religious pilgrims to a holy place, not as pioneers bent on founding a new nation. To the orthodox Jew, the worship of God exists for its own sake; it is a sacrilege to view it as a means to a secular end, even if that end is the preservation of a people. Jews have a meaning only as servants of God, not as an ethnic group.

The Zionists were wrong. Religion was not a substitute for nationalism. Religion was positive, self-determined, unequivocal. Nationalism, however, was an anchor of identity for the Jew who had lost his religion. Nationalism was in some ways a Jewish reaction to rejection by the non-Jewish environment. It was a frustrated assimilation.

The issues raised in these long-ago debates have not been resolved by the passage of time. Rather, the Zionist "solution" has proved to be faulty on several counts.

First, a majority of the Jewish people did not wish to emigrate from North and South America to the Jewish homeland, thus casting doubt on the idea of a dispersed nation with an age-old yearning for a homeland. There has always been a dedicated Zionist hard core, and this was the group that founded Israel, led it and governed it. But many Jews go to Israel simply because they have nowhere else to go. When they do have the choice, as in the case of Jewish emigrants from the Soviet Union, they prefer America. Indeed, most Jews leave their countries only under pressure, and Israel is one of their last choices for a destination. The continuing Diaspora is thus a matter of preference, not of necessity.

Second, the promise of Israel as a "haven for the Jewish people" has been proved false. Apart from occasional outbreaks of anti-Semitism elsewhere in the world, Israel is the only country (except Argentina and the Soviet Union) where being a Jew is dangerous, and it is the only Jewish community in the world that calls on other Jews to save it from "another Holocaust," a threat its founding was supposed to avert.

Third, the establishment of Israel was supposed to make the Jewish people economically self-sufficient and more productive. Jews would have their own national economy, with a full range of occupations open to them. The Israelis did indeed create a national economy, and quite a modern one at that, but the country is sinking deeper and deeper into foreign indebtedness and has been dependent since its inception on the largess of Jews abroad and on aid from the U.S. government.

The greatest paradox relates directly to Israel's lack of a cultural identity. No genuine Jewish national culture has yet developed in Israel. Israeli culture has little connection with the Jewish past; immigrant literature is an evocation of the "old country" rather than an expression of a living tradition. The culture of Israel is essentially the culture of a new nation, shallow in many respects, as cultures of new nations tend to be. Any sense of cultural continuity is apparent mainly among the religious, and this obviously means a religious continuity, not a nationalistic one. Indeed, in the residential areas of some Israeli cities one has a feeling of being not in Israel but in some Eastern European *shtetl*. Among secular Israelis, there is a strong feeling that Jewishness is irrelevant. Some of them identify themselves as "Israelis," not "Jews," while others debate whether they are "Israelis first and Jews second," or the reverse. So the return to the Jewish homeland, far from "making the Jew whole again," as the early Zionist thinkers predicted, made it possible to be an Israeli while ceasing to be a Jew. And in Israel there is none of the reinforcement of identity that comes from living in a non-Jewish world that regards one as Jewish. In fact, the claim of many Israelis that they are Zionists is unintentionally misleading. They use the word to denote patriotism, not an acceptance of an ideology.

The paradox is compounded by the fact that there *is* a secular, national Jewish culture, the Yiddish culture of Eastern Europe, whose most prominent spokesman is Isaac Bashevis Singer. The culture is carried on in the work of American (and European) Jewish writers, but it simply does not exist in Israel, and all attempts to revive it there have failed.

The present situation calls then for a re-examination of basic assumptions, which I can do only briefly here. In my view, the basic flaw in Zionism is the concept of "normalization." Significantly, Herzl himself gave the game away in his utopian Zionist novel *Altneuland*. The ideal Jewish state he described must win approval from a non-Jew, a haughty visiting Prussian nobleman, through whose eyes we observe the Jewish utopia and by whose values we judge it. As his book shows, Herzl viewed Jewish identity in the mirror of the gentile world, and what he saw reflected there made him become a Jewish nationalist. His values were those of the non-Jewish world, and by that standard Jews were obviously "abnormal" and had to be "normalized."

The very idea of "normalization" was a symptom of the loss of Jewish identity and the acceptance of the values of the non-Jewish world, and so Zionism meant nothing more than "nation building." A more realistic view of the Jewish situation necessitates discarding value-laden words like "normality" or "abnormality," and historical-philosophical speculations about the "genuine national characteristics" of the Jewish people, and recognizing that any group of people who adopt freely any way of life are just as "normal" as anybody else. The Jewish situation in the Diaspora is "abnormal" only by outworn rationales used to justify the nineteenth-century European nation-state.

But once it is established, a nation must follow the internal logic of self-preservation and perform certain basic functions. It must maintain law and order, be responsible to and for its citizens, refrain from interference in the domestic affairs of other nations, defend itself, honor its international obligations and develop its own identity and a sense of solidarity. Yet Zionism, which gave birth to the state of Israel, now interferes with its carrying out the functions of a proper state.

The modern state, whether it be a capitalist democracy or a Communist "popular democracy," comprises the totality of its citizenry. Being English or French is not an *ethnic* identity. Israel, by officially characterizing itself as a Jewish-Zionist state, placed its non-Jewish citizens in an ambiguous and in some ways inferior position. (In this, Israel resembles the ethnic states of Central and Eastern Europe that were created after World War I, whose inherent instability was one of the causes of World War II.) There also arose the problem of defining who was legally a Jew. The determination of Jewishness has devolved upon the rabbis (many of whom, ironically, are either non- or anti-Zionist), which contradicts the Zionist precept that Jews are a nation rather than a religion. (The religious aspect of the state also undermined Zionism's claim to have created a haven for persecuted Jews. For the definition of Jewishness in Adolph Hitler's Nuremberg Laws was quite different from the orthodox rabbinical one. As a result, many of the Jews murdered by Hitler would not be recognized as Jews under the Israeli Law of Return.) A permanent state of tension between the religious and the secular Jews in Israel was thus created.

Despite the political upheaval and legal contention this grave tension has engendered since the establishment of Israel, a precarious balance was maintained until the 1967 war. But the addition of 1.5 million non-Jews in the occupied territories, which Prime Minister Menachem Begin vows to incorporate permanently into the state, has radically distorted the country's social structure. The Palestinian Arabs, who make up about 35 percent of this group, are treated as a subject population with no political rights. If they wish to become citizens, they must swear allegiance to the Israeli government, despited their own sense of nationalism. Needless to say, they are kept under Israeli control not by consent but by force, and their resentment further destabilizes Israeli society.

In addition, foreign Jews, who are not Israeli citizens, have a status and influence in the country that non-Jewish citizens do not have. Rabbi Meir Kahane of the Jewish Defense League could thus bring his American hoodlums to Israel and aggravate tensions on the West Bank with near impunity. Non-Jewish Israeli citizens like the Druzes, who serve in the Israeli Army and who have suffered many casualties in Israel's wars, are not permitted to buy residences in the Jewish quarter of Jerusalem's Old City, where noncitizens who are Jewish are welcome. Such practices, of course, dilute the sense of citizenship and territorial cohesion and undermine the country's political structure. They create a nonterritorial nation, and this contradicts the idea of the state as a territorial entity.

Finally, the Israeli authorities feel morally justified in demanding the allegiance of Jews everywhere. As a result, American Jews petition their government on Israel's behalf and mobilize Congressional support for it. Israel could hardly survive without Jewish-American support, while American Jews could get along without Israel. This again reverses the role of a Jewish state envisioned by the Zionists, who assumed such a state would "normalize" the Jewish people. Now it is the Jewish state that has become "abnormal."

Some would argue that if Israel was founded by an "abnormal" people, it cannot itself be "normal," and that it must be accepted in its uniqueness, which reflects the uniqueness of the Jewish people. What I have tried to show is that such a uniqueness is contrary to the very nature of the nation-state and necessarily undermines it. The unresolved question of which comes first, Jewish interests or Israeli interests—and how to distinguish between the two, for that matter—makes it difficult to define Israel's true national interests.

For example, Prime Minister Begin says that the West Bank is vital to Israel's security. On the other hand, the inhabitants of the areas to be annexed are hostile to Israel, and the effort to "pacify" them is a constant drain on Israel's human and material resources. There is also the inevitable brutalization of conqueror and conquered. Any territorial gain is thus outweighed by its political, moral, and social costs. Reasons of state would call for an attempt to reconcile the Palestinians to Israeli rule by granting them full political and civil rights, making them equal to Israeli Jews and fully integrating them into Israeli society. But equal rights would mean that the Arabs were entitled to their own Law of Return, which would permit the refugees of 1948 and 1967 to come back to their former homeland. In view of their much higher birthrate, even without the refugees, Arabs would equal or outnumber Jews within two decades, meaning the end of Israel as a Jewish state. Such examples could be multiplied indefinitely. In Israel's case, the term "national interest" depends then on what you define as "the nation."

Reason should teach us that the national interest is whatever promotes and strengthens Israel as a normal state. The national interest would seem to call for full equality of all citizens before the law, irrespective of race, origin or creed (Israel would not thereby lose its distinctive character any more than France has ceased to be French and America American) and the integration of the state into the international community. Such a course would lead to Israel's development as an independent entity, connected with the rest of the Jewish world in the same way that the United States has cultural and emotional affinities with the rest of the English-speaking world, but not obliging it or being obliged by it. If Israel had followed such a course, relying in the last analysis on its inherent interests and capabilities and not resorting to Jewish help except in emergencies, I believe that it would never have tried to settle and annex the territories conquered in 1967. It would have realized that its resources were inadequate for such an undertaking. It would have tried instead to reach the kind of settlement with its neighbors that it reached with Egypt—peace in exchange for territories.

The continuation of present policies, aggravated in particular by Begin's Messianic obsessions, could lead to disaster for Israel and the region. If Jewish public opinion abroad were not so deferential to the Israeli government and dared to voice the criticisms that many Jews do have toward Israel, perhaps we Israelis would have long ago adjusted to reality, for our own good.

Aid to Israel, then, and identification with Israel by Jews living abroad, appear contradictory. Such aid and identification were essential at the earlier stages of Israel's development, for without them Israel could never have absorbed mass immigration and undertaken the development of its economy while at the same time maintaining a large defense establishment against the hostile Arab world. But this devoted, unquestioning support has (in spite of signs that the Arab world may be ready for some kind of accommodation with Israel, as exemplified in the Camp David accords) more recently enabled the Begin government to launch its settlement policy, to refuse to compromise on the issue of the Palestinians, to take steps toward the annexation of the West Bank and the Golan Heights and to maintain the enormous military machine necessary for the implementation of these intransigent policies.

Yet these very policies are plunging Israel into ever-deepening debt and political isolation, and they are causing the cessation of Jewish immigration and a steady flow of emigrants from Zion. Thus the more Israel is "supported," the further it sinks into the mire, and the more "abnormal" it becomes. Before the 1967 war, there were already prospects that Israel might soon become economically independent. But postwar aggrandizement has plunged the country into hopeless economic and political dependence.

To understand how the Israeli government was able to achieve control over the opinions of Jews abroad, I shall refer to Herzl's Prussian nobleman's standards as the yardstick of the ideal Jewish state. Jewish support of Israel derives from feelings of solidarity, responsibility and pride, as well as a desire to expiate the guilt some felt for not having done enough to resist the Holocaust. But would the feelings of identification and pride, particularly among those for whom Israel has become the focus of Jewish identity, have been as intense if Israel were a peaceful, prosperous, uneventful, "normal" country, a Middle Eastern Switzerland, peacefully engaged in commerce and industry and needing no help from Jew or Gentile? What really arouses the enthusiasm of so many Jews, it seems to me, is the constant drama of danger, war and military success, the very features that the imagined Prussian

Junker would presumably most admire in the Jewish state. This
warrior image, which had traditionally been antithetical to the
very concept of Judaism and was held in contempt by generations
of Jews, has become the most cherished characteristic of Israel in
Jewish eyes.

Now Diaspora Jews, for all their admiration of this warrior
state, prefer to live in safer, more comfortable and less "exalted"
environments. But by identifying with the Israelis ("we are one
people," as the slogan goes), they become heroes by proxy. This
enhances their self-respect, because they believe that the non-
Jewish world has always respected force above everything else. In
short, their sense of identity depends on their reflection in the eyes
of others. The extent to which some orthodox Jews have unconsciously fallen for these alien values, which have fused with the
ancient sense of Jewish exclusivity to produce a particularly intolerant nationalism, is evidenced by the phenomenon of Gush Em-
munim [movement to settle occupied areas] in Israel and its
religious supporters abroad.

If my conjectures are right, the reason that Israel has such a
strong hold on Jews abroad is that it enables them to lead a vicarious existence and provides them with a borrowed identity. It re-
leases them from the task of figuring out themselves what
Jewishness really means in the here and now. Instead, they identify with an image of an idealized Israel that can do no wrong (like
the old Communist true-believer for whom Russia could do no
wrong) and that in reality is antithetical to traditional Jewish values. This visionary Israel is designed to show the non-Jewish
world that Jews are as good at the power and violence game as
non-Jews. The real, though unconscious, message Diaspora Jews
intend to convey to non-Jews, particularly in America, is that
their values are the same, that they have "an old country" too,
which is as adept at the power game as the other "old countries"
(or their adopted new countries). In short, this vicarious identification with Israel and Israeli military might is a roundabout way
to a more complete integration (or "normalization") in their host
societies.

Diaspora Jews pay for these emotional compensations with
lavish financial and political support for Israel, encouraging Israel

to act out the "superman" role for which it is being paid. But this role prevents Israel from working out its own identity in its own way. This, in turn, prevents the Jewish nation from achieving a real "normalization" and plunges it into the graver dangers outlined above. Both Israelis and overseas Jews are playacting roles instead of addressing themselves to the important questions of their real interests and identities.

Jews abroad should review their support for Israel and reconsider what its aims should be. Israel is now so desperately dependent on their aid that it would face disaster if it were withdrawn. Jews abroad should determine how their support is used, and they should speak their minds and direct their assistance in ways that will enable Israel eventually to dispense with it, instead of becoming increasingly addicted to it and corrupted by it.

Vicarious living could be psychologically harmful to Diaspora Jews in the long run. But the effect on Israel of playing a role contrary to its true nature and interests, which prevents it from becoming a normal nation, could be more than psychological; it could be a matter of life and death.

FAIR GAME[6]

On Israel's Borders

Everybody knows that Israel has a border problem. The problem, in a nutshell, is too many borders and not enough Israel. There's nothing like seeing such a nutshell for oneself, and I had the opportunity to do that a few weeks ago, along with a group of journalists on a 10-day visit, subsidized in part by the American Zionist Federation. The Zionists, considerate hosts, did not assault us with heavy preachments—no brainwashing, at most a rinse or two. They transported us to all parts of the small country,

[6] Magazine article by Walter Goodman. *New Leader*, 65: 6-7. Ap.19, '82. Reprinted with permission from The New Leader. Copyright the American Labor Conference on International Affairs, Inc.

introducing us to a variety of opinions, not counting those of the Palestinian refugees. Among all the achievements of Israeli agriculture, nothing can match the Jewish State's crop of diverse opinions.

It was my first visit. I went as a friendly critic and returned with my feelings of friendship enhanced and my critical tendencies somewhat chastened. Yes, the Zionists were wise to let the land work its spell.

But to get back to those borders. We visited the town of Yamit, in the Sinai, as the last Jewish settlers were moving or being moved out, in pursuance of the Camp David agreements. Their presence on Egyptian soil, or sand, was intolerable to Cairo. Those who remained were in large part people who had come to the area only within the past few months, not to settle but to protest. Their strategy was simple—to make this withdrawal so uncomfortable politically that withdrawal from the West Bank would become unthinkable.

Still, the settlements created out of the desert have been disbanded, the oil fields that would have assured Israel's energy needs for years given up, the airfields and other military installations that provided security against the most important Arab state dismantled. All in exchange for peace with Egypt. Whether this bargain, made with a ruler who was assassinated for his efforts, will prove a good one for Israel depends now on an Egyptian President who would rather not be assassinated—and on the U.S., whose interests in the Middle East are not confined to Israel.

We visited the Gaza Strip during a time of tension over harsh measures by the Israeli occupation forces reacting to agitation by Palestinian refugees. A stone shattered a window of our bus; the kid who threw it has a career ahead as a pitcher for the PLO Patriots.

At the Golan Heights, lately annexed by Israel in what critics of Prime Minister Menachem Begin's style consider a needlessly provocative gesture, we prowled about an Israeli bunker, one of several designed to hold back for a day or two any attack from Syria. Before the 1967 War, such positions, exemplary observation points for an expanse of Israeli territory, were held by the Syrians, the most intransigent of Israel's enemies. From here Syrian riflemen could make life hot for Israeli settlers in the plains directly below. If there exists an Israeli who is inclined to give up the Golan again prior to the appearance of the Messiah, we did not encounter him.

We crossed into Lebanon through the "good fence" used by Lebanese with jobs in Israel or in need of medical attention, and met with Major Sa'ad Haddad, the Lebanese Christian whose 2,000-man Army, financed by Jerusalem, serves as a buffer between Israel and the PLO forces. Haddad may be just another Third World military hustler or he may be bloated with *grandeur*—he is said to think of himself as the de Gaulle of Lebanon—but he is apparently giving the Israelis good value for their money. Those who live on the northern border need all the protection they can get from terrorist incursions.

The Arabs Within

In the Arab town of Jatt, we talked with several school teachers who complained of discrimination against them by the Israeli establishment. After earning degrees in science or sociology at a university, they had been consigned to the low-status job of teaching in Arab schools. It is a truism that as long as these citizens feel themselves to be outsiders in their own country, discontent will fester, particularly among intellectuals. Yet, can they be brought into the mainstream as long as their brothers throughout the Arab world are at war with Israel? It would be astonishing if there were no sympathy for a Palestinian State and for the PLO and its more adventurous offshoots among Israel's Arabs. For now, they live in a sort of limbo, suspect in the view of many Israelis and contaminated in the view of many Arabs. Their unenviable condition is tied to the much disputed future of the West Bank.

We visited Israeli settlements there, in the areas once known as Samaria and Judea, where some 800,000 Palestinians live as a sort of occupied nation. Military occupation is no healthier for the moral condition of the occupiers than for the physical condition of the occupied. Such power is always a temptation to ruthlessness. It is easy for the occupier to see his subjects as an inferior breed, to interpret every sign of discontent as a security threat, and to respond with available force at the clenching of a fist. The inevitable stifling of opinion and restrictions on daily life feed discontent among the occupied, which in turn feeds anxiety among the occupiers—and here comes another crackdown. Emotions are always at the boil, and during our visit Israeli administrators, troops and settlers were stoking the fires.

Israeli spokesmen, some of them a touch embarrassed by what is going on, maintain that tough actions against PLO sympathizers, broadly defined, are necessary to give a chance to the majority of Palestinians to cooperate in progress toward "autonomy." It is an explanation that evokes uncomfortable memories of other occupation forces in other periods and climes. Since World War II, people who cooperate with the occupiers of their land have been know as Quislings. As for "autonomy," the word is no better defined today than it was at the Camp David signing. The Israelis are near-unanimous in opposing any PLO-run Palestinian state on the West Bank—but that only sets the issue.

Are those hundreds of thousands of Arabs to be kept indefinitely within the boundaries of Israel as a subject people? Can a democratic state exist with such an anomaly? If they are accepted as citizens, however, with all the political rights now enjoyed by Israeli Arabs and with a much higher birthrate than the Jews, what will happen to the idea of a Jewish State? A binational state being neither a Zionist ideal nor a political reality, solutions are elusive. At a meeting with Foreign Minister Yitzchak Shamir, I asked how the Begin government saw the long-term resolution in the West Bank. He responded only with the hope that given five years of "autonomy," some sort of "federation or confederation" could be worked out that would offer the Palestinians substantial self rule, something different from either incorporation into Israel or a state of their own.

The Labor Opposition, although agreeing that no Palestinian state can be tolerated in the present territory of the West Bank, parts from the Begin line that not an inch of the historical lands can be given up. Former Labor Prime Minister Yitzchak Rabin outlined for us, again in a vague way, a proposal that would put a portion of the West Bank, along with the bulk of the Palestinians, under Jordanian control (where they were before the 1967

War), leaving to Israel most of its settlements and the territorial security they provide. Such a solution remains highly problematic, given the careful game being played by King Hussein, who is publicly committed to a Palestinian state, yet maintains less public contacts with Israel, and in all circumstances is determined to protect his precarious throne.

The Arabs Without

If there is anything amusing about the situation in the Middle East, it is the enthusiasm with which the Arab powers support the PLO, as long as it does not operate too close to home—Arab homes, not Israel's. Since being driven out of Jordan in 1970, the PLO has managed to shatter Lebanon. That once-democratic state where Moslems and Christians lived more or less tolerably together also enjoyed peaceable relations with Israel, but its government was too weak to resist a takeover by the PLO and its Syrian patrons. Although a truce reigned on the Lebanese border, the common feeling was that if the Israeli military did not act today, they would have to act tomorrow.

In the years between 1948-1967, when the lands now occupied by Israel were held by the Arab countries, there was no international outcry for a "home" for the Palestinians. There was no talk of "autonomy." Nor were there any efforts at cultivation that can match what Israel has accomplished since 1967. Whatever one's sympathies for the Palestinians, it becomes instantly and dramatically clear to the new visitor that wherever the Israelis have settled, they have built, developed, produced, finding remarkable ways to salvage the land, capture the waters, harness the sun. (These days Israelis joke wryly about how long it will take the Egyptians to turn the Israeli-made gardens in the Sinai back into a desert.) Farms in Jordan have adopted some of the ingenious agricultural methods use in the kibbutzim, and Israel invites Jordan's participation in its visionary plans for turning the Dead Sea into a great solar pond. All this constitutes an oasis of reason amid nationalist and religious passions. Not a novel point, yet a basic one that needs periodic reiteration.

The Begin regime's discrimination against Israeli Arabs and its suppression of the Palestinians add no credit to the principles on which Israel is built. But, as ever, the country is at war, and even in that uncivil circumstance, its treatment of potential enemies is more benign than Moslem dissidents can hope for in any Moslem state.

In a region of closed societies, Israel remains open to a degree that rivals and in some ways surpasses our own. Every crackdown by the Begin regime has been met with opposition in the Knesset, in the press, in the streets. Despite the existence of a politically potent ultra-Orthodox minority bound to medieval practices, the country is a fount of innovation. For the American visitor its lack of ceremony and irreverence toward authority reminds one of an earlier America, less entangled in the trappings of power. If one can separate the geopolitical considerations of the hour from the values America is presumably dedicated to, then in all the Middle East it is surely Israel that holds the deepest claim to our continued support, admiration and affection. Not that it requires a visit to reach that position.

INTERNATIONAL LAW AND THE ISRAELI OCCUPATION[7]

Since 1967, Israel has governed the West Bank as well as the Gaza Strip as a "belligerent occupant," a legal concept recognized by international law and codified in the Geneva and The Hague Conventions. The law of belligerent occupation views the seizure of territory as a tactical but temporary necessity of war; until a peace treaty is signed and the territory is returned, the law tries to balance the military needs of the occupying power with the human needs of the inhabitants of the occupied territory. While recognizing the occupier's complete control over the land and the

[7] Magazine article by Michael Reisman, teacher of international law, Yale Law School. *Nation.* 233: 616-19. D. 5, '81. Copyright, 1981, by The Nation Magazine. Reprinted by permission.

people it has conquered, the law limits the exercise of *legal* power there to actions that are consistent with military necessity and that maintain the status quo. These actions should facilitate the peaceful resolution of the conflict and the return of the territory to the government from which it was seized. In the case of the West Bank, there are many complications.

After the 1973 Yom Kippur War, the Arab states explicitly recognized the Palestinians as the rightful owners of the West Bank. Jordan, which had annexed this area in the 1948 war, and many members of the United Nations have accepted that decision and have insisted that the territory be turned over to the Palestine Liberation Organization as the representative of the Palestinian people. But because the PLO is publicly committed to the destruction of Israel, Israel, not surprisingly, refuses to recognize the legitimacy of the PLO's claim to the land. That roadblock has political advantages for Israel, which has its own claims to the West Bank. Intensely religious groups of Jewish settlers have established a presence there, and substantial domestic support for retaining the area has developed in Israel. Nonetheless, in the Camp David accords of September 1978, the United States, Israel and Egypt agreed on a transitional regime for the West Bank and Gaza, lasting no more than five years and aimed at providing "full autonomy to the inhabitants." The accords also stipulated a withdrawal of the Israeli military government and civilian administrators as soon as a self-governing authority was freely elected and outlined a procedure for reaching a final resolution of the West Bank issue after five years. This was unusual not only because Israel and Egypt had taken it upon themselves to make the final disposition of the West Bank but also because they were contemplating options—for example, Israel's retention of the area—that are not countenanced by the law of belligerent occupation.

Egypt believed that Camp David and the peace treaty were the necessary first steps to securing Israeli withdrawal and the creation of a Palestinian state. But most other Arab countries denounced the agreements, ostracized Egypt and vilified Anwar el-Sadat for concluding a separate peace with Israel and betraying the Palestinian cause. Many openly exulted at Sadat's assassination. Jordan, though courted ardently by the United States and Egypt, refused to participate in the Camp David negotiations or their aftermath. Israel continued its settlement policy on the West Bank and insisted on a very limited form of autonomy, all of which confirmed the worst fears of many Arabs, made intransigence seem the proper course and drove an even deeper wedge between Sadat and other Arabs.

Another complicating factor in Israel's occupation of the West Bank is that new developments in international law have changed some basic rules of the game. In the past, the belligerent occupant was required to maintain the status quo in the occupied territory so as to facilitate its return to the state from which it was taken. But the scope of international law has expanded in recent years to include such areas as human rights and economic development. Thus an occupying power may have to do more than maintain the status quo; it may be called on by the international community to initiate reforms. Some of these reforms—extensions of the franchise, increased access to courts, economic development and reallocation of natural resources—will inevitably affect the eventual reversion of the territory that international law requires. Nor can an occupier deny the inhabitants' right of self-determination, for it is a fundamental postulate in international law.

The International Commission of Jurists is a private organization that has distinguished itself in human-rights matters. All human-rights organizations must become embroiled in politics to some extent, and the I.C.J. has not avoided controversy. In 1980, it published a study by Raja Shehadeh and Jonathan Kuttab, Palestinian lawyers in Ramala, on the West Bank. The study, "The West Bank and the Rule of Law," presented the authors' conclusions about how well Israeli military authorities have observed the international laws governing belligerent occupation. Shortly after the study appeared, the Israeli section of the I.C.J. protested that the Israeli government had not been given the opportunity to comment on the report and published a rebuttal titled "The Rule of Law in the Areas Administered by Israel." It was prepared by lawyers in the military reserve performing their required active duty by serving with the occupation forces on the West Bank; the lawyers were assisted by the head of the international-law branch of the Israeli Advocate-General's unit.

While papers prepared by the opposing states in international disputes make one think of civil cases in which the judge, after hearing each party's presentation of the facts, wonders whether the plaintiff and the defendant were involved in the same accident. The occupying authority, ruling by military force and possessed of almost unlimited powers, is invariably astonished and enchanted by its own near-saintly self-restraint in the face of unremitting provocation. On the other side, the occupied population sees the occupation as unmitigated tyranny and regards any action the authorities take, however grave the provocation for it, as automatically cruel and unjustified. Generous acts are studied for conspiratorial motives. From the perspective of the occupied, the only good thing an occupier can do is to leave.

As legal documents, both studies are seriously flawed. The I.C.J. report ignores the doctrine of belligerent occupation, which permits the occupier to disregard local law when military necessity requires it. Indeed, there is almost no mention of military necessity in the report, which is essentially a catalogue of alleged violations. But Israel is still at war, and so it may invoke military necessity in justification of its actions. The Israeli rebuttal, on the other hand, does not take into account the international laws on human rights, certain precepts of which are considered inviolable. (If the I.C.J. report virtually ignores military necessity, the Israeli reply often speaks of it in the same talismanic way that Richard Nixon used the words "national security.") And the rebuttal is sublimely oblivious to the Arab nations' fears that Israel intends to annex the occupied territories.

Not surprisingly, the I.C.J. report portrays darkly many things the Israeli military authorities have done, while in the Israeli rebuttal these same actions are refulgent. The I.C.J. study does praise the Israeli government for abolishing the death penalty on the West Bank, but it criticizes reforms that are cited with pride in the Israeli report. Since 1968, for example, Israel has permitted West Bank residents to bring suit against the military authorities in Israeli courts. But the I.C.J. views this concession with alarm, charging that it undermines the West Bank's indigenous court system. The Arabs' lack of confidence in the impartiality of Israeli judges in matters affecting Palestinians is understandable.

Disagreements on the "facts" abound. The outsider lacking firsthand knowledge of life on the West Bank (as I do) cannot evaluate the truth or the falsity of the conflicting claims. Even the documentation is suspect, and some documents are apparently not available. The secretary general of the I.C.J. wrote in the preface to its report that copies of the legislation and the rules passed by the Israeli occupying authorities were unobtainable. "Nowhere is a complete set available," he wrote, "and efforts even by lawyers to obtain copies of missing orders are usually unsuccessful." In their rebuttal, the Israelis claim that volumes of "the collection of proclamations and orders are distributed free of charge to all those included in the general distribution lists. . . . Anyone else requesting copies from the military government receives them immediately." Whom does one believe?

And what of the extralegal acts of the military that go unrecorded? The I.C.J. paper alleges, for example, that Israeli soldiers frequently seize identity papers, which West Bank residents need to travel within the region, and hold them for periods up to several weeks as a form of punishment. The Israeli reply does not mention this allegation.

There is much else on which the parties disagree. The I.C.J. report is alarmed by Israel's expropriation of Arab lands and water rights in the occupied territories, which takes on a crucial importance in an agrarian society. The Israelis, for their part, claim they strictly adhere to the law, and deny many of the charges regarding water policy. They do, however, concede that Arab land is often taken for settlements. The I.C.J. report is highly critical of Israel's education policy in the territories, charging censorship, invasion of school premises, closing of schools, restrictions on private universities, deportation and harrassment of teachers and discouragement of research. The I.C.J. does not consider, however, if these actions were justifiable under the doctrine of military necessity. The Israeli reply claims that there have been substantial improvements in education and seems to imply that Israel is responsible for the new private institutions of higher learning.

In addition to the factual disputes, there are a number of sharp exchanges on legal matters. In some of these, the claim of military necessity does not help the Israeli case. For example, the I.C.J.

report criticizes the Israeli authorities for destroying houses belonging to people who associated with, or were suspected of associating with, Palestinian guerrillas. The Israeli rebuttal concedes that Article 53 of the Geneva Convention prohibits "any destruction by the occupying power of real or personal property belonging individually or collectively to private persons. . . . " (This prohibition does not apply in cases where the destruction is, as one authority puts it, "rendered absolutely necessary to military operations.") The Israeli reply cites a lawyer with its Ministry of Justice who has expanded the concept of military necessity to include the need "to create effective military reaction." But, of course, military reprisals against civilians are simply illegal.

Nor is Israel's practice of using deportation as a punishment defensible under international law. Article 49 of the Geneva Convention prohibits "individual or mass forcible transfers, as well as deportations." Yet Israel has deported Palestinians for what it has called "security reasons." The Israeli Supreme Court has interpreted Article 49 broadly, and a former Israeli attorney general, who is now a justice of the Supreme Court, has justified the deportations by citing public statements made by some of the deportees about their subversive activities on the West Bank. But the Geneva Convention and relevant provisions of the U.N.'s International Covenant on Civil and Political Rights quite clearly prohibit this practice.

Human rights apply to individuals; one must not lose sight of the trees for the forest. It is important to protest specific violations of belligerent occupation law, even when it can be argued that, overall, the occupation is a relatively benign and lawful one. Hence the valuable contribution of organizations like the I.C.J. But it is equally important not to lose sight of the forest. Ultimately, any appraisal of the lawfulness of activities on the West Bank depends on whether Israel is engaged in a belligerent occupation or an incremental annexation. If the former is true, then according to one's political taste, one can praise particular instances of Israeli generosity and lawful behavior or protest particular instances of Israeli violations of international law, assured that, at the appropriate time, the land will be either returned to Jordan or turned over to its Palestinian inhabitants. But if annexation is the goal, then each instance of departure from the law of belligerent occupation takes on a graver significance.

The Israeli government has not formally declared its intention to annex the West Bank. Since 1967, it has proclaimed a policy of abiding by The Hague regulations and the Fourth Geneva Convention (though on occasion the Israeli Supreme Court has evaded application of the latter on technical grounds). But Israel's Prime Minister and its current Minister of Defense, Ariel Sharon, have made no secret of the fact that they consider the West Bank an integral part of Israel. Other members of Menachem Begin's government have strongly supported retaining the West Bank on religious, imperial or strategic grounds. In 1968, Professor Yehuda Blum, now Israel's representative to the United Nations, published an article, widely circulated by the Israeli government, arguing that since Jordan was not really entitled to the West Bank, Israel's claim to the territory was as good as, if not better than, others. "Since," wrote Blum, "no State can make out a legal claim that is equal to that of Israel, this relative superiority of Israel may be sufficient, under international law, to make Israel[i] possession of Judea and Samaria virtually indistinguishable from an absolute title. . . . " The claims of the Palestinian inhabitants and their right to self-determination were not mentioned.

Legal arguments aside, both the Labor and the Likud parties support a settlement policy that seems to rule out eventual withdrawal. In a recent public-opinion poll, 52.8 percent of the Israelis surveyed expressed no reservations about Israeli settlements on the West Bank. In this context, Begin's repeated reference to "Judea and Samaria" and his characterization of Israeli Jews as "Palestinians" should not be dismissed as mere pedantry. They may represent an important step in the direction of appropriation: first symbols and names are taken over and then everything else. On the other hand, these are, after all, only words, an abundant resource in Middle East politics. Former U.S. Attorney General John Mitchell's cynical advice has relevance here: "Watch what we do and not what we say." Since 1967, eighty-nine Israeli settlements have been established on the West Bank, some in populated Arab areas, and they are now organized into ten regional councils. The Jewish National Fund, an Israeli group, has been quietly purchasing land on the West Bank. It is unclear exactly how many Israelis have settled in the area. Some American accounts have placed the number at more than 100,000, but it is probably less than 20,000. *Newsweek* reported in August that Israeli settlers owned one-third of the land and 90 percent of the water rights on the West Bank, but the source of these figures is obscure.

In October, Sharon, a champion of grandiose schemes of Israeli settlement on the West Bank, began to transfer power there from the military to a civilian governor. He also sought to neutralize resistance to an increased Israeli presence by bypassing pro-PLO mayors and city councils and creating indigenous governmental organizations. These are, to say the least, innovations in belligerent occupation law. Their purpose, however, is not hard to divine. The Camp David accords do not provide for a plebiscite for self-determination after five years of autonomy. Instead, the agreement reached by Israel, Egypt and Jordan will be voted on "by the elected representatives of the West Bank and Gaza." Sharon, it would appear, is making sure who those representatives will be.

If these examples augur an Israeli policy to retain the West Bank permanently, with a "military-civilian administration" having power over the Arab inhabitants, as long as there are any, Israel would no longer be a temporary belligerent occupant but a colonizing power. The West Bank would be transformed into a Middle Eastern Bantustan.

Certainly, recent steps the Israelis have taken are legally controversial. Paragraph 6 of Article 49 of the Fourth Geneva Convention states that "the Occupying Power shall not deport or transfer parts of its own civilian population into the territory it occupies." The Israeli rebuttal to the I.C.J. report interprets this as prohibiting only migration into the occupied territory that results in the displacement of the local population or that is encouraged by the state. It does not apply to voluntary movements of individuals, "as is the case with the Israeli settlers who live in these new settlements." This artful interpretation is inconsistent with the basic principles of belligerent occupation, and it conveniently overlooks the role the Israeli government has played in the creation of the settlements. It also ignores the settlements' potential

effect on moderate Arabs, who watch the Camp David process to
see if its promise of autonomy and self-determination for the Palestinians is real or a sham.

Obviously no one wants his country to be occupied. But the
prospect of a slow de-facto annexation of the West Bank is even
worse—for its Arab inhabitants, for Israel and for all the rest of
us whose security is increasingly intertwined with the politics of
the Middle East. One must not forget that the PLO's stated goals
are unacceptable and must be changed. Until the PLO indicates
its willingness to accept Israel's existence, and until a general
peace is forged, Israel is legally entitled to continue its belligerent
occupation. But is is not entitled to undertake an incremental annexation.

An Israeli government—Likud or Labor—is thus caught in
a cruel dilemma. In the absence of a comprehensive peace, Israel
has no choice but to remain on the West Bank, where international law requires it to introduce some reforms. But given the am-
biguity of its ultimate objective, every such reform must remain
suspect. The longer Israel occupies the West Bank, the more Israeli political elements, who justify its retention on mystical and
security grounds, will settle there. This in turn will convince the
Arabs that Israel is bent on expansion, making peace more difficult to achieve and making Israeli withdrawal an even more im-
probable task. Annexation will almost certainly doom efforts to
negotiate a peace and eventually lead Israel to either create its own
Northern Ireland or undertake a massive expulsion that would
stir intense international protest and create new instabilities in the
region. Nor will it end there. If Israel is entitled to the West Bank
under revisionist Zionist theories, it may also be entitled to
"Eastern Eretz Israel." There will be no end to expansion.

It is obvious that there cannot be a resolution of the Middle
East conflict without Israeli withdrawal from the West Bank and
the creation of some sort of territorial community for the Palestinian people. Israel may certainly provide for its own security, and
it may validly insist on appropriate guarantees and defensive arrangements. But not more. Unfortunately, indecision in Washington and confusion among groups in America sympathetic to Israel
about the real security issue have made it easy for extremists to

shape a policy that many Israelis know is profoundly wrong. The key to change is the United States.

Withdrawal from the occupied territories was the policy expressed in U.N. Resolution 242, at one time a keystone of American and Israeli policy, but now interpreted in innovative and obscure ways by the Begin government. The peace treaty with Egypt indicated that if there is a promise of a settlement of the issue of a Palestine homeland, peace can be purchased by returning the territory seized in 1967; without withdrawal and palpable progress on the Palestinian problem, no resolution is conceivable with Syria, with Jordan, with the Palestinians and with the rest of the Arab world. This view, widely held in Europe and slowly winning converts in the United States, still has little support in Israel. One hopes that ultimate disengagement and withdrawal become clear Israeli policy and that, in the interim, Israel remains nothing more than a scrupulously legal belligerent occupant.

THE "PERFECT LOGIC" OF MIDEAST WAR[8]

Another war in the Middle East. And all perfectly logical, too. The PLO is Israel's sworn enemy. The PLO has been building its military force in Lebanon. Sooner or later, someone would strike, and Israel has always favored sooner. The Arab states are in disarray over the Iran-Iraq conflict. Egypt has not yet digested the Sinai. The West's leaders are on the road. Why wait?

All perfectly logical, at least in that cold-blooded logic—which the Israelis, it should be noted, did not invent—of Mideast survival. The logic has its limits, however. It cannot insure that the fighting in Lebanon will not mushroom into a larger war: at this writing, the response of the Syrians is still in doubt. Nor can logic resolve an old problem for militarily successful nations—getting in is easier than getting out. How can the Israelis prevent the PLO from reconstructing its military infrastructure, except by occupy-

[8] Magazine article by the Editors. *Commonweal.* 109:355-6. Je. 18, '82. Copyright, 1982, Commonweal Publishing Company. Reprinted by permission.

ing Lebanon indefinitely? But what the logic of the Lebanese invasion avoids entirely is the impasse that is at the root of the problem.

The Camp David accord specified that the 1.3 million Palestinian Arabs living on the West Bank and the Gaza Strip should be granted "autonomy," a limited form of self-administration, during the five years in which the final status of the Israeli-occupied territory is to be negotiated. But it is becoming increasingly clear that Israel has no intention of giving up the territory it won by force of arms in 1967. In the weeks before the Lebanese incursion, more Arab mayors on the West Bank were dismissed from their posts by their Israeli overlords, more and more previously "moderate" Palestinians were drawn into the resultant protests, and more and more Arab youths were being shot by Israeli soldiers and quick-on-the trigger, ultra-nationalist Jewish settlers. Asked about the possibility that his country would annex the West Bank, which he calls by its Biblical names, Prime Minister Begin is quoted as saying: "You cannot annex your own country. Judea and Samaria are parts of the land of Israel, in which our nation was born." Speaking a few days later at the opening of the Israeli parliament's summer session, he affirmed that Israel would demand national sovereignty over the West Bank and the Gaza Strip at the end of the five-year transition period prescribed by Camp David. At the same time he vowed that no Jewish settlement in the area would be dismantled as the result of any future peace negotiations. In one sense there is nothing new in this; Mr. Begin has always considered the West Bank to be an integral party of Eretz Israel—the Land of Israel. But according to David K. Shipler of the *New York Times,* ever since Israel's withdrawal from the Sinai Mr. Begin has taken to referring to Israel and the West Bank and the Gaza Strip as "Western Eretz Israel." Ominously, this phrasing revives the notion of the Revisionist Zionist movement, to which he belongs, that the historical land of Israel also included the East Bank of the Jordan river, which is Jordanian territory. How far do Mr. Begin's ambitions go? How much effective opposition is there to his policies inside Israel? And what kind of alternatives does the Labor party offer? Not many so far.

At least as disturbing as Mr. Begin's rhetoric and the general political situation in Israel are the rumors about the plans of one of his potential successors, Defense Minister General Ariel Sharon. If anyone could make Begin look like a moderate, it is Sharon. It is he who is responsible for much of the pressure for additional Jewish settlements on the West Bank and for the increasingly heavy-handed and inflammatory work of the Israeli civilian administration of that area. Many Israelis fear for the future of their Jewish state if Israel annexes the West Bank and Gaza with their 1.3 million Palestinian Arabs. But Sharon is said to have an answer for that: make life so uncomfortable for the Palestinians on the West Bank that many will pack up and leave, including most Palestinian leaders. And it is reported to be Sharon who pushed hardest for an all-out assault on the PLO in Lebanon, already called by many in Israel "Sharon's war"—with what is rumored to be an almost unbelievable scenario in mind: decimate the Palestinians in Lebanon, with a few swipes at the Syrians by the way, pushing the remainder of the PLO completely out of the country and into Jordan; there they will in turn overthrow the moderate King Hussein, take over the country and turn it into a Palestinian state, thus removing the international pressure on Israel for a Palestinian state on the West Bank. Far-fetched, yes, but in the Middle East today nothing is impossible.

It should be clear that neither side in this dispute is blameless. Messrs. Begin and Sharon provide deadly provocation to the PLO almost every day; the PLO in turn regularly arouses Israeli wrath by terroristic actions and inflammatory statements. The PLO and most of the surrounding Arab states remain officially as unreconciled to Israel's existence as the Begin government is to genuine Palestinian self-determination. The difference is that the Israelis are in a position to put their one-sided view into practice; the Arabs are not, and the Israelis are understandably loath to test whether Arab "rejectionism" is as strictly verbal as sometimes claimed.

In a sensitive area where the two superpowers could easily come eyeball to eyeball, both Israelis and Palestinians need a firm and impartial arbitrator if the risk of all-out war is to be avoided. Instead of playing this role, the U.S. has vacillated irresponsibly.

We sell the AWACS to Saudi Arabia, then sign a strategic memorandum with Israel, then void it after Begin's move in the Golan Heights, hint at renewing it in the face of Iran's recent victories (which Israel has aided), talk of new arms for Jordan, and even while remonstrating in Washington with Mr. Sharon send him home with massive military and economic grants. It is time that we, too, concentrate on the core problem, unmistakably indicating that we reject Mr. Begin's notion of autonomy on the West Bank, pushing hard for an open PLO affirmation of Israel's right to exist, but also ending our fruitless policy of refusing to talk to the PLO. The immediate task is to contain the Lebanese fighting, but a new initiative on the Palestinian issue is the very next order of the day. Mr. Begin is buying time in Lebanon, but losing time on the West Bank. And the world with him.

EDITOR'S INTRODUCTION

A continuous and intense rivalry for possession of the Holy
Land has existed since before the dawn of the Christian era. In
examining the Palestinian claim to the West Bank from an historical point of view, the first article in this section, written by the
editors of the Foreign Policy Association, observes that "painfully
aware of their own tragic histories, both Israeli and Palestinian
have often been strangely uncomprehending of the other's
suffering." Through the years, this conflict has sporadically erupted in terrorism and violence, with the consequent dispersal of the
Palestinians from their ancient homeland. The second article, a
short excerpt, from *Israel and the U.S.*, indicates the countries to
which the thousands of Palestinians fled and describes the formation of the PLO and its leading faction, under Yasir Arafat.

Expelled from Jordan because of its disruption, a radical element of the PLO found sanctuary in neighboring Lebanon, where
sectionalism and violence were already rampant. The third article
in the section by William Haddad, reprinted from *Current History*, describes the anarchic conditions in Lebanon—the many religions, sects, political factions, and neighboring nations vying for
control of the country. The author calls it "a country of people divided against each other," and he describes PLO provocations that
led to the Israeli invasion of Lebanon. In the fourth article, a
newspaper report from the *New York Times*, Thomas Friedman
analyzes the apparent helplessness of the divided Arab states and
their disappointing failure to back the PLO militarily against the
Israelis in Lebanon.

The June 1982 Israeli invasion of Lebanon generated an
abundance of emotion and disagreement worldwide. The next
three articles, all from the *Nation*, provide a variety of opinions
on the underlying reasons for the invasion and discuss both Israeli
and world reactions to the war. In the eighth article, William

Buckley Jr. of the *National Review,* maintains that aggrandizement, and not security, was Israel's reason for invading Lebanon and claims that the Israeli case for a homeland should also apply to the 4.4 million Palestinians.

In the ninth and tenth articles, both the *Economist* and the *New Republic* editors are optimistic concerning the outcome of the war and the evacuation of the PLO from Lebanon. The *Economist* magazine notes that Israel's success in wresting additional security is grounds for considering "home-rule" for the Palestinians. The *New Republic,* calling the PLO "hijackers," is hopeful that with the enforced absence of PLO terrorism from Lebanon, attention will be paid to the Israeli-Palestinian question and "there will finally be a chance for accommodation on the West Bank and Gaza."

The last two articles in this final section deal with the actual peacemaking phase of the conflict. The *New Republic* applauds President Reagan's September 1, 1982, peace plan, which "completes Camp David," comparing it to the Arab Fez Plan. He concludes that while giving up the West Bank and Gaza is an anathema to Israel's present government, recognition of Israel and the need to face up to the requirements for making peace may be intolerable for many Arab governments. Finally, Harold H. Saunders, former Assistant Secretary of State for Near Eastern and South Asian Affairs, writing in *Foreign Affairs,* spells out the necessary steps for getting the opposing parties together and lists the compromises that will have to be made on both sides in order to settle the Palestinian conflict.

WHO ARE THE PALESTINIANS?[1]

Like the Israelis who claim the same strip of land between the Mediterranean Sea and the Jordan River as their ancestral home, the Palestinian Arabs have ancient ties to the land. The problem

[1] Excerpt from *Great Decisions '82,* a book by the editors of the Foreign Policy Association. p 39-42. Copyright, 1982, Foreign Policy Association, Inc. Reprinted by permission.

has been not between a right and a wrong, but between two peoples who have forcefully asserted their competing rights to the same land.

There are similarities in the history of the Jewish people and the Arabs of Palestine. Both have known the loss of their homeland; both became merchants and professionals in their adopted homes. During their two-millennia exile the Jews suffered inquisition, pogroms and the death of 6 million in the Holocaust; since 1948 the Palestinians have suffered exile and hardship at the hands of Israel as well as of the Arab states. Because of their experiences, both have forged a fiery nationalism. From the Jewish diaspora, the Zionist dream transformed an ancient people into a new one—the Israelis. From the refugee camps of the Arab world, the dream of return transformed the exiled Palestinians into nationalists.

Painfully aware of their own tragic histories, both Israelis and Palestinians have often been strangely uncomprehending of the other's suffering. And fully possessed of their own national dreams, both today fail to acknowledge any legitimacy in the other's political claims.

Palestine's Tangled History

Palestine saw conquerors come and go during antiquity; the list includes Egyptians, Assyrians, Babylonians, Persians, Greeks, Seleucids and Romans. Unlike the others, the Hebrew tribes formed lasting ties to the land, and they were in possession of much of it by 1100 B.C. Although never the sole occupants of Palestine nor always its masters, the Jewish people called it their home for the next 1200 years. In A.D. 66 the Jews revolted against Roman rule, and after seven years their rebellion was crushed. Jerusalem itself was later destroyed and plowed up by the Romans, and most surviving Jews were sold into slavery and scattered throughout the Roman world.

The Palestinian Arabs claim their descent from the Canaanites, who also were ancient inhabitants of Palestine. In Arabic, the land is called Filastin; the Philistines are a people well-known to those familiar with the Bible. During the seventh century the armies of Islam swept through the area; the populace, largely Christian at the time, converted to the faith of Mohammed. In the Middle Ages, Christian crusaders from Europe fought to regain the Holy Land from the Muslim "infidel"; they established short-lived Crusader kingdoms, the last of which succumbed in A.D. 1291. The Ottoman Turks captured Palestine in the 16th century, and they held it until World War I.

The beginning of the modern conflict over Palestine was foreshadowed in late 19th-century Europe. Theodor Herzl, a Jewish journalist born in Budapest, Hungary, was one of the founders of a movement named Zionism, which called on Jews to return to their ancient home, Zion, in the land of Palestine. Zionism was part of the tide of nationalism which swept 19th-century Europe; it was also a reaction against the deep-seated anti-Semitism manifested during France's Dreyfus Affair (1894-1906) and the pogroms of Czarist Russia. As early as 1880, Jews began to emigrate to Palestine to join the scattered thousands who had lived continuously in the land of their ancestors. By 1914, 85,000 Jews lived in Palestine, in addition to some 560,000 Arabs.

During World War I, a British Army captured Palestine from the Turks, and with the help of Arab armies advised by British Colonel T. E. Lawrence, the British captured Damascus, sealing the Turks' defeat. In exchange for Arab support, Britain promised the Arabs independence after the war. The nature and territorial extent of these promises, however, were deeply ambiguous, and were further clouded by the Balfour Declaration of 1917.

The British Mandate in Palestine

British Foreign Secretary Arthur James Balfour was concerned with keeping the Russians in the war and with securing the support of the American Jewish community. He thought these ends might be served by a declaration in favor of Zionism. In a 1917 statement to Lord Rothschild, head of the English branch of the banking firm, he wrote: "His Majesty's Government view with favor the establishment in Palestine of a national home for the Jewish people, . . . it being clearly understood that nothing shall be done which may prejudice the civil and religious rights of existing non-Jewish communities in Palestine. . . . " The Balfour Declaration served as a guideline when the League of Nations granted Britain the Palestine mandate.

News of the Balfour Declaration and its meaning for the Arabs resulted in serious anti-Jewish rioting in Palestine in 1921. Tensions eased somewhat later in the 1920s as Jewish immigration slowed. But when immigration increased again because of depression in Europe and Nazi persecution, violence between Arab and Jew increased as well. By the outbreak of World War II, a three-cornered fight among the British, the Arabs and the Jews was in full progress. The Arabs opposed British plans to partition Palestine; the Jews opposed British plans to limit future Jewish immigration.

After the war, the British gave notice that they intended to quit Palestine, and they brought the issue before the United Nations. In November 1947 the UN agreed, after heavy lobbying by the United States, to a partition of Palestine. The Jewish Agency, which represented the Jewish community, rapidly agreed to the plan, which called for the establishment of two independent states in Palestine, one Jewish and one Arab. The Arabs rejected partition as they had ten years previously, and fighting rapidly escalated. On May 14, 1948 Israel declared itself a sovereign state, and the next day British troops left Palestine, and Arab armies from Egypt, Syria, Jordan and Iraq invaded. The state of Israel, outnumbered by its Arab neighbors, nonetheless managed to field a bigger—and better—army. Israel triumphed.

While the UN partition plan had allotted Israel 55 percent of the Palestine mandate, the armistice lines of January 1949 left Israel in control of 78 percent of the territory. The remainder was occupied by Jordan and Egypt. Population changes in Palestine were striking. At the beginning of the war, 1,320,000 Arabs and 640,000 Jews lived there. But between 600,000 and 700,000 Palestinian Arabs were displaced from their homes. At first, many left at the urgings of the Arab leaders. Later, many fled in fear of Jewish reprisals. Like all wars, this war was marked by cruelties and atrocities.

The war's end brought rejoicing in Israel. The new state was decidedly Jewish in character, bolstered by the influx over the

next three years of 500,000 immigrants, many of whom were survivors of the Holocaust or had been expelled from Arab lands. The
Arabs who remained were offered Israeli citizenship.

For the Arab refugees from Palestine, the end of the war
marked the beginning of a long period of misery in camps in Lebanon, Jordan, Syria and Egypt's Gaza Strip. Israel and the Arab
states denied responsibility for the refugees, and only Jordan integrated the refugees into its own society. The refugees themselves
for the most part refused attempts at resettlement, fearing that
their claim to a lost homeland would be forgotten.

The Politics of Exile

The Palestinian leaders of 1948 had been killed, dispersed or
discredited. Their cause, however, was taken up by Egypt's "Free
Officers," who overthrew King Farouk and came to power in
Egypt in 1952. Gamal Abdel Nasser, a pan-Arabist who became
Egypt's premier in 1954, viewed Israel as another European colo-
ny, another Crusader kingdom implanted in the heart of the Arab
nation. Nasser's pan-Arab and revolutionary doctrine appealed
strongly to young Palestinian intellectuals at the American University in Beirut, Lebanon. Led by Dr. George Habash, these intellectuals viewed Arab unity as the only means of confronting the
powerful new Jewish state.

A second political response developed among young Palestinians living in the Gaza Strip. A Palestinian commando unit from
Gaza, including Yasir Arafat, fought with the Muslim Brotherhood against the British in Suez in 1952-53. These Palestinians,
however, became suspicious of Egypt's commitment to their cause
after they were forced to leave Gaza during a crackdown on the
Muslim Brotherhood in 1954. In Kuwait, Arafat and several com-
panions in 1957 founded Fatah, which became the foremost of the
Palestinian resistance groups. Fatah accepted aid from all the
Arab states but offered allegiance only to its own nationalist goals.

Other clandestine Palestinian organizations sprang up in the
Arab world in the late 1950s and early 1960s. The Arab leaders
feared that these secret groups would undermine their own rule,
and so they created the PLO in 1964 as a means of controlling the

Palestinians. The rhetoric of the PLO was white-hot: its leader, Ahmed Shuqairy, called on the Arabs "to drive the Jews into the sea." The Arab states, however, tried to curb guerrilla activity, fearing that the PLO would provoke a war with Israel for which they were ill-prepared. As Arafat has pointed out, the first Fatah guerrilla was killed not by Israeli troops, but by a Jordanian border patrol. Only in Syria did the guerrillas get treated with much sympathy in the 1960s, and escalating raids across the Syrian frontier contributed to the outbreak of the June 1967 Six-Day War.

Israel soundly trounced the Arabs. In just six days it seized the whole of the Sinai Peninsula and Syria's Golan Heights and the remainder of the former British mandate of Palestine—the West Bank of the Jordan and the Gaza Strip. Another 200,000 refugees, mostly Palestinian, fled across the Jordan river. Many Palestinians dismissed all hope that the Arab states would be their saviors, particularly after Nasser and Jordan's King Hussein agreed in November 1967 to UN Resolution 242. The resolution called on the Arab states to make peace with Israel in exchange for Israel's withdrawal from occupied territory; it made no reference to national rights for Palestinians, who were treated as refugees.

Failure in war discredited the PLO leadership, and the guerrilla groups took "armed struggle" against Israel into their own hands. Terrorism was by no means unknown before the 1967 war, but its pace increased substantially afterward. Most of the PLO raids were foiled, and Israel exacted a punishing toll on the guerrillas. But the 1968 battle of Karameh in Jordan boosted guerrilla morale and the flow of recruits. Thus strengthened, Fatah and the other guerrilla groups won control of the PLO in 1969.

In Jordan the PLO's presence was hardly well received by Hussein. Over one-half of Jordan's inhabitants are Palestinians, and Hussein saw the PLO guerrillas, particularly as they grew in strength and independence of action, as a direct challenge to his throne. After a series of provocations, Hussein took action in September 1970. His Bedouin army killed thousands of PLO guerrillas during "Black September"; the rest were driven across the border into Syria and Lebanon. The enmity ran so deep that when fighting resumed briefly the following year, guerrillas waded across the Jordan river to surrender to Israeli border patrols rather than remain in Hussein's kingdom.

Black September also became known to the world as the name of the offshoot Palestinian terrorist group which seized the Israeli compound and killed 11 Israeli athletes at the Munich Olympics in 1972. Palestinian terrorists also sponsored other grisly international attacks. The PLO disavowed Black September's actions, saying that it opposed terrorist tactics outside of the Middle East. But given the PLO's own record of terror, its disavowal was treated most skeptically.

The October War and Its Aftermath

The PLO and its small army of 10,000 or so played no significant role in Egypt and Syria's attack on Israel in October 1973. Nonetheless, the PLO was a major political beneficiary of the October war because of the oil embargo which the Arab oil producers imposed on the United States and the Netherlands. Western Europe and Japan, deeply dependent on Arab oil imports, expressed new sympathy for the Palestinian cause.

With world attention newly fixed on Middle East politics, the PLO scored major diplomatic successes. At an October 1974 Arab summit conference in Rabat, Morocco, it was recognized as "the sole legitimate representative of the Palestinian people," and in November of that year Arafat was invited to speak before the General Assembly of the UN, which gave the PLO observer status—just short of outright recognition.

The PLO's fortunes, seemingly in the ascendant, plummeted rapidly because of the civil war in Lebanon the following year. Lebanon had long been able to keep out of the Arab-Israeli conflict, but in 1975 it was drawn in against its will. Under Lebanon's Constitution, political power had been divided between Christian and Muslim communities on the basis of a 1932 census, with the Christians holding the greater power. Yet by the 1970s the Muslims claimed they had surpassed in number the previous Christian majority, and in 1975 the Palestinian guerrillas in southern Lebanon made common cause with leftist and Muslim opponents in a war against the Christian-controlled regime.

Syria's President Hafez al-Assad feared that a Palestinian and Muslim victory would both bring to power left-wing elements hostile to his own regime and provoke another war between Israel and Syria. Therefore, he intervened in June 1976 with a Syrian force of 25,000 on behalf of the Lebanese Christians. In a war of strange bedfellows, Syria and Israel both offered support to the Christians, and the PLO fought bitter, pitched battles against its own nominal ally, Syria. The PLO even found itself fighting its own forces, the Saiqa commandos who were attached to the Syrian army. The civil war cost 60,000 lives and it destroyed Lebanon; the PLO itself was badly battered.

The Palestinians and Jimmy Carter

When President Jimmy Carter entered office, he did not shy away from Middle East politics; he and his advisers felt that there could be no peace without some recognition of Palestinian rights. In March 1977 Carter spoke of the need for a Palestinian "homeland" in addition to peace and security for Israel. In October 1977 the United States issued a joint statement with the Soviet Union which called for a peace conference in Geneva to resolve the key issues, including "insuring the legitimate rights of the Palestinian people." The statement met a wave of domestic opposition, and U.S. plans for a Geneva conference were dramatically altered in any event by Egyptian President Sadat's historic trip to Jerusalem in November 1977. Instead of the Geneva format, the United States backed Sadat's initiative.

The visit to Jerusalem raised both hopes and fears among the Palestinians. As one West Bank mayor put it, "People here want what Sadat is preaching, but they don't believe Israel will give it." The Camp David accords of September 1978 and the Egyptian-Israeli peace treaty of March 1979 seem to have confirmed most of the Palestinians' fears. The treaty gave Israel peace with Egypt; for the Palestinians it offered negotiations to provide "full autonomy" for the Arab inhabitants of the West Bank and Gaza Strip. But autonomy did not mean recognition of Palestinian national rights or a commitment by Israel to the eventual withdrawal of its troops from occupied territory. Jordan and the Palestinians of the West Bank boycotted the autonomy negotiations, and the PLO and the other Arab states greeted them with derision.

For the Palestinian Arabs, "autonomy" was little different from Israel's previous offers of local Arab administration. Israel intended to maintain control over internal security, land and water resources, radio and TV, prisons and traffic arteries; the plan contemplated no Palestinian legislative powers. As the editor of *al-Quds,* the Arab newspaper in Jerusalem, noted: "The Israeli view of autonomy is far from what the most moderate Palestinian would accept. It just means that some Arab will take over from an Israeli officer but still carry out his orders."

So far, the Palestinian autonomy negotiations between Egypt, Israel, and the United States have failed to reach agreement. The May 1980 negotiating deadline came and went; in December 1980 Sol M. Linowitz, President Carter's special envoy to the Middle East, summed up his mission noting that "very crucial questions were still not settled." Under the Reagan administration, autonomy talks formally convened in September 1981, and after Sadat's assassination, President Mubarak and Israeli Prime Minister Menahem Begin pledged to continue them. But few expressed any optimism about early results.

. . . No other Arab leader has followed Sadat's lead; none has recognized the existence of Israel. No Palestinian has come forward to join U.S., Israeli and Egyptian negotiators in their efforts to devise a "self-governing authority" for the Arab inhabitants of the territories occupied by Israel. These negotiations on Palestinian "full autonomy" in the West Bank and Gaza Strip have achieved little so far; Egypt and Israel themselves are at odds over autonomy's definition. Without some resolution of the Palestinian issue, peace in the Middle East, many believe, will be impossible.

WHERE ARE THE PALESTINIANS?[2]

. . . The PLO remains a loose umbrella organization, and
its numerous factions—pro-Syrian, pro-Iraqi, Marxist-Leninist,
and Arab revolutionary—are often openly hostile to each other
and to Arafat's Fatah, the PLO's leading faction which is strictly
nationalist and otherwise nonideological in its politics. Though
the PLO's military power is largely concentrated in southern Lebanon, Palestinians remain scattered throughout the Arab world
[and the U.S.]:

Jordan	1,161,000	Saudi Arabia	127,000
West Bank	818,000*	U.A.E.	35,000
Gaza Strip	477,000	Qatar	35,000
Israel	531,000	Iraq	20,000
Syria	216,000	Libya	23,000
Lebanon	347,000	United States	10,000
Kuwait	280,000	Others	175,000

*Including 100,000 in East Jerusalem
Source: Al Fajr and Palestine Institute of Statistics

DIVIDED LEBANON[3]

The past . . . months have been difficult for Lebanon; in
many ways the present situation is worse than the 1975-1976 civil
war. At that time, there were fronts that one could avoid, but today
sniping and car bombs bring death with no defense. The number
of killings is averaging 100 per month, even in the period since
July, 1981, when the latest cease-fire took effect.

[2] Excerpt from *Israel and the U.S.: Friendship and Discord,* a booklet by the Editors of the Foreign
Policy Association. p 5. Copyright, 1982, Foreign Policy Association, Inc. Reprinted by permission.

[3] Magazine article by William Haddad, associate professor of history, Illinois State University. *Current
History.* 81:30-5. Ja. '82. Copyright by Current History, Inc. Reprinted by permission.

Until August, 1980, Lebanon enjoyed a two-year respite from fighting. That period of relative calm fell between the March, 1978, Israeli invasion of the south and the Israeli strike in August, 1980, against Beaufort castle, a Palestinian stronghold near the Litani River. The Israeli attack signaled an increase in military activity and Lebanon was again the victim.

What is particularly depressing for the Lebanese is that there seems to be no way out of the fighting. The number of groups struggling in Lebanon is over 100. This number increased arithmetically in the 1970s and in a perverse Malthusian manner increased Lebanon's problems geometrically. The internationalization of the fighting means that the very real domestic causes for the civil war seven years ago have been subordinated to outside interests. The President does not control his palace; the government does not even control its offices. In what other country could thugs stop a Prime Minister's car and confiscate the weapons of his bodyguards with impunity? Because of this anarchic condition, one begins to feel that Lebanon, the nation, no longer exists.

If one looks at a map of Lebanon, one can see how the country has been divided during the last five years. In the south is "Free Lebanon," ruled by a renegade Lebanese army officer, Sa'd Haddad, who acts as Israel's surrogate. North of Free Lebanon is territory under the nominal control of the 6,000-man United Nations Interim Force in Lebanon (UNIFIL). Along the coast, Palestinians have control from the UNIFIL area north, plus the cities of Tyre and Sidon. The eastern half of Lebanon is controlled by the Arab Deterrent Force (ADF), which at this time contains only Syrian soldiers.

The Lebanese Right controls the territory to the west of the ADF area and north of Beirut. Around Tripoli, former Maronite President Suleiman Franjieh has carved out a small section. He broke with the largely Maronite Right in 1978 and continues to be a Syrian ally.

Beirut, the capital, is chopped into many fiefdoms. One usually speaks of Beirut as being divided into east and west but this only tells part of the story. The Leftist alliance, for example, which controls West Beirut is itself divided into innumerable factions.

Lebanon's social structure is a legacy of the Ottoman Empire. Then called the millet system, the organization of the population according to religious groups was institutionalized in the Lebanese National Pact of 1943, which allocated power and responsibilities to different sects. Under this "confessional" system, based on a census taken in 1932, there are 15 recognized sects in Lebanon, and they regulate most aspects of a citizen's life. Although originally it was liberal in intent, because it allowed religious and social freedom for all, the confessional system hindered the development of a sense of Lebanese nationalism, froze in place each group's political power and kept alive Lebanese clannishness.

Furthermore, because Lebanon was divided into religious groupings, leading families from Lebanon's feudal era were able to maintain themselves in power. For example, the Karami in Tripoli and Usayran in the south were old feudal houses that emerged as powerful political forces in the new republic. The Maronites, who held a plurality in the 1932 census, were given the most powerful positions, including that of the presidency, and were able to use their power to enrich themselves. However, over the course of 30 years the demographic situation changed dramatically. The Shiites, the third largest sect in 1932, had grown to be the largest by the mid-1970s. When they (and others) called for a change in the National Pact to reflect population shifts, those groups which had benefited most from the confessional system's rigidity refused.

A Lebanese wrote in 1970 that Lebanon was a country composed of people divided against each other. This created social and economic problems, and the very rigidity of the system mitigated against their solution. Economic planners called for an equitable distribution of wealth but never said how that should be achieved. Lebanon's laissez-faire economics brought in a great deal of capital that never reached the poorest elements of society. Slowly, the country became an economic pyramid, with large gaps separating the few wealthy at the top from the many poor at the bottom. That the system lacked compassion is illustrated by the fact that throughout the 1970s no single major public works program was designed to help the southern third of Lebanon, where most of the poor lived. They felt abandoned by the government in Beirut and the opulence they saw in that city made them angry. Whenever the disadvantaged demanded a greater share of the nation's wealth, the wealthy resorted to violence. When the civil war began in 1975, a good deal of the early fighting centered around looting, gunrunning and smuggling.

Added to this dismal picture were high inflation in the early 1970s and wages that did not keep pace. After 1973, when oil prices climbed, petrodollars came pouring into Beirut, adding to the upward pressure on prices. The change between 1970 and 1974 was dramatic. For a poor Lebanese, or one on a fixed salary, it became virtually impossible to live in one's own country. On the other hand, many in power benefited from the lively business atmosphere. In 1974, the disenchantment of the poor materialized in labor disputes—50 strikes in one 30-day period. The resulting war was largely economic in origin, although some poor fought with the Right and some rich fought with the Left.

Westerners, and some Lebanese, preferred to interpret the war in a religious context, but this did not stand under close scrutiny. The Lebanese Right, champions of the status quo and dominated by Christians, received support from Muslim Arab countries and from Sunni Lebanese. On the Left, many Christians fought with the Muslim majority. Today, 40 percent of Lebanon's Christians live in areas controlled by the Left.

Even if the Lebanese civil war of 1975-1976 was largely economic in origin and would have occurred no matter what the circumstances, the presence of the Palestinians on Lebanese soil acted as a catalyst. The Palestinians went to Lebanon in 1947 as refugees. Numbering over 100,000, they were placed in refugee camps that were often located near factories where they provided cheap labor. When they organized, realizing that if they were to return to their homeland they had to struggle, they came into conflict with the Lebanese authorities. With the formation of the Palestine Liberation Organization (PLO) in 1964, the stage was set for tension.

As part of its sovereignty, a government wants to assert authority over all its territory. On the other hand, a revolutionary movement operates outside the law; it must be able to work clandestinely and to move covertly across national borders. Perhaps

Lebanon could have accepted this if the Israelis had not held Beirut responsible for controlling Palestinian guerrilla acitivity. This was explicitly demonstrated when an Israeli raid destroyed Lebanon's commercial air fleet in 1968. In effect, Israel was asking the Lebanese to choose whether to fight Israel or control the PLO. The Lebanese Right decided on the latter course, while the Left defended the Palestinians. The Israeli attack made greater the already existing differences amongst the Lebanese people. An attempt to work out a modus vivendi resulted in the Cairo Agreement of 1969 whereby the Palestinians gained control of their camps and, in return, agreed to limit their activities against Israel to certain kinds and from certain areas in Lebanon.

The civil war in Jordan in 1970-1971 doomed the fragile Cairo Agreement. Many Palestinians were forced out of Jordan into Lebanon, which they viewed as their final refuge. Today, there are perhaps 400,000 Palestinians in Lebanon and it is the only territory from which they launch guerrilla operations. As they see it, the Cairo Agreement limits their ability to act in the only territory where they have some freedom. Palestinian frustration increased in 1974 and 1975 with the signing of Sinai I and II between Egypt and Israel. Because Sinai II renounced the use of force, thus effectively neutralizing Egypt in the Arab-Israeli conflict, the Palestinians felt abandoned by Egypt and realized that their national interests were to be subordinated to Egypt's desire to regain the Sinai peninsula, which it had lost in 1967. Feeling deserted by Egypt and bombarded by Israel, the Palestinians found a natural ally in the poor Lebanese of the south, themselves forgotten by Beirut. Thus was born an alliance of the "have-nots" of the Middle East.

In January, 1975, Israel was attacking almost daily into Lebanon. As a result, Pierre Gemayel, leader of the Right and head of the Phalangist party, called for a popular referendum on the PLO's prerogative to operate out of Lebanon, arguing that a majority of Lebanese would vote no. In February, the government announced that it would give a license to a fishing company to be headed by former President Camille Chamoun, a leader in the Rightist alliance. The issuance of this license gave rise to Leftist demonstrations in the city of Sidon, because fishermen there feared that the building of a modern fish processing facility would mean the end of their livelihoods. The demonstrations ended in violence, with the death of the parliamentary member representing the town.

As the alliance of the poor and the Palestinians, the Left saw Gemayel's demand for a referendum and the violence in Sidon as Rightist attempts at suppression. The Left responded by calling for increased participation of the have-nots in the Lebanese political and economic arena, focusing attention on increasing Leftists in Parliament and calling for a new census. The Right responded that the National Pact of 1943 was inviolable, that there were no problems the Lebanese could not solve if left alone, and that Lebanon's problems were brought about by the unwanted presence of Palestinian foreigners.

In April, 1975, the Phalangists attacked a bus, killing all the Palestinian riders. This signaled the beginning of the civil war, which did not end until October, 1976. Though the fighting began for economic reasons, ultimately economics became unimportant. The Right consistently argued that the only problem was the presence of the Palestinians. Though it tried to stay out of the early fighting, the PLO later entered on the side of the Left.

The Arab states played a destructive or neutral role. Some Arab governments, regarding the PLO as a hindrance to a peaceful solution of the Arab-Israeli conflict, supported the Right. Other Arab governments wanted the Left to win because they supported revolution or thought that a Leftist victory would be an Islamic victory. Still others favored any movement that would end Western influence in Lebanon.

The United States played no visible role during the conflict. Its position was difficult; its refusal to recognize the PLO meant it had little influence with the Left. One might argue that West European nations could have taken a stronger stand, but their good relations with Arab governments, which themselves were divided, mitigated against any decisive role.

When the Lebanese army, reflecting its society, disintegrated into factions and sects, the fighting became horrendous. Since the beginning of the fighting, 80,000 people have been killed in a country of 3 million.

One might ask, who was paying for the war? The answer is largely foreign nations. And once the war was funded by outside interests, they demanded loyalty to their respective causes. Lost were the original reasons for the war. The existing militias, or newly created militias, were being used as proxies to contest all the ideologies, national antagonisms and personal animosities that permeate the region.

In order to stop the carnage, the United States supported an agreement between Syria and Israel. Israeli Foreign Minister Yigael Allon sent a letter to the United States in March, 1976, outlining the conditions under which Israel would accept Syrian intervention in Lebanon. The letter was passed to Syria. One may speculate with some certainty that Syria was to have free reign in the northern two-thirds of the country while Israel was to have control of the skies and a sphere of influence in the southern third, below an imaginary "Red Line" where its enemy, the PLO, was concentrated.

In line with the agreement, the Syrian army marched into Lebanon. On one level, there was considerable satisfaction that the Syrians had arrived to end the bloodshed. But to end the war, they had to stop the Left (which by the summer of 1976 was winning the war) because one Syrian aim was to restore a balance between the two sides. The Arab League legitimized the Syrian army's presence by calling it the Arab Deterrent Force, which numbers 22,000 men.

The end of the fighting in October, 1976, saw Beirut divided between Left and Right, with the Left and its Palestinian allies holding West Beirut. Most of the PLO forces, however, returned to the south to face their traditional enemies, the Israelis.

Renewed PLO and Israeli hostility reached a peak in March, 1978, when Israel attacked the Palestinians by invading south Lebanon. The United Nations condemned the invasion and created UNIFIL to supervise the Israeli withdrawal and return south Lebanon to the Lebanese government. UNIFIL has been unable to fulfill its mission, because Israel turned over a seven-mile-deep enclave to the Rightist, Sa'd Haddad. Israel and Haddad argued that giving their buffer zone to UNIFIL would mean the return of the PLO and its attacks into Israel. The creation of "Free

Lebanon" in 1978 was an embarrassment to the Lebanese government. Its official position is that Haddad (who was officially dismissed from the army in April, 1979) and his Israeli allies are resisting the reassertion of government control over all Lebanese territory.

Haddad receives training, arms and other supplies for his 2,000-man force from the Israelis. In order to enter Haddad-land one goes through Israel. To publicize his view that Lebanon is occupied by foreigners, largely Palestinians and Syrians, Haddad has established two radio stations, which play American country and western music when they are not broadcasting Rightist propaganda. In February, 1981, "Free Lebanon" acquired a television station. The money for this $1-million enterprise came from High Adventure, a Christian fundamentalist organization in California associated with George Otis.

Whatever Haddad's protestations, it is clear that he serves Israel by keeping Palestinians from the Israeli border. That this policy has won over some Lebanese cannot be denied. Only 40 percent of the 100,000 people under Haddad's control are Christian. Many Muslims have come to believe that the PLO brings nothing but problems for them in the form of Israeli attacks, and they have shown a willingness to join Haddad's forces. There is also some fear that the Palestinians may ultimately be settled in the south and the Lebanese may therefore lose their land.

UNIFIL is caught between the PLO and Haddad. More than 60 soldiers of the United Nations force have been killed since 1978. Whenever UNIFIL attempts to increase its control in the south and to turn territory over to the Lebanese government, Israel and Haddad open fire.

The tacit agreement reached in 1976 between Syria and Israel yielded benefits for both countries. The Israelis gained influence in the southern third of Lebanon, and the Syrians were able to prevent the Left from gaining a victory which would have led to a pro-Palestinian government in Beirut. The Syrian government would like to see a negotiated settlement and does not want to become embroiled in another conflict with Israel, which a Leftist government in Beirut might have precipitated. Furthermore, by controlling two-thirds of Lebanon, Syria gained control of an area that might be traded later for the Golan Heights.

However, the congruence of interests that linked Israel and Syria in 1976 ended with the Israeli invasion of 1978 and Israel's subsequent alliance with Haddad and the Lebanese Right. Horrified by the possibility of a Rightist victory in a renewal of the war, Syria switched its support to the Left and the PLO.

The Leftist alliance is bound together by its commitment to an economically and politically restructured Lebanon that is not so Western-oriented as in the past and that supports the Palestinian revolution. Among the more important groups of the Left are the *Murabitun* under the leadership of Ibrahim Qulaylat, who is loyal to Damascus; the Iraqi branch of the Baath party; the Lebanese Communist party; the Syrian Socialist Nationalist party; the Progressive Socialist party (PSP), under the leadership of Walid Junblat, which represents the Druze; remnants of the Lebanese army; the PLO; and al-Amal, the Shiite organization. There is tension among the partners in the National Movement, as the Left calls itself; witness the fighting between al-Amal and pro-Iraqi forces, reflecting the hostility caused by the Iran-Iraq war. Pro-Syrian forces have also attacked pro-Iraqi forces, mirroring the tension between their respective champions.

Particularly crucial to the Left is al-Amal, which is loyal to Ayatollah Ruhollah Khomeini. The PLO has distanced itself from the leader of the Iranian revolution as Iran moves closer to civil war. As a result, tensions between the PLO and al-Amal have increased. The Shiites are arming themselves rapidly, willing to engage PLO forces, and rumored to be receiving arms from the Right, and they would probably align themselves with whichever side helps them gain more power.

The Lebanese Front, as the Right calls itself, is also composed of many groups. The most important are the Phalangists, under the leadership of Pierre Gemayel and his sons, Amin and Bashir; the Free Nationalist party of Camille Chamoun; the Maronite Order of Monks led by Charbel Kassis; the Marada (Giants) of Suleiman Franjieh and factions of the Lebanese army. The Right is committed to a Lebanon that is Western oriented and has the Christian flavor that orientation implies. If possible, it would support the Palestinians only on the political level. Therefore it calls for the control of guerrilla activity on Lebanese soil and the withdrawal of the ADF or the requirement that it become a truly inter-Arab force.

As Syria became supportive of the Left after 1978, cracks within the Rightist alliance appeared. Former President Franjieh, always loyal to the Syrians, broke with the Right in 1978. He has reconciled himself with the traditional Sunni leadership in Tripoli and has carved out with them a territory that is loyal to Syria. In July, 1980, the two strongest factions within the Rightist alliance fought for supremacy, and the Phalangists emerged victorious over the Free Nationalists. In essence, Pierre Gemayel and his son Bashir, leader of the Phalangist militia, rule unchallenged throughout the Rightist-held areas. Israel has supplied the Phalangists with 40 American-made Sherman tanks and has provided extensive training to the Phalangists' 15,000-man force.

Since Beirut is far and away the most important area in Lebanon, it has been the focus of fighting since 1975. In the past year, the capital has been plagued by inter-Arab squabbles, as well as by hostilities between Syria and the Right and the PLO and Israel. Emboldened by its closer ties with Israel, the Right began in 1981 to call for the "liberation" of all Lebanon. The desire to be rid of the Palestinians and the Syrians resulted in heavy fighting in April and May, 1981.

Though the fighting between the PLO and Israel is usually focused in the south where the Palestinian guerrillas are located, the war often erupts in Beirut. The PLO has its command structure in Beirut, its political activities emanate from that city, and several refugee camps are located in the area.

In its ongoing fight with Israel, the PLO had acquired long-range artillery and multiple-barrel Katyushas capable of firing 40 rockets simultaneously, which enabled the PLO to bombard villages in Israel. With both sides escalating the warfare, Israel announced in 1979 that its activities in Lebanon would no longer be retaliatory but rather preemptive.

We are on the offensive. We are the aggressors. We are penetrating the so-called border of the so-called sovereign state of Lebanon and we go after them [the Palestinian guerrillas] wherever they hide.

The violence culminated in the Israeli bombing of West Beirut on July 17, 1981, in a raid that killed 300 people and wounded at least 800 more. This attack on a civilian area severely embarrassed the United States and brought international condemnation of Israel. The administration of President Ronald Reagan reacted by extending the freeze on the shipment of American jets to Israel, a stay that had been imposed because of Israel's destruction of the Iraqi nuclear reactor in June.

The inability of Prime Minister Menachem Begin's government to end the shelling of northern Israel and the international uproar over its bombing of Beirut left Israel with two unpleasant choices. The first was to repeat the invasion of March, 1978, to stop the PLO. This had not worked in 1978 and presumably would not work in 1981. The second choice was a cease-fire between the PLO and Israel. This was accomplished on July 14 and was even extended to the Syrian-Rightist confrontation. The PLO hailed the cease-fire as an international public relations victory because by agreeing to it Israel indirectly recognized the PLO.

In September and October, 1981, urban terror returned to Beirut in the form of car bombings, mostly in Leftist Beirut, which were apparently directed at the PLO. The Palestinians claim that the terror wave is Israeli-inspired, though no one has claimed responsibility. Thus as 1981 came to a close, tension remained high in Beirut and throughout the country.

Seven years of fighting have taken a tremendous economic toll. The central government is unable to collect taxes on a regular basis and depends on foreign aid from Saudi Arabia, France, the United States, and others. Since 1975, the road system has deteriorated because few roads can be repaired. The government is working with Sweden on the telephone system, which was never good even in the best of times. Supplies of water and electric power are often erratic. The government, however, is operating under difficulties.

The deterioration of the economy has been accelerated by the flight of professionals and technicians, particularly in medicine and merchandising. Yet the Lebanese seem to have money. The foreign powers involved in the fighting pay their forces well. Lebanese abroad continue to remit $100 million a month. Deposits in Lebanon's banks have grown by one-third in the last three years. Many merchants, their stores destroyed, are still trying to reap advantage from adversity. Push carts filled with goods may be seen as far south as the UNIFIL held area. Small ports controlled by one or another militia collect "tariffs" and allow contraband to enter the country. There is a thriving business in perfume, cigarettes, hashish, guns and stolen cars.

The Biqa' Valley

The international community fears that the fighting in Lebanon will get out of hand, escalate to involve Syria and Israel, cause the failure of the Israeli-Egyptian peace treaty, and lead ultimately to a confrontation between the superpowers. Such a sequence almost occurred in the summer of 1981. The crisis began when the Phalangists widened and paved a dirt road from Zahlé westward over the Sannin Mountains, to connect the provincial capital of the Biqa' (Bekaa) Valley with the Rightist heartland on the western side of the mountains.

This was an action the Syrians could not tolerate for a number of reasons. Zahlé was in a Syrian-controlled area and the loss of the town would have been a serious blow to Damascus. Near the city is Riyaq airbase and the town of Shtura, both of which served as headquarters for the Syrian-dominated ADF. Zahlé also overlooked the Beirut-Damascus highway, a critical supply and communications line. Furthermore, control of Zahlé meant control of the Biqa'. The Syrians believe that, for their own defense, they must control the valley because a drive northward through it leads to the Syrian city of Homs, the headquarters of Syrian communications. (Also, in 1973, Israeli jets had flown up the Biqa' before heading east to attack Damascus.) Finally, if the Phalangist plan was successful, the Syrians believed they would be caught in a pincer movement—the Right attacking from the northwest and Israel attacking from the south.

The Syrians reacted by surrounding Zahlé on April 1, and throughout the month they attacked the Phalangists above the city. By the end of April, the ADF was able to move the Rightists out of the hills and to concentrate their attention on forcing the

Phalangists out of the town. Israel reacted on April 28 by downing two Syrian helicopters. Israeli Prime Minister Menachem Begin argued that he would not allow the Christians to be annihilated in Lebanon; apparently he had been looking for an opportunity to be "tough," to impress the electorate before Israel's June elections.

On April 29, Syria moved three batteries of SAM-6's, surface to air missiles, into the Biqa'. Though the missiles are defensive, their position in Lebanon was viewed by the Israelis as a severe escalation of the conflict. Israel feared that the SAM-6's ultimately would be moved into Palestinian areas to protect the PLO and to limit Israel's reconnaissance flights. Syria argued, on the other hand, that the Israeli downing of its helicopters was a violation of the agreement that had allowed Syrian intervention in 1976.

The United States was so worried that activities would escalate into a major war that it dispatched Philip Habib, a retired State Department official, to defuse the situation. Habib remained in the area for 21 days in May. Crucial to Habib's mission were the Saudis, who were underwriting the costs of the ADF and giving additional foreign aid to Damascus. Saudi pressure on Syria and American leverage on Israel defused the crisis. Habib believed that the real issue was not the missiles but the tension between the Rightists and the Syrians. While urging the Israelis not to attack the SAM's, he worked for a suitable end to the seige of Zahlé, which ended on June 30 after 90 days. Though the Phalangists were able to gain international media coverage, the Syrians seemed to be the winners. They retained control of the Biqa', and their missiles are still in place.

The future of Lebanon, at least in the short term, appears bleak. If it were simply a matter of national reconciliation, the problem could perhaps be solved. When it began to lose the civil war, the Right expressed a willingness to increase the power of the Left. In this light, the contacts between the Right and the Shiites are important.

Even a national consensus on the PLO may be emerging. At the Islamic summit meeting in Saudi Arabia in January, 1981, President Elias Sarkis asked the PLO to abide by the Cairo Agreement, arguing that the Palestinian resistance operates only out of Lebanon, that Lebanon is punished by Israel for this, and that "Lebanon is no longer able to bear the death, destruction and displacement of its people." Earlier, the President told a group of ambassadors, "If the Palestinian problem is sacred, it is self-evident that Lebanon's unity, integrity, sovereignty and independence is [sic] also sacred. . . . " No Lebanese group opposed either of his statements.

The Palestinians, of course, are not willing to leave Lebanon, their last refuge, unless it means returning to their homeland. In March, 1977, United States President Jimmy Carter called for such a Palestinian entity. And in 1981 as they were returning from President Anwar Sadat's funeral in October, he and former President Gerald Ford urged the Reagan administration to open negotiations with the PLO.

Even if a Palestinian homeland were established and if the Lebanese were reconciled, Lebanon's problems would not end. Israel controls the southern third of the country and has often said that its more natural "boundary" with Lebanon is the Litani River. Israel also controls the skies and the sea lanes and is the protector of the Rightists. Presumably Israel would not give up these advantages unless it could gain something in return.

Israel may also believe that a continuation of the Lebanese conflict is in its best interests. As long as there is conflict in the country, Arab and world attention is diverted from Israel's settlement policy on the West Bank and its annexation of Jerusalem. For Syria, as well, there is some advantage in remaining in Lebanon, because its prestige grows when it is the only Arab country willing to stand up to Israel.

Some Lebanese military leaders are suggesting another solution. Lacking a political settlement, these officers are suggesting that the country should be forcibly united. This seems unlikely. The army would have to be doubled from its current size of 20,000 and it would have to be accepted by all Lebanese. The army is still perceived as basically a Christian militia, an image that was not enhanced in the April, 1981, fighting when some units sided with the Right. Weak, perhaps divided, and with little popular following, the army does not appear to provide an answer.

If one were to ask a Lebanese how he would end the hemorrhaging, he might ask for West European intervention. This does not seem likely either, because of the East European opposition it might cause. Thus Lebanon may well continue in its present state for the foreseeable future.

ARAB INACTION ON LEBANON[4]

The absence of an effective response by Arab nations to the Israeli onslaught against the Palestinians in Lebanon is attributed by many Arabs to their overwhelming sense of helplessness.

"The Israelis counted on the inter-Arab divisions when they launched their invasion," an official of the Palestine Liberation Organization said. "And they were right."

In the light of the Arab inaction, it is hard to tell here sometimes whether the Palestinians are angrier at the Israelis for overrunning their bases in southern Lebanon or at the Arab nations for sitting idly by while it happened.

"I don't understand how the Arabs can be so ineffectual when the Israelis are knocking at the gates of an Arab capital," Yasir Arafat, the PLO chairman said in a radio address last week as Israeli forces were poised in the southern outskirts of Beirut.

"The submissive and indifferent Arabs," added Mr. Arafat's chief deputy, Salah Khalaf, "will be brought to account for their attitude."

The virtual silence of the leaders of Arab nations over the last two weeks speaks volumes about the political changes that have overtaken the Middle East since the Camp David accords were signed in September 1978.

The removal of Egypt from the ranks of enemies of Israel and the disagreements over the Iran-Iraq war have left the Arabs too weak militarily and too divided politically to act in concert either regionally or internationally. The Arabs' military weakness is

[4] Newspaper article by Thomas L. Friedman. *New York Times.* p A1. Je. 21, '82. © 1982 by The New York Times Company. Reprinted by permission.

largely a result of the fact that two of the three main Arab armies have been removed from the Arab-Israeli military equation.

Egypt had been at the forefront of every Arab-Israeli military campaign since 1948. But with its signing of a peace treaty with Israel in March 1979, Egypt was no longer available as a fighting force for the Arabs. This neutralized the only Arab army the Israelis respected on its own.

Making matters even worse, the Iraqi Army, which had always contributed men and matériel to every battle with Israel, became tied down in a losing war with Iran.

With Jordan not about to go to war to save the PLO and with the other Arab nations lacking any threatening armed forces, only Syria was left. No one was more aware of this than the Syrians.

Syria's Dangerous Game

Damascus played a very dangerous game with the Israelis, trying to protect as much of its area of control in Lebanon as possible without becoming embroiled in a full-scale, one-to-one fight with Israel. Once this balancing act started to become impossible after the Israeli invasion June 6, the Syrians agreed to a cease-fire, leaving the Palestinians to fight on their own.

On the diplomatic front, the Arabs have never been more divided at anytime since Israel's creation. The lines of division run along two axes.

Since the Egyptians made peace with Israel, the other Arab nations have been groping for a unified strategy on how to deal with Israel. Moderate oil-producing nations have rallied around the peace plan offered by Saudi Arabia as an alternative to Camp David. The plan offered by Crown Prince Fahd, who is now King, calls for Israeli withdrawal from all occupied Arab territories, the establishment of a Palestinian state and the recognition of the right of all states in the area to live in peace.

Hard-liners led by Syria and Libya rejected even this approach, but they did not offer any alternative military or diplomatic strategy. The result has been months of verbal jousting between the two camps, producing nothing but suspicion and bad feelings.

The Split Over Iran

There is, however, an even deeper fissure running through the Arab world, and it emanates from the Iranian capital of Teheran. The threat that a militant, Islamic revolutionary regime under Ayatollah Ruhollah Khomeini might overwhelm the Arab oil nations has refocused the attention of the Saudis and other Persian Gulf Arabs from the Palestinian problem to their Gulf problem. Although it was Iraq that fought the war to contain Iran, it was the Gulf Arabs who underwrote it, for a total of $24 billion so far.

But where the Saudis and Kuwaitis saw a threat, the Syrians, Libyans and other hard-liners saw an opportunity. The Iranians were a revolutionary force for change, and their enemies, particularly Iraq, were also the enemies of Damascus and Tripoli. Hence the Syrians and Libyans began aiding Iran in its war effort, incurring the wrath of the other Arabs.

All of these divisions boiled over at the Arab summit meeting in November in Fez, Morocco. Since then, the Arab leaders have been unable to get together around one table, even when the Lebanese Government appealed for a summit meeting on the first day of the Israeli invasion.

Being unable to do anything collectively, the Saudis, Kuwaitis and others have tried to act independently, pressing Washington to restrain Israel. But even these independent initiatives came in the second week of the war, and the motivation for them was not entirely altruistic.

The Arab oil nations have always been of two minds about the PLO. On the one hand, they identify with its cause. But on the other, the guerrillas have always represented a force with nothing to lose in a region of wealthy oil producers that have everything to lose.

Whatever his image in the West, Mr. Arafat is viewed by the Saudis as a moderate within the PLO and as a restraining force on the radicals in his coalition of eight groups.

It is noteworthy that the PLO as such does not have an office in Saudi Arabia. The Saudis always dealt with the organization through a personal representative of Mr. Arafat's Al Fatah, the mainstream group in the PLO. They rarely had dealings with radical members such as Dr. George Habash, leader of the Popular Front for the Liberation of Palestine.

"When the Saudis warned Israel . . . against attacking the PLO headquarters in west Beirut," a PLO official here said, "they were also warning them against wiping out the only thing preventing the PLO from breaking up into smaller, uncontrollable units that would wreak havoc on the ruling Arab elites."

MR. BEGIN'S NEW FRIENDS[5]

Amid all the reporting of Lebanese turbulence and Palestinian vacillation, the press found little space for a small but significant story from Jerusalem. On July 25, the ranks of Menachem Begin's Likud Party government were augmented by the three members of the Tehiya Party. This brings Begin's Knesset majority to eight. It also makes rather clearer the real objective of his war on the PLO in Lebanon.

The Tehiya Party represents the extreme right in Israel. Its leader, Guela Cohen, was the author of the bill that annexed Jerusalem as Israel's "eternal and indivisible" capital. By adding the Tehiya to his parliamentary strength, Begin has insured that the Israeli rejection front is part of the government.

We have argued before that the chief purpose of the invasion of Lebanon is the consolidation of Israeli rule on the West Bank. And, according to the BBC World Service, the price the Tehiya asked (and got) for its support was several thousand new homes and seven new settlements on the occupied West Bank. General Sharon, the designer and executor of the Lebanese war, is also the sponsor of the Israeli settlement movement at home.

Of course, the main argument of the past week has been about the ambiguities of Yasir Arafat. Though he is clearly continuing in his years-old policy of adapting to the existence of Israel, he has not quite uttered the phrases that are demanded of him. Is it not

[5] Editorial in *Nation*. 235:97. Ag. 7, '82. Copyright 1982 by the Nation Associates, Inc. Reprinted by permission.

incredibly, tragically unwise for the Israeli government to choose this precise moment to incorporate its own rejectionists more fully into power? If Tehiya and Likud get their way and the West Bank is annexed by Israel, there will be nothing for Arafat to negotiate about and the whole exercise of coaxing him toward recognition will have been in vain.

MIDDLE EAST COMMENTS[6]

To see the Israeli invasion of Lebanon for what it really is, one needs a vision that combines (a) Menachem Begin's lifelong ambition to bring all western Palestine (*Eretz Israel* in Hebrew) under Jewish domination—to achieve which he must break down Palestinian resistance; (b) Ariel Sharon's view of Israel as a superpower whose strategic interests range—as he put it in an interview published last December—from northern and central Africa via the Levant to the Persian Gulf and Arabia; (c) Chief-of-Staff Gen. Raphael Eitan's idea that a splendid war machine, such as the Israeli Army has become under his command, must be used if it is not to grow rusty.

The combination of these three concepts led to the war in Lebanon, incredibly named "Peace for Galilee"—which region, incidentally, has experienced nothing warlike since the cease-fire agreement with the PLO in July 1981.

I shall not go into the military and political implications of the siege of Beirut, the end of which, as I write these words, is not in sight. What is becoming discernible is the effect of the war on Israeli society. In the 1967 war, although Israel took the initiative, it was in response to direct threats by Gamal Abdel Nasser. In 1973, it was Egypt and Syria which struck first. The present war caught the Israeli public, no less than the Lebanese, by surprise. Its prolongation beyond the originally stated objective of clearing

[6] Magazine article by Yael Lotan, an Israeli writer and editor; formerly managing editor of *New Outlook*. *Nation*. 235:100-101. Ag. 7. '82. Copyright 1982, by the Nation Associates, Inc. Reprinted by permission.

the PLO out of a forty-kilometer area north of the border, and the high number of Israeli casualties, have shaken the confidence of large segments of the public in the government. Setting aside leftist and peace groups, many Israelis who in the past never questioned the rationale behind the government's belligerent acts—including the so-called "Litani Operation" in 1978 and the bombing of the Iraqi nuclear reactor in 1981—have now grown very thoughtful, and some are already voicing their reservations about the entire operation.

Protests abroad are generally dismissed as hypocritical, motivated by either oil and petro-dollars or anti-Semitism. But the disaffection—which is also found among soldiers in the field—is unmistakable, and is pointed up by the fact that the government has seen fit to organize demonstrations in support of its position. Perhaps for the first time since 1976, Israelis are beginning to wonder if military might alone can resolve the fundamental problems of their country's relations with its neighbors, and to realize that underlying it all is the Palestinian problem. To keep driving these wretched refugees from pillar to post through all eternity does not seem like a plausible answer after all. And it has become disconcertingly clear to many Israelis that whereas in the past it was the declared ambition of the Arabs "to drive Israel into the sea," today it is Israel which seems to be trying to do this to the Palestinians. Only the very gung-ho or the very naïve believe that this can be done and that the Palestinian national movement and its leadership can be crushed. The rest of the public is finding this hard to swallow. Does that mean there is a profound change of heart in Israel, a disenchantment with Begin and his policies? It's too early to say. It is not impossible.

MIDDLE EAST COMMENTS[7]

For a generation now, I have been deeply troubled by the chauvinistic assumptions and repressive effects of Israeli nationalism. I have experienced the war on Lebanon as a turning point in Jewish history and consciousness, exceeded in importance perhaps only by the end of the Second Commonwealth and the Holocaust. I have resisted the idea for more than thirty years, but the war on Lebanon has now made clear to me that the resumption of political power by the Jewish people after 2,000 years of Diaspora has been a tragedy of historical dimensions. The state of Israel has demanded recognition as the modern political incarnation of the Jewish people. To grant that is to betray the Jewish tradition.

The state of Israel and its supporters have probably been right all along in arguing that political power comes at the price of the normal detritus of the nation-state. But I am not disposed to await the outcome of debates by politicians and theologians on whether the threat from the Palestine Liberation Organization was sufficiently clear and present to justify the killing of so many Lebanese and Palestinian men, women and children (or of *only* so many). I will not avoid an unambiguous response to the Israeli Army's turning West Beirut into another Warsaw Ghetto.

I conclude and avow that the price of a Jewish state is, to me, Jewishly unacceptable and that the existence of this (or any similar) Jewish ethnic-religious nation-state is a Jewish—i.e., a human and moral—disaster and violates every remaining value for which Judaism and Jews might exist in history. The lethal military triumphalism and corrosive racism that inheres in the state and in its supporters (both there and here) are profoundly abhorrent to me. So is the message that now goes forth to the nations of the world that the Jewish people claim the right to impose a holocaust on others in order to preserve their state.

[7] Magazine article by Henry Schwarzschild, who fled Nazi Germany in 1939. *Nation*. 235:100-101. Ag. 7, '82. Copyright, 1982, by the Nation Associates, Inc. Reprinted by permission.

I now renounce the state of Israel, disavow any political connection or emotional obligation to it and declare myself its enemy. I retain, of course, the same deep concern for its inhabitants—Jewish, Arab and other—that I hold for all humankind.

I remain a member of the Jewish people—indeed, I have no other inner identity. But the state of Israel has now triumphed over the Jewish people and their history, for the time being at least. I deem it possible that the state, morally bankrupted and morally endangered by its victories, is essential to the survival of the Jewish people. Therefore, it may take the Jewish people with it to eventual extinction. Yet I believe that the death of the Jewish people would not be inherently more tragic than the death of the Palestinian people, which Israel and its supporters evidently seek or at least accept as the cost of the "security" of the state of Israel. The price of the millennial survival of the Jewish people has been high; I did not think the point was to make others pay it. That moral scandal intolerably assaults the accumulated values of Jewish history and tradition.

If that is where the state of Israel chooses to stand, I cannot stand with it. I therefore resign all connections with Jewish political and public institutions that will not radically oppose the state and its claim to Jewish legitimacy.

THE ISRAELI BLUES[8]

The British historian Alistair Horne, whose work has brought him great renown, has for many years publicly and privately argued the case for Israel. Moreover his sympathy for Israel crystallized notwithstanding the personal tug of his own experiences. As a young officer in the Coldstream Guards he was assigned to duty in Palestine and there two of his 19-years-old subordinates were ambushed and hanged by terrorists of the Irgun, which organization was at the time headed by Mr. Begin himself. It is important

[8] Article from *National Review* by William F. Buckley Jr., editor. 34:253. Mr. 5, '82. Copyright 1982 by Wm. F. Buckley Jr. Reprinted by permission.

in passing to re-record that Mr. Begin's activities were specifically condemned by the Israeli leadership, so that it becomes less easy to say, as Jesse Jackson likes to do, that Israel has no right to criticize the terrorism of the PLO given "Israel's" history. It wasn't Israel's history, but the present danger is that Israel's history and Begin's fanaticism may merge.

This point, made by Mr. Horne, threatens to infect the basis of Israel's support, which has all along been one part geopolitical, and nine parts moral. In England, Horne reports, the feeling grows that Mr. Begin has no intention at all of coming forward with any strategic plan for a Palestinian "entity," as President Mubarak now calls it, since everyone is afraid of pronouncing the word "Palestinian state." The essence of the Israeli case has always been the right of a people to a homeland, sanctified in the case of the Jews by tradition and by the special ties the Jewish people have felt for Jerusalem. But the right of a people to a homeland is, at root, impartial. The Palestinians are also entitled to a home. It was the purpose of the Camp David meetings to build on the great initiative of President Sadat, who proffered reconciliation with Israel. One chapter of that initiative is scheduled to close successfully when Israel returns the balance of the Sinai to Egypt. But the uncharted second chapter greatly threatens the initiative of Sadat in 1978, which looked not only to the repatriation of his country's territories, but to the settlement of Palestinian hopes.

Now although PLO leader Arafat is thoroughly objectionable, and although the Palestine National Council persists in declining to accept the existence of Israel, supporters of Israel are increasingly embarrassed by the failure of the Begin government to articulate *terms* on the basis of which something on the order of a homeland might be established. The anti-Israeli crowd have all along insisted that Mr. Begin never had any intention to give up the West Bank or the Gaza Strip, that he would come up with excuse after excuse for not doing so. And that in the meantime he would encourage an increase in the settlements in the area. And now the critics are in a position to add that the time may come when Begin will do to the West Bank what he did two months ago to the Golan Heights: simply annex the area.

Now, intransigence in the matter of the security of the state is one thing. If it disguises a form of aggrandizement, it is something else again. Horne's point, and I agree with it, is that Begin is diminishingly plausible as someone who seeks Israeli security within the old frontiers. Increasingly he fits the mold of the Zionist impelled by Biblical appetites to settle as a part of Israel the area once known as Samaria. And the problem for Israel—recognized as a problem by many Israeli leaders and sympathizers—is to distinguish between Begin, who is only a single political figure, however seized he appears to be by his afflatus, and the State of Israel. It is their ambition that the latter should survive the former.

What's needed? Surely the precedent of Austria in 1955 is useful.

The Austria Peace Treaty resulted in the single voluntary retreat by the Soviet army from territory occupied during the World War. But the terms were tough: Austria would remain neutral. The armed forces of Austria would be restricted to what was needed to police the country. Although Austria is for obvious reasons emotionally attached to NATO rather than to Warsaw, in fact it has presented no threat to Russian satellites.

A Palestinian state without the right to an armed force would not come into being as an emasculate. The Palestinians would simply have to accept the humiliation of having no army or air force, or other potential that might threaten Israel. But in other respects, such a state would have sovereignty to make its own laws: and these laws should grant the same rights to Israelis living in Palestine as the Israelis grant the Palestinians living in Israel. Only a gesture by Begin in the direction of such an agreement would repristinate the enthusiasm that Alistair Horne and others have felt for so many years for Israel. The present course is deeply dangerous. Imagine an Israel in which Teddy Kollek of Jerusalem were President, and Shimon Peres Prime Minister. One can dream.

THE HABIB OPENING[9]

The chance created by Mr. Philip Habib and his co-negotiators in Beirut must not be lost. To look for certainty in the Middle East is to walk on egg-shells. But by Thursday morning, August 12th, [1982] the main obstacles to an agreement removing the Palestine Liberation Organization from Lebanon had probably been overcome. Mr. Arafat's PLO at last seemed willing to go. The necessary number of reluctant Arab governments had at last agreed to provide another exile for the PLO's leaders and guerrillas. And Israel was probably ready to settle for the PLO's evacuation rather than the extermination some bloodier-minded Israelis had appeared to hanker after. . . . Mr. Habib and weary company have turned a shambles into an opportunity.

The removal of the PLO from Lebanon opens a window that had long seemed jammed shut. In most places where people are in conflict with each other, the psychological factors—suspicion, fear, self-mistrust—are as important as more measurable things like territory or borders. In Israel's 34-year-old confrontation with the Arabs, the psychological factors have been overriding. The Israeli itch for physical expansion has to a large extent, though by no means entirely, been the distorted image of the Israeli yearning for physical security. No lasting peace is possible in the region until the Israelis feel that they can live in safety. Properly handled, meaning vigorously and firmly handled by the United States, the PLO's withdrawal from Lebanon can be the start of a process which makes Israel feel safe without sitting on large numbers of Arabs. It can lead to a secure Israeli land short of Mr. Begin's unnaturally and unjustly expansionist Old Testamentarian Land of Israel.

[9] Magazine article from *Economist.* 284:9-10. Ag. 14, '82. Copyright The Economist Newspaper Ltd., London, 1982. Reprinted by permission.

Let Safer Mean Bolder

For the first time, almost all of Israel's frontiers could soon be at peace in practice, if not yet in theory. With Egypt a formal peace treaty has already been signed. A similar peace should be possible with post-PLO Lebanon: since the 1947-1948 war which brought Israel into existence, it is only the PLO's state-within-a-state in Lebanon that has led to fighting across that border. King Hussein's Jordan has had a hands-off arrangement with Israel since 1967. Only Syria, which touches Israel along the 40 miles of the Golan heights, is still in a state of heartfelt enmity, and Syria is in no shape at the moment to do anything about that thumb's-width of dispute.

Those are the physical frontiers. Even more important is the shadow-frontier of fear and hatred that separates Israel from the Arabs of the West Bank and the Gaza Strip, whom it has controlled since the war of 1967. The scattering of the PLO, if Israel is made to think calmly about it, should disperse some of that shadow.

The great majority of Israelis, not just Mr. Begin's band of religious-nationalist zealots, rejected the idea of a fully independent Palestinian state in the West Bank and Gaza, under a PLO government, because they said that this would in the end be incompatible with the survival of Israel. They observed, correctly, that the PLO was only a loose confederation; they argued that the parts of the confederation which were willing to live in peace with Israel would not be able to control those which were not. This is why even many Israelis who disagree with Mr. Begin were stubbornly unwilling to allow any autonomous Palestinian political life to develop in the occupied territories, lest that give the PLO its foothold. The defeat of the PLO should help to banish this nervous Israeli immobility.

Whether the dispersed PLO holds its confederation together, or splits up into its component parts, its campaign for an independent Palestine has taken a fearful blow. So has its influence over the West Bankers and the Gazans. The Palestinian problem has not changed: the Palestinians are still people living under Israeli orders, or refugees huddled in Jordanian and Lebanese camps, or exiles dotted deeper around the Arab world. What could change is Israel's attitude towards the core of the problem, the Palestinian heartland in the West Bank and Gaza. With the weakening of the PLO, Israel has not even half-plausible reason not to let these two areas have a genuine system of home-rule.

Home-rule is different from independence, in that Israel or Jordan or Egypt (or combinations of them) would still supervise the peace in the West Bank and Gaza. But the inhabitants would otherwise be free to pass and administer their own laws. They could regain the use of much of the land which a PLO-obsessed Israel has put under its army's control. They could have a fairer share of the all-important water supplies.

Provided, that is, the Reagan administration jumps vigorously into the next stage of the proceedings. The United States has the inclination to nudge Israel towards genuine Palestinian autonomy. Mr. Reagan himself, pro-Israeli though he is, has said that there is right on both sides; and in Mr. George Shultz and Mr. Caspar Weinberger he has two ministers who want to remove the Palestinian obstacle to better American relations with the Arab world.

The United States also, without doubt, has the power to nudge. The Americans are hamstrung when they wish to extract sudden changes of policy from Israel (as when they asked it to pull back in west Beirut earlier this month), because they have armed Israel so thoroughly that it can always afford to defy them for a time. But their command over the Israeli purse, and much of the Israeli armory, certainly gives them the power to urge slower, quieter changes of direction. America has not used this power to insist on a fully independent Palestine because most Americans have shared most Israelis' fears of where that might lead. For a better definition of home-rule the power could, and should, be used.

There are booby-traps waiting to be trodden on. In their despair, some parts of the PLO will plunge into new experiments in international terrorism, or subversion of insufficiently sympathetic Arab governments; and some Israelis will claim this as a new reason for doing nothing about Palestine. The Begin part of Israel, clinging to its historical dream, will argue that the United States cannot afford to take risks with its Israeli friend in a Middle

East which also contains its Ayatollah Khomeini foe. The answer is that, if nothing at all is done for the Palestinians, the Middle East may before long contain two, three or four Khomeinis; and Israel cannot indefinitely live with itself if its only policy towards the Palestinians is to keep them a subject people without any political rights.

An opportunity to avoid this may now be emerging, as big as the opportunity created by Sadat's trip to Jerusalem in 1977. The road by which it was reached has been horrible. When the truth eventually emerges, or something close to it, the number of people killed in Lebanon in the past 10 weeks may be smaller than first reports suggested; but there is a sense in which a political opportunity cannot be "bought" by any number of lives. The business of statesmen is to make the best they can out of the wreckage created by human hatreds: to convert, where they can, bad into somewhat better. In different ways, the governments of America and Israel are now challenged to do that.

MIDEAST IRONIES[10]

The Middle East has long been a greenhouse for ironies, but none quite as striking as the one now flowering in Beirut. For eight weeks the West, and particularly the United States, has engaged in a massive effort to rescue the PLO, an organization that has warred on the West for fifteen years, a Soviet client with irredentist claims that promise the Middle East no peace until either it or Israel ceases to exist.

Why has Philip Habib engaged for two months in extraordinarily complicated negotiations to save the PLO? Why has the U.S. made its prestige contingent upon Mr. Habib's ability to produce a peaceful PLO exit from Lebanon? For the vast majority of Americans, and for this Administration, the answer does not lie in any sympathy with the PLO. They recognize that Yasir Arafat

[10] Magazine article by the editors. *New Republic.* 187:7-9. Ag. 30, '82. Reprinted by permission of The New Republic, © 1982 The New Republic.

called for armed struggle, got armed struggle, and now has lost the armed struggle. They also remember the particular type of armed struggle that the PLO has waged. Unlike Israel, which despite its precautions has killed civilians in pursuit of enemy soldiers, the PLO has always made the killing of civilians an end in itself. Can anyone remember a single PLO attack in the last fifteen years on an Israeli military installation? The athletes in Munich and the schoolchildren of Maalot were not unfortunate innocents who happened to be living near Israeli artillery batteries, ammunition dumps, or military targets. They *were* the military targets.

To be sure, there are some, mostly in Europe, who want to save the PLO for its own sake, who want to support the fight against Israel to the last Palestinian. By and large, they are romantics caught up in national liberation mythology, or else they still believe—after fifteen years of evidence to the contrary—that the PLO will bring dignity and peace to the Palestinians. But most Americans know the PLO's record—know what it has done to others and what suffering its false promises and empty bravado have brought to the people it claims to represent.

Americans, like Israelis and Lebanese and Palestinians, would like to see Mr. Habib succeed and the war end without any more deaths on either side. But the PLO's interests are different. Had it been interested in ending the war with a minimum of bloodshed, it would have evacuated Beirut weeks ago. It discovered that by prolonging the fighting and multiplying the casualties it could both make political gains and an historic name for itself as the heroic band of fighters who held out against the Israelis longer than any other Arab army. (But then, Arab armies do not hide behind civilians.) The PLO's decisions in Beirut continue a longstanding policy of trying to exploit civilian deaths for its own political gain. Whether the corpses are Arab or Jewish seems to matter little to the PLO. But now two things have changed in the PLO political calculus. First, Arafat's men believe they have garnered all of the political capital to be gained from prolonging the battle for Beirut. And second, the Israeli thrust into west Beirut in the beginning of August, much decried in the West for "complicating" negotiations, seems to have concentrated PLO minds on the advantages of getting out. Negotiations speeded up remarkably after the Israeli move, a coincidence largely ignored by the State Department and the media. . . .

But the ironies abound. First, the Administration sent Mr. Habib to the Middle East and kept him there, all the while using extraordinary pressure and threats to restrain Israel, on the grounds that it is necessary in order to win the favor of moderate Arab regimes like Egypt and Saudi Arabia. There were dire predictions, mostly from American "Middle East consultants," of an end to the "peace process" or a cut-off of oil unless the U.S. forced an Israeli pullback. Yet Egypt has not even recalled its ambassador to Israel, and the OPEC meeting that took place immediately after the Israeli move into Lebanon voted to *raise* production ceilings—as always, for sound economic reasons. While the U.S. tries to save the PLO to please our Egyptian and Saudi friends, they refuse to allow them into their own countries, a sign of their regard for the PLO. Our attempts to get Syria to accept the PLO are even more ironical. In this case, we are imploring one Soviet client, implacably hostile to the U.S., to accept the defeated remnants of another Soviet client, even more hostile to American interests. And the Syrians are reportedly demanding a price *from the U.S.* for doing so—that the U.S. acquiesce to the Syrians' occupation of the Bekaa and northern Lebanon as the price for saving their PLO brothers. Most amazing, the U.S. sees nothing unusual in this transaction.

The most recent draft of the Habib plan calls for French troops, followed by Italians, to be stationed in Beirut to protect the PLO during its evacuation. The irony here cannot be more stark. Only last week Direct Action, a French terrorist group which is reported to be armed and supported by George Habash and the Popular Front for the Liberation of Palestine, one of the major PLO groups, threw a grenade into a Jewish restaurant in Paris and machine-gunned survivors and passersby. President Mitterrand attended a service for the dead, only a few days after supporting the U.N. resolution to embargo arms to Israel—arms that Israel uses to put George Habash out of the terrorism business. And now France will be sending troops to make sure that Habash escapes from Beirut to carry out his activities from some safe haven in the Arab world.

And yet it cannot be otherwise. The Israelis don't want to go into Beirut, with the attendant suffering for their own soldiers and for innocents in Beirut. They are prepared to see the PLO leave Lebanon in exactly the same way one is prepared to see hijackers receive safe passage from airplanes in order to save the civilians, even though safe passage assures that they will have the capacity to hijack again. For what is happening in Beirut is a hijacking, not a siege. Israel has no desire to conquer Beirut, to subdue it, or to keep it. Its only object is to get to a group of fighters hiding inside. That is precisely what happens in a hijacking. Security forces have no territorial claims on the plane. They only want to get the hijackers out.

But we must not underestimate the cost in future lives and political instability of saving the PLO. The *New York Times* recently noted the need to engage Jordan in the next stage of negotiations. But the presence of the PLO in Jordan can only make that prospect more uncertain, and increase the risk to King Hussein of moving in the direction of peace. Similarly, the rescue of George Habash and others dedicated to random terror will guarantee that there will be more killing in the months and years to come.

Thus the moral and political calculus of evacuating the PLO from Beirut is a complicated one. Nevertheless, the eviction of the PLO will have large positive consequences for the Middle East. It will allow Lebanon to restore its delicate system of internal accommodations that had been disrupted by the PLO and Syria. It will mean that there will be no more raids and counterraids across the Lebanese-Israeli border, and that Galilee and southern Lebanon will live in peace. And it will make possible for the first time a solution to the problems of Lebanon and the Israeli-Palestinian conflict. For Lebanon it will mean that negotiations can begin for a withdrawal of both Syrian and Israeli troops under conditions that will ensure that Lebanon will not be used by either to attack the other. As for the Israeli-Palestinian question, there will finally be a chance for accommodation on the West Bank and Gaza. Unless, that is, cynics in the West combine to try to revive the PLO and its irredentist imperative to make Israel's fate, and not that of the West Bank, the ultimate question. Under those circumstances, negotiations on the West Bank are doomed.

On the other hand, if the Palestinians on the West Bank can finally overcome their tragic history of following leaders with maximal demands producing less than minimal results, and can decide that the time has come to compromise with Israel, there is a chance for peace. Such an event would be comparable to Anwar Sadat's flying to Jerusalem. Sadat's stroke was a permanent refutation of Arafat's contention that recognition of Israel is the last trump card. Sadat proved that it is the first card, that it has a dramatic and overwhelming effect on Israel's desire for peace, and that it can produce revolutionary changes in Israeli opinion overnight. In the end, he proved that recognition—genuine, unconditional, and guaranteed—can lead to an accommodation that satisfies both sides.

It is true that Menachem Begin and a minority in Israel would prefer to annex the West Bank. It is also true that Mr. Begin is intent on pursuing a settlement policy that might eventually make an accommodation impossible. But he can pursue his settlement policy only because of the absence of any Palestinians to bargain with. If it is true that no government of Israel could negotiate with the PLO and survive, it is also true that no government of Israel could refuse a West Bank offer of accommodation and coexistence—and survive. A Palestinian leadership willing to compromise with Israel would find a vast reservoir of Israelis sick of war and eager to live in peace and mutual respect.

We are wounded and troubled by the suffering of innocent civilians in Beirut. We are also wary of those who are ready with instant solutions for the dilemmas posed by this war. As Saul Bellow has noted, the Middle East has become the moral resort area of the West. The moral sunbathers call for a ceasefire in place and the restoration of normal services to west Beirut. That is a call for stalemate, and in the middle of a war, a prescription for indefinite bleeding, shelling, raiding, and suffering. It is also a guarantee that the PLO, which stalled for eight weeks and used every tactic to stay in Beirut, will stay indefinitely, that the war will continue, and that Lebanon, which has demanded that the PLO leave so that it can breathe again, will not be restored to life.

War is monstrous. And war against terrorists who specialize in shooting civilians while hiding behind other civilians is all the more monstrous. This war will end when the PLO realizes that it cannot rely on misguided American moral sentiment or American misperception of its own interests to permit it to stay in Beirut. A final irony of this tragedy is that it took Israel's advance into West Beirut, over frenzied objections in the West, to send the PLO that message. Now that it has been received, there is a chance for peace in Lebanon.

GOOD IDEA, BAD START[11]

In the entire history of the conflict between Israel and the Arabs—more specifically, between Jewish nationalism and Palestinian nationalism—there has been only one good and fair idea for the resolution of the conflict, and that is partition. The peace plan that President Reagan put forward on September 1 is based upon the idea of partition, and it deserves praise.

The President, in a sensitive and sophisticated speech, made his position clear: "The United States will not support the establishment of an independent Palestinian state in the West Bank and Gaza, and we will not support annexation or permanent control by Israel." Of course this has been the American position for a long time. But the President did more than say what he will not support; he said what he will support. This was a break with the past. The United States had always withheld its views about the final disposition of the disputed territories, for the sake of its role as an "honest broker" between the parties. No more. The United States now has a goal not only for the beginning of the peace process, but for its end as well. That goal is "self-government by the Palestinians of the West Bank and Gaza in association with Jordan."

This does not contradict Camp David so much as it completes it. The linkage with Jordan that the Administration envisages is perfectly consistent with the concept of autonomy outlined at

[11] Magazine article from *New Republic*. 187:7-8+. O. 5, '82. Reprinted by permission of The New Republic, © 1982 The New Republic.

Camp David. The Palestinians, according to the Reagan plan, will start with the five-year period of autonomy, the "transitional arrangement" prescribed by Camp David, and after five years they will remain autonomous, but under the authority of Jordan. The autonomy that the President has in mind, however, like the autonomy conceived at Camp David, is no trifling matter. It is a considerable political enfranchisement—"the peaceful and orderly transfer of domestic authority from Israel to the Palestinian inhabitants of the West Bank and Gaza," as the President put it. This is "full" autonomy, that is, the administration of virtually all of the people's affairs by the people themselves—social, political, economic, and cultural self-government, and "progressive Palestinian responsibility for internal security." It stops short only of sovereignty.

That is the plan for the people. There is also a plan for the land. President Reagan defined its principles as "an exchange of territory for peace." He invoked U.N. Resolution 242, the proof text for all Middle East peace plans, in this connection. But he did not do so mechanically, without proper regard for the gravity of the withdrawal from the West Bank for Israel. First, he made it clear that the territory that is returned will be returned only to Jordan. Second, he agreed that the 1967 borders are unacceptable, that the security of Israel requires more strategic depth than it had before 1967, and that the final border will be determined in negotiations. Third, and most impressively, the President declared that "our view on the extent to which Israel should be asked to give up territory will be heavily affected by the extent of true peace and normalization" of the five-year period of transition, and by "the security arrangements offered in return." This last provision demonstrates that the President has understood Camp David well. The purpose of the five-year plan was precisely to normalize relations between the men and women on both sides of the 1967 lines, to take the poison out of the air; and the political and military arrangements that would be made after five years would be determined precisely by how much poison had been removed. In other words, Israel will be asked to remove its troops from most of the West Bank only in a situation in which such removal seems plausible from the standpoint of its security.

These are the broad outlines of what *The Economist* called "Camp Santa Barbara." For the beginning of the peace process, and for the fate of the occupied people, the President concurred with the thinking of Menachem Begin; but for the end of the peace process, and for the fate of the occupied land, he concurred with the thinking of Shimon Peres. "Camp Santa Barbara" is Camp David plus the Labor Party. Those familiar with the views of the Labor Party will recognize its ideas of "territorial compromise" and "the Jordanian option" in the Reagan plan. We have argued for these ideas many times in the past, and we will continue to argue for them. They are the contemporary incarnation of the idea of partition, corrected for thirty-five years of war and terrorism. Israel cannot dominate or absorb the Arab population of the West Bank and Gaza without debasing itself morally or politically, and it has no need of all the territory that it seized when it saved itself in 1967; but it cannot ignore its experience of its neighbors' enmity. Partition is not as simple now as it was then, though the principle is still just. Israel must eventually return most of the land only to an Arab authority that has no designs upon Israel.

Not surprisingly, Prime Minister Begin was swift to scorn the Reagan plan. It flies in the face of much that he believes. It called for a "settlement freeze" (the President has apparently been impressed by the popularity of the metaphor), whereas Mr. Begin contends, in his Cabinet's communiqué, that "such settlement is a Jewish inalienable right and an integral part of our national security," and that "settlements are legal." (On the latter point the President, and most students of history and law, have already agreed.) The Reagan plan called for "full" autonomy, whereas Mr. Begin, in all the negotiations since Camp David, has advanced a definition of autonomy noteworthy mainly for its parsimony; he would allow the Palestinians of the West Bank and Gaza to take charge of only the pettiest and least political of their affairs. And the Reagan plan called for the evacuation of the West Bank and Gaza, and the renunciation of Israeli sovereignty over the area, which is exactly what Mr. Begin lives to oppose. As he wrote in a letter to Mr. Reagan a few days after the plan was presented, "the truth is that millenia ago there was a Jewish kingdom of Judea and Samaria where our kings knelt to God, where our prophets brought forth the vision of eternal peace." What God gives, in other words, no President can take away.

Mr. Begin's government's rejection of the Reagan plan has won a great deal of attention. The Prime Minister is cast in his customary role as the spoiler. Israel, say the makers of opinion, is being intransigent again. Mr. Reagan, if his plan is to succeed, must stand up to Mr. Begin, and so on. What this leaves out, as usual, are the historical and political contexts in which judgments about "Palestine" must be made. The prospects for the Reagan plan must be seen against the background of the Arab-Israeli conflict, which shows clearly that if the plan is to succeed there is more work to be done on the Arab side than on the Israeli.

The plan has many things going for it in Israel. There is, for example, the splendid political system of the Jewish state. The foreign policy of Israel must be acceptable to its citizens, who debate its merits vigorously and vote on it. Mr. Peres, in what may be his greatest challenge in opposition, has announced that the Labor Party will launch a major national debate about the American proposals. And Mr. Begin, a pious Jew with profound parliamentary habits, has also declared his willingness to take these proposals before the Israeli public; he appears to be seriously contemplating a new national election as a referendum on the Reagan plan. And there is the American Jewish community, which is rather less muzzled than its critics habitually contend. The heads of the B'nai Brith, the American Jewish Committee, and the American-Israel Public Affairs Committee (the infamous Israeli lobby) have all praised the President's plan, differing dramatically with the government of Israel whose puppets they are said to be. American policymakers can take heart from the democratic manner in which the Jews, American and Israeli, conduct their public affairs. But they must not attempt to manipulate the debate, as a report in *The Washington Post* by John Goshko suggests they might, by threatening the Israeli public with "isolation from the United States." That will doom the Reagan plan as surely as Mr. Begin's Bible. The Administration has put its plan before the Jews, who are considering it. Now it must be patient.

It need not be quite as patient, however, with the Arabs. Where there is no democracy, foreign policy is easily made. According to press reports, the Administration is "working on the assumption that Jordan will eventually cooperate." Jordan is required, naturally, for the Jordanian option. But is Jordan there for the United States? "We didn't have a clear green light," according to a high Administration official, "but we did have an amber light." That is King Hussein: forever amber. The Reagan plan, he says, is "very constructive" and "very positive"; and the Fez plan is "a very dramatic step," and "a very important development." And it was in Fez, not in Amman, that the Arab response to the Reagan plan came. There the light was not even amber. In Fez there was no light. The heads of twenty Arab governments adopted a peace plan of their own, known as the "Fez Charter." It specifies "the withdrawal of Israel from all Arab territories occupied in 1967, including Arab Al Qods" (East Jerusalem) "the dismantling of settlements," the "establishment of an independent Palestinian state with Al Qods as its capital," the recognition of the PLO as "the sole and legitimate representative" of the Palestinians, and a "Security Council guarantee [of] peace among all states of the region including the independent Palestinian state." In sum: if you liked the Fahd plan, you'll love the Fez plan. Its last clause is the most recent Arab formula for recognizing Israel without recognizing Israel. (Secretary of State George Shultz is more sanguine about it. "So that is a breakthrough," he told the Senate Foreign Relations Committee, "a genuine breakthrough.") The clause before is particularly damaging to the American plan, which requires the repeal, or at least the revision, of the resolution at Rabat in 1974. As King Hussein observed this week, the Arabs at Fez made it clear again that Jordan cannot negotiate the future of Palestinians. Only the PLO can do that. Indeed, by bringing the PLO to the fore, and by calling only for "peace" for all states in the region where the Fahd plan spoke of "rights," the Arabs at Fez have made the maximalism of Fahd more maximal. The Fez plan is really a refinement of the Fahd plan [see "Arab Inaction on Lebanon" on page 177] for the sake of the rejectionists. It appeases Yasir Arafat, and Hafez Kassad; and it repudiates the Americans.

The Fez Plan will not be placed before the Arab masses. No Arab government will be endangered by it. The Reagan plan, in

short, does not have a chance in the Arab world. The reason for
this may be found in the history of the idea of partition. In 1947
the Jews agreed to partition Palestine, and thereby agreed to a
Palestinian state in an area much larger than the West Bank and
Gaza. The Arabs did not. Instead, they attacked. The Palestinian
state did not come into being as a consequence of the Arab attempt
to prevent the Jewish state from coming into being. The idea of
partition, then, has no political or ideological basis in Arab nationalism. It is the political and ideological basis, on the other hand,
of the major current in Jewish nationalism. The Zionism that
built the state believed in partition. There was a Zionism, to be
sure, that did not, and the leader of that Zionism is now in power.
Before 1977, when the Likud won a plurality in Israel's election,
in some measure because the Arabs made Begin seem right, Israeli
governments accepted partition and Arab governments did not.
Since 1977 neither of them do. That is all that has changed. It was
not a change for the better, but it is a change that may be reversed.
A greater change, and one that is less easily managed, must take
place among the Arabs. It is an Israeli idea, after all, that the
United States has adopted. What was televised from the studios
in Burbank was the Allon plan. (After the 1967 war Yigal Allon
proposed that Israel keep a military presence on the outer reaches
of the West Bank, but return all the populated areas of the disputed territory to Jordan.)

The hardening at Fez, however, does not exhaust the Arab reaction to the President's plan. Egypt was not present at Fez—it
is suspended from the ranks of these Arabs who want peace because it made peace—but its president was quick to establish that
he preferred the American plan to the Arab plan. The Fez proposals, he observed, are impractical, while the Reagan proposals are
based upon a peace process that already exists. The former won't
work, in other words, while the latter might—this is the sensible
view of a man who really wants a solution, and not merely sentiments. Another such man, Mayor Elias Freij of Bethlehem, took
the same position. He wrote Mr. Reagan to congratulate him for
his plan "to end the sufferings of the Palestinian people and to
bring peace and security for all the nations of the Middle East."
And he, too, immediately interpreted Fez as a new reason for Pal-

estinian hopelessness, and rejected it. (We hope he does not lose his job.) The Fez plan may be known, then, by its Arab opponents. The pragmatists will not hear of it.

By revealing what it wants for the West Bank, the Reagan Administration has transformed the American role in all future negotiations. This is a large risk, because all future negotiations will require the good offices of the United States. The risk will be worth it only if the Administration is prepared to do what must be done to make its plan work, and bring pressure where pressure must be brought—upon the Arabs. Unfortunately Secretary of State Shultz seems to think differently. According to the *The Washington Post,* the strategy he has outlined for selling the President's plan focuses almost exclusively upon "trying to moderate Begin's hard-line policies." Nothing could be less productive. It is Jordan that he must deliver. Whatever Mr. Begin may think, no Israeli government will last long that keeps King Hussein waiting at a negotiating table. The Administration must prove that it is serious about peace, and not merely about its standing in the Arab world. Reagan's plan is truly a plan for peace, if he makes every effort to persuade the Arabs, who are the oldest obstacle to peace; but if he does not it is only a plan for putting the screws on Israel yet again, and for showing the Saudis that America's hands are clean.

Mr. Begin's patter about prophets and kings must be sharply distinguished from his legitimate concerns about security, even if they are sometimes confused in his own mind. A good test of U.S. understanding for these concerns will be Lebanon. Mr. Reagan's speech implied that events in Lebanon are no longer a danger to Israeli security, and all attention must now go to the West Bank and Gaza. The war in Lebanon, however, may not be over. The assassination of Lebanon's President-elect Bashir Gemayel may have destroyed the best chance for peace and reconstruction in Lebanon. Mr. Gemayel was no saint, but he was determined to recreate a sovereign Lebanon, free from foreign armies, and at peace with Israel. He was killed by those for whom the prospect of such a Lebanon was intolerable. The explosion of a 440-pound bomb expertly detonated in a heavily guarded building indicates that this was not the work of amateurs or random assassins. His ascendancy had been a blow to Syria, the PLO, and extreme Moslem factions in Lebanon.

But Mr. Gemayel's death will do more than abort Lebanon's reconstruction. It sends a message to any Arab leader, like King Hussein, who dares contemplate peace with Israel. Gemayel's assassination is now added to that of Abdullah, Hussein's grandfather, and Anwar Sadat, earlier victims of "the peace process." The rhetoric of Fez cannot obscure the fact that in the Arab world, even after thirty-four years of war, contemplating peace with Israel is still a capital crime.

AN ISRAELI-PALESTINIAN PEACE[12]

. . . The purpose of this article is to assess the balance of forces in the aftermath of the war, to identify next steps in Lebanon, to analyze what an Israeli-Palestinian peace process requires, and to suggest the elements of a comprehensive U.S. strategy for helping to move toward an Arab-Israeli-Palestinian peace. It may seem absurd to write of an Israeli-Palestinian peace process just after Israel has tried with all its power to destroy the structure of the Palestinian movement in the West Bank and Gaza, as well as in Lebanon. But how the Israeli-Palestinian conflict is dealt with now will determine whether Israelis and Arabs capture a last chance to negotiate peaceful relations in this generation. The alternative is another generation of conflict which could well end in a nuclear holocaust.

The question after any war is what the new balance of forces is and how it can be used to build something positive from the rubble. Opportunity does not automatically spring from that rubble. Opportunity comes out of destruction only when statesmen with a vision of peace and growth work with greater creativity and tireless diligence to fashion hope from the ashes.

[12] Article by Harold H. Saunders, former Assistant Secretary of State for Near Eastern and South Asian Affairs; now resident fellow at the American Enterprise Institute. *Foreign Affairs.* 61:103-21. Fall '82. Copyright 1982, Council on Foreign Relations, Inc. Reprinted by permission.

At this moment, it is by no means clear that the 1982 war has ended: there remain serious possibilities that fighting will be renewed, and a high probability that isolated actions will continue. Let us assume, however, that there is no renewal of organized military conflict, and look candidly at the impact of the war on the principal actors.

First, this war has again demonstrated that, in Arab words, "Israel is the superpower of the Middle East." With Egypt absent, there is no Arab military constraint on Israeli leaders who are willing to use their power to the fullest and who seem to believe that Israel's future can be assured by force alone. As just noted, Israel's attack on Syria's Soviet-supplied air defense missiles seemed designed to show that the Arabs could not rely on Moscow for help. Israel's open dismissal of President Reagan's repeated appeals to stop the bombardment of Beirut and to give the negotiations conducted by Ambassador Philip Habib a chance seemed designed to show the Arabs that they could not expect the United States to impose peace on Israel.

In Arab eyes, Israeli military encirclement of an Arab capital and the related Israeli objective of remaking the political life of an Arab country imposed a new character on what they see as Israeli expansionism. Thoughtful Arabs, looking to the future, put high on their agendas the need to show Israel that it cannot count on getting its way by force. In the end, most Arabs still look to the United States to reestablish some restraining influence over an Israel they regard as out of control.

Second, a central question is how the Palestinians will emerge. If an organized Palestinian movement survives in the aftermath of the war, preserving what institutions exist in the Palestinian community and able to play a political role, a peace process could begin sooner than if the movement is atomized or divided by internecine struggles. If Palestinian leadership were eventually to settle in Cairo rather than Damascus, it would receive greater support in pursuing a political course. Whether leadership committed to peace or to a continued guerrilla campaign emerges from the crisis, and whether most Arab states will agree that Palestinian military action from Lebanon and terrorism elsewhere should cease, will depend heavily on whether Palestinians and other Arabs see a real diplomatic alternative.

Ambassador Habib, to his great credit, seems to have kept the door open to Palestinian leadership to build a new future. The Palestinian movement is not dead politically. In some Arab eyes the PLO has emerged from the crisis as the only heroic party, having demonstrated that Israel with all of its power could not destroy the symbol and the organization of Palestinian nationalism. Whether the leadership will pull itself together and show its ability to act with a coherent strategy on the diplomatic stage, only time will tell.

Third, with the headquarters and military arms of the PLO gone, Lebanon can return to dealing with the problems which were already beginning to divide it before the new PLO influx that began in the early 1970s. It is now being said in many quarters that the enlarged and militarized PLO presence in Lebanon was the sole cause of the armed conflict there that began in 1975-76 and continued at substantial levels of violence thereafter. Even in Lebanon it has not been popular to say that there are grave Lebanese problems which have only been exacerbated by the PLO presence. But the plain fact is that many Lebanese have voiced concern privately for more than a decade that the 1943 French-influenced compact underlying Lebanon's political organization and integrity was disintegrating—and that Lebanese leaders in a position to restore that integrity were more interested in enhancing their own power than in strengthening the unity of Lebanon.

With the organized Palestinians a less significant factor, Israel and Syria are still in positions to inhibit free and constructive Lebanese efforts to build a new Lebanon. A critical issue as the new balance of forces is shaped will be whether Lebanon is freed of international intervention so that Lebanese will have a fair opportunity to reestablish the integrity and independence of their state, or whether Israel and Syria will try to enhance their own power by carving out semi-permanent positions for themselves in Lebanon. That option is already being discussed in Israel, and many Arabs are already anticipating such an Israeli move.

Fourth, it is necessary to assess carefully the attitudes of the Arab states. The war has not changed the readiness of Egypt, Jordan, and some other moderate Arabs to pursue peace with Israel on a reciprocal basis or to work with the United States toward that end, but it has caused all of them to question seriously whether Israel will negotiate a just peace and whether the United States will take a position independent of Israel's. It is widely believed that the United States acquiesced in Israel's invasion of Lebanon, and few Arabs believe that the United States could not have prevented Israel's heavy bombardments.

It may still be possible to produce a statement by moderate Arab nations of their readiness to make peace, but it seems unlikely that the entire Arab world could unite on such a position. The moderates will probably have to move on their own. Iraq could well move toward the moderates, given its dependence on moderate Arab support against Iran. There will, however, continue to be a small group of states like Libya, South Yemen, and some of the more extreme Palestinian groups, who will reject any initiative to make peace with Israel. The positions of Syria and Algeria remain question marks. The position and leadership of the United States will be an important factor in the decision of each Arab state.

Much has been made of the reluctance of Arab states to accept the PLO apparatus now being evacuated from Beirut. And it is clear that each of these states will be careful to assure that the PLO does not come close to achieving within its borders the independent strength it achieved in Jordan in 1970 or subsequently in Lebanon.

But this does *not* mean that Arab support for Palestinian self-determination and a state in the West Bank and Gaza, or for the PLO as the only organization which speaks for the Palestinians, has declined. Even those Arab governments and groups that have come to accept the existence of Israel, within essentially its pre-1967 boundaries, likewise accept and support, however belatedly in historic terms, the reality and force of Palestinian demands for a homeland of their own. In their view, that homeland should include the West Bank and Gaza, which would be freed if Israel withdrew from territories occupied in the 1967 War. In the wake of the 1982 war, there is already much evidence that underlying Arab support for the Palestinian cause has been increased by Israel's conduct of the war.

Moreover, there are often practical reasons for such support from Arab governments, especially those with large Palestinian populations. They see a dispersed Palestinian people as a politically disruptive force as long as their aspiration for a homeland of their own is unfulfilled. For that reason, among the others just stated, they will continue to press for an Israeli-Palestinian peace. Iran's military success over Iraq and its strong support of some factions in the PLO give moderate Arab leaders added incentive for wanting to develop a political alternative for the Palestinians that has a realistic chance of producing results.

In sum, the war has created, or intensified, attitudes that are often conflicting and that could now move in either direction. On the one hand, they could be channeled to produce a new process leading toward an Arab-Israeli-Palestinian peace. The Administration in Washington is again becoming directly engaged in the problems of the Middle East. Israel has demonstrated clearly what its objectives are, and has posed sharply for the United States the question of what the U.S.-Israeli relationship has become. The PLO has been forced to face the fact that its only hope for achieving its objectives is through political and diplomatic effort. Moderate Arab governments are deeply enough concerned about the radicalization of the Middle East that they may be prepared to support a Palestinian peace inititive.

Peace can come, however, only if statesmen work hard at it. The new balance of forces if left alone could more likely harden into the causes of a new and more terrible conflict before the 1980s end. After each major conflict—in 1949, 1956, 1967, 1973— opportunities have briefly existed for leaders of vision. The psychological humiliations in 1949 and 1967 made it harder for Arab leaders to negotiate. Limited Arab successes in 1973 opened the door to negotiation. If Israel's crushing military actions were now to be followed by a continued application of force by Israel in Lebanon, and the unchecked continuation of Israel's present policies in the West Bank and Gaza—so that there existed no apparent possibility of movement toward a negotiated resolution of the Palestinian issue—the 1982 war will have left the parties further apart than ever. We could look forward only to all the possibilities and dangers this would entail, including Arab alienation from the

United States and progressive radicalization in the Arab world, and organized and unorganized violence growing both in the Middle East and elsewhere.

Restore Lebanon's Integrity

A critical step in achieving a balance of forces conducive to peace will be restoring Lebanon's political and territorial integrity and its self-government. This is of overriding concern for the sake of the people of Lebanon, who have suffered too long.

Obviously, there is an immediate need for a massive program of humanitarian and economic aid to help the Lebanese rebuild their country, and this should be undertaken by the widest possible group of nations, with the United States playing an important role. However, such a program will not have lasting effectiveness unless there is a new political consensus within Lebanon.

Restoring Lebanon's integrity is essential also in establishing the basis for a wider peace. Israel must withdraw quickly and completely before its occupation of south Lebanon hardens. Israel's remaining credibility as a nation claiming to want a negotiated peace with its neighbors on the basis of respect for each other's sovereignty depends on it. Consolidation of Israel's position in Lebanon will be a final confirmation that Israel with U.S. support intends to resolve issues by force, not by negotiation. Israel's withdrawal is not an issue for compromise.

Moreover, there will remain in any circumstances a Palestinian population of at least 500,000 in Lebanon. If that population (which is bound to include some remnants of the PLO military and political apparatus) sees no prospect of movement toward a Palestinian homeland—and especially if it sees Israel acting to deal with the West Bank and Gaza by pressure and force—it is bound to become again a serious disruptive force within the political structure of Lebanon.

It follows that, while there may be a tendency to think of the issue of foreign forces in Lebanon as a "Phase II" of negotiations to wind up the 1982 war, and of the Palestinian issue as "Phase III," in practice the two issues must be addressed simultaneously. There will be pressures, and a clear Israeli interest, to pursue the two problems in sequence. This must be avoided, from every standpoint and because the issues are in fact interlocked. Moreover, we should keep in mind the vivid lesson of 1974-75, when the issues of immediate withdrawal from Egypt and from the Golan Heights were addressed while the Palestinian issue was put to one side. The result, of course, was the Rabat decision of late 1974 that installed the PLO as the only Arab-backed negotiating partner of the West Bank and Gaza, removed Jordan from the play, and generally hardened Arab positions on the Palestinian issue. It was a mistake that must not be repeated.

If Israel is to withdraw safely, two steps related to Lebanon will be required. First, a strengthened peacekeeping force must be put in place quickly, with an effective mandate to assure a zone of peace above Israel's northern border until a Lebanese force is able to do so. Second, all parties to the conflict must support a new compact for Lebanon. Syria and Israel must end their intervention in Lebanon's internal affairs. Syrian and Israeli withdrawals should be worked out on parallel but separate tracks because the backgrounds of their respective involvements raise quite different issues. Lebanese factions need to agree to reconstitute a workable central government. This will require agreement on new relationships among them, reviewing and revising the 1943 compact as they think necessary.

Finally, it is important to move quickly to help both the Lebanese and the Palestinian homeless. The Palestinians pose a special problem because their plight raises the question of how and where they should be provided new housing and new communities. Confronted now with resettling a fourth (1948, 1967, 1970, 1982) wave of Palestinian refugees, the United Nations and those who support its Palestinian relief program face again the question of building "temporary" housing for several hundred thousand people. Israel is already insisting that camps should not be rebuilt in southern Lebanon.

If there is to be a real effort to resolve the Israeli-Palestinian conflict, housing could be truly temporary. If not, perhaps these people are entitled to more than makeshift quarters. Whatever is done about their housing, it has long been agreed that those refugees who cannot or do not want to return to property in Palestine are entitled to compensation for property lost. Israel will then raise the separate question of the claims of Jews who lost property when they left Arab countries.

In short, as the world deals with another group of Palestinian refugees, it must consider whether now is not the time to establish a framework for dealing with the refugee problem in the context of an Israeli-Palestinian peace process.

Changing Attitudes

If we were going to try to develop an Israeli-Palestinian peace process, it is important for us to understand what such a process will involve. In 1977-78, the United States was dealing with two negotiating partners, Israel and Egypt, who were prepared to work on a negotiated approach to the issue of the Palestinians in the West Bank and Gaza, even though they clearly differed on the ultimate political solution for the area. Now, however, it is clear that there does not exist a willingness on the Israeli side to seek a true negotiated approach, and that the Arab side does not see any possibility of progress in the face of Israeli attitudes. Moreover, the Arab states other than Egypt have declined to participate in the Camp David peace process, and only Egypt and Jordan have made clear their acceptance of the existence of Israel.

In short, after several years of detailed Egyptian-Israeli negotiation, we are now back near the beginning of an Israeli-Palestinian peace process, in a pre-negotiation phase dealing with attitudes that block negotiation. We are used to running in third and fourth gear. Now we need to shift directly back to first. Unless we understand that the first need is to change basic attitudes rather than to negotiate texts, any next steps to launch an Israeli-Palestinian peace process will start us up a dead-end street.

Today the government of Israel is seen, with reason, as pursuing a peace imposed by force and by the passage of time rather than a negotiated peace. As one Egyptian speaking this July put it in retrospect, "The fifth Arab-Israeli war started within days after Camp David, when Prime Minister Begin announced that the government's policy of building new settlements in territories occupied in 1967 would continue." This signaled that key issues would be dealt with unilaterally outside negotiation. Anyone who has seen the massive concrete blocks of settlement apartment buildings in the West Bank and ringing Jerusalem will understand the impact of the Israeli government's actions. Step by step, the Begin government extended its control over land, water, administration and the movements of daily life in the West Bank and Gaza.

In August 1981, when the second Begin government was formed and Ariel Sharon became Defense Minister, the government announced openly that its policy was to assert Israel's claim of sovereignty over all the land west of the Jordan River—not to negotiate a peaceful and just settlement of the Palestinian problem in all its aspects as agreed at Camp David. The Israeli administration in occupied territories intensified its campaign to restrict the authority of democratically elected Palestinian officials and, eventually, to remove them from office, to break their ties with the Palestinian national movement outside the occupied territories, and to set up an alternative group of compliant local Palestinian administrators.

The Israeli invasion of Lebanon, to repeat, was designed to destroy once and for all any hope among the people of the West Bank and Gaza that the process of shaping the Palestinian people into a nation could succeed. It was designed to break any final resistance to total Israeli control and to pave the way for making life so difficult for those who valued their freedom and political self-expression that they would eventually leave for Jordan.

For their part, neither the Arab states (apart from Egypt and Jordan) nor the PLO have been prepared formally to accept Israel's existence as a state. Such acceptance of Israel is indeed central to peaceful resolution of the conflict.

A critical missing ingredient in the peace process is a clear-cut statement by Arab and Palestinian authorities of their readiness to make peace with Israel provided Israel will make peace with them. Attitudes within the PLO and Arab governments have moved toward acceptance of Israel. In contrast to the Arab position adopted in 1967—no peace with Israel, no recognition of Israel, no negotiation with Israel—a number of important Arab leaders today will state privately that they are prepared to live at peace with Israel. Their formal public positions, however, are evasive on that point and do not present Israelis with an offer of peace Israelis can call realistic.

Moreover, the PLO and Arab governments except Egypt rejected the two-stage negotiating process agreed to at Camp David and refused to start negotiations unless the outcome of the negotiation was assured before the negotiation began. When Saudi Crown Prince Fahd, in August 1981, put forward a position including both a stated objective and a transitional process for achieving it, Arab leaders could not agree to support it, and the Saudi government itself would not authoritatively and unequivocally say the plan provided for recognition of Israel.

No one with any experience in the Middle East can minimize depth of feeling on both sides that lies behind these attitudes. They date back to the creation of Israel and the division of Palestine in 1948, and although there has been a great deal of change in the 1970s in underlying Arab attitudes, those in Israel have tended to harden since 1977. The essential point of disagreement is whether Israel and the Palestinians each have valid claims in the area defined in 1948 as Palestine.

Today, in *Israel,* there may be serious challenge to a definition of the Palestinian problem which acknowledges both Israeli and Palestinian claims *in the same land.* Many Israelis fear that accepting a Palestinian claim would dilute their own claim to all the land west of the Jordan River. Again and again in Israel one hears the sincerely stated view of early settlers that the Palestinians were doing little with the land when the Jewish settlers came. In their view, the Palestinians became active only when they wanted to share in gains the Israeli settlers were achieving. Arab states, they recall, either did not regard the Palestinians as a separate people or did not support them in establishing a state of their own when Jordan controlled the West Bank, and Egypt controlled Gaza, from 1949 until 1967.

Palestinian nationalism, in their view, is the product of terrorism and intimidation by the PLO under Yasser Arafat, and with the PLO's defeat in Lebanon, Palestinian nationalism will decline as an effective political force. The Israelis from the beginning of Jewish settlement in Palestine have either set aside the question of their long-term relationship with the Palestinian Arabs or have vaguely envisioned some kind of coexistence which Israel would dominate. Even those who are prepared to accept partitioning the land west of the Jordan River between Jews and Arabs for the most part see the Arab role being played by Jordan and not by Palestine Arabs acting independently. Most Israelis have never thought of a negotiated settlement with Palestinian Arabs as an equal partner.

At the same time, Israelis are not monolithic in support of their government's plan to assert Israel's claim of sovereignty over all the land west of the Jordan River. Many other Israelis see Israel facing an impossible future if they pursue that course. Incorporating 1.2 million Palestinian Arabs within Israel along with those already there, with appropriate civil and political rights, would eventually produce a large enough Arab population to destroy the Jewish state. Incorporating those Palestinians without civil and political rights would require measures that would violate the principles and practice of human rights which are at the heart of Jewish tradition. And driving large numbers of Palestinians out of the West Bank and Gaza by force or pressure goes against the moral code and self-image of their country held by many if not most in Israel, as well as among its supporters abroad.

Palestinians and other Arabs, wherever they are, strongly hold the view that Israel will achieve peace only when Israel comes to terms fairly with the Palestinian people and respects their right to self-determination as the Jewish people have enjoyed their own. The rights of Palestinians as a people are belatedly recognized in some form by a majority of the world's governments. Palestinians do not want a state in Jordan, because it is not the land of their fathers. They do not understand why Zionists, who rejected a Jewish homeland in Africa, fail to comprehend why Palestinians want a homeland in the land where their homes have historically been. They do not understand how an Israeli Prime Minister who led violent resistance against British rule can credibly voice moral outrage at the people Israelis displaced when those people assert their rights through the means available to them. They do not understand how a Jewish government with centuries of persecution behind it could think that attacking several thousand Palestinian fighters could destroy the nationalist determination of almost four million people. They do not understand how Jews, of all people, can be insensitive to what it means to be a stateless person.

In short, the attitudes that must now be brought together have deep roots, and it will take enormous effort to bring them to the point where a serious negotiating process could get underway. At a minimum, Israel must demonstrate its willingness to accept a negotiated approach, and its abandonment of the present policy of seeking a de facto solution in the West Bank and Gaza by force—while the PLO and the Arab states must join Israel in reaffirming their support of the basic territorial provisions of Security Council Resolution 242 of 1967, as well as declaring formally their acceptance of Israel within essentially its pre-1967 boundaries.

In essence, both sides must perceive that the attitudes and formal positions of the other side now make a negotiating process more promising than any realistic alternative. It is *not* essential, at least for the renewal of a serious negotiating process for both sides to agree at the outset what the ultimate result would be. This, and the ways to move to it, are exactly what the negotiation would be about.

U.S. Leadership

How, then, can the necessary changes in attitude come about? Here the position of the United States is central. An active U.S. role is vital in helping to establish the basis for negotiation, and it is essential for the United States to reaffirm its own view of the Palestinian problem.

The issue is whether the United States supports a just settlement for the Palestinian people or whether it buys the argument of Begin's Israeli and American supporters that the Palestinian people are an artificial creation and that peace is only possible if they are dispersed and suppressed by force. Now is the time to thrash out among ourselves our answers to the questions that are endlessly argued. Are the Palestinians a people who will remain an effective political movement? Can they be destroyed or controlled by force? Can they be settled outside Palestine, or will their irredentist objective persist with growing support from most of the world? Can the United States or world Jewry support an Israel built on subjugation and dispersal of another people?

For years after 1947, the United States approached the "Arab-Israeli" conflict in terms of relations between existing states. After the partition, Jordan had assumed the Arab role in the West Bank and Egypt in Gaza, while the leadership and many members of the Palestinian Arab community were dispersed and the institutions of that community disintegrated under the impact of the war and dispersion. The Arab states did not support the creation of a Palestinian state.

Then, in 1967, the situation began to change—although Resolution 242 reflected the viewpoint of the past in referring to the Palestinians only as refugees, not as parties to the conflict or parties to the peace. Only in the late 1960s did it become abundantly clear that there was a strong Palestinian national sentiment, so that the United States, along with others, came again to think of the "Palestine problem" as a central part of the Arab-Israeli conflict. That problem, simply stated, is how two peoples—two national movements reflected in Zionism and Palestinian nationalism—can live together in peace and security with claims in the same land. Palestinian national rights gained increasing recognition internationally, as did the PLO itself.

Yet throughout these 35 years the position of the United States has been totally clear on the territorial question. In 1947, the United States voted for the U.N. resolution to partition the Palestine Mandate west of the Jordan River into a Jewish state and an Arab state, with Jerusalem set aside as a separate entity. After the 1967 War, when Israel occupied all the land west of the Jordan, the United States voted for Resolution 242, which called for Israeli withdrawal from territories occupied in the conflict, in the context of peace and recognition. In 1978, the United States was partner to negotiating the Camp David Accords, which reaffirmed Resolution 242. The question today is whether the Administration stands by that position and is prepared to use its influence to reaffirm it as the basis for peace negotiations.

If the United States holds to its longstanding position, while Israel continues to assert the position now taken by Prime Minister Begin and his government, then Israel and the United States clearly have a difference vital to their relationship. The United States can in no way interpret Resolution 242 or the Camp David Accords as endorsing Israeli sovereignty—whether de facto or by formal claim—imposed by force over all the land west of the Jordan River.

A sustained U.S. dialogue with Israel is thus essential to reestablish a relationship of mutual respect based on common interests. A collision is in neither nation's interest. There is no question about the fundamental U.S. commitment to the security of Israel. As of the summer of 1982, however, there was no understanding between the United States and Israel of what "Israel" the United States is being asked to support, or what American interests in the Middle East must be protected if the United States is to remain able to support Israel over the long run.

For almost 30 years, Israel and the United States operated on the shared premise that Israel should be accepted as a Jewish state in Palestine and that the land west of the Jordan River should be divided between Israel and an Arab entity. Since 1967, the United States has strongly supported negotiation as the only realistic way to produce an Arab-Israeli settlement. That was also a shared objective until the recent period. When two friendly nations begin operating from widely different premises without talking seriously with each other about where they are going together, they are jeopardizing their relationship. There has not been a real discussion of these fundamental, long-term issues for at least two years.

In Lebanon, Israel appears increasingly to have acted without regard or respect for the interests of the United States or the expressed concerns of its President. In fairness to Israeli leaders, they may have thought over the past year that they had the silent assent of, or even a green light from, Washington, at least for their initially stated war aim. Now the war in Lebanon has forced the Administration to define for itself and for Israel somewhat more precisely what the limits of its support for Israel are. Until the United States makes absolutely clear in word and deed, in a spirit of mutual respect and commitment, what it will and will not support in resolving the Israeli-Palestinian conflict, the United States will continue to look like an Israeli satellite and will risk a historic collision with Israel.

No one can say whether or how far the present government in Israel would alter its position in the face of a reaffirmed U.S. view. There are those who say flatly that Begin will never give up the West Bank—and clearly it would take not only formal statements but extensive actions to persuade the world, the Arab states or the Palestinians that Israel had in fact abandoned the objective of maintaining absolute and permanent control in the West Bank and Gaza. It is essential that Israel return convincingly at least to the negotiating position of 1977-78, although it may not be necessary at the outset for Israel to commit itself to a Palestinian homeland west of the Jordan.

In parallel with the enunciation of a firm U.S. position and a new and visible dialogue between the United States and Israel to the above ends, it is incumbent on the Arab states and the PLO to make the necessary declarations of acceptance of Israel and willingness to make peace. Today Israelis who would be willing to negotiate peace on the basis of withdrawal from territories occupied in 1967 can point to no Arab position that offers a basis for negotiation. Authoritative, unequivocal statements by the Palestinians, Jordan and Saudi Arabia, with Egyptian and other Arab support, could begin to change Israel's own perceptions of its alternatives. The Israeli people would have to decide between trying to negotiate peace and retaining territory through another generation of conflict—a choice they faced after President Anwar Sadat's visit to Jerusalem in late 1977.

Many reasonable Arabs question why the Arabs should make this first move, before Israel commits itself to Palestinian self-determination or a Palestinian homeland west of the Jordan. The response is simply a practical question of whether they want to seize the initiative in an effort to break the present impasse. It is difficult for them to do so when they feel they are acting from a position of military inferiority. What they have not yet understood is that an offer of peace could be far more effective than military weapons in changing the balance of political forces within Israel as well as in the United States.

There are strong Arab voices in the wake of the war in Lebanon—at least in Egypt, Jordan and the Palestinian movement—arguing for such a move. Moderate Palestinian leaders—both in the PLO and in the West Bank—were seriously talking this July about how to make clear at least to the United States their readiness to negotiate peace with Israel. Their problem was to do so in a way that would not make them look as if they were capitulating at Israeli gunpoint. Having now withstood the onslaught of vastly superior military power and having proved that Israel cannot destroy the Palestinian movement or impose a solution by force, the time may be at hand for them to declare a political victory and to capitalize on it by seizing the high ground on the diplomatic front.

At the same time, moderates in those countries are virtually pleading with the United States to promise convincingly that it would respond positively to such an initiative and put its weight on the scales on the side of a negotiated settlement of the Israeli-Palestinian conflict. Moderates need some sign to show radical opposition and doubters that a political course can produce results. If they can show no such evidence, they deeply fear a sharp increase in radical or Islamic fundamentalist influence in their countries.

In sum, once the United States has reaffirmed that its aim is peace between the Israeli and Palestinian peoples, the first objective in launching an Israeli-Palestinian peace process is a convincing commitment on both sides to mutual acceptance and to a negotiated settlement rather than one imposed by force or by exploiting the passage of time. The support of the United States is critical in crystallizing such commitments.

A Camp David Framework

The changing of attitudes on both sides is central to the resumption of any Israeli-Palestinian peace process. But at the same time it is useful to look briefly at the possible mode and participation for negotiations, and at objectives that should initially be sought.

The obvious existing framework is of course that of the Camp David Accords of 1978. Israel and Egypt then agreed that "the parties are determined to reach a just, comprehensive, and durable settlement of the Middle East conflict through the conclusion of peace treaties based on Security Council Resolutions 242 and 338 in all their parts." This affirmation of purpose, subsequently ratified by the Israeli Knesset, remains important, and could indeed— if reaffirmed in credible fashion—be itself part of the declared change in attitudes required.

That half of the Camp David Accords that provided for an early peace treaty between Egypt and Israel has now been carried into effect. However, the second half, concerning the West Bank and Gaza, has not.

It is important to recall what was agreed at Camp David both concerning the Palestinians and concerning the specific stages of agreement and action for the West Bank and Gaza. First, it was specified that the parties

> recognize that for peace to endure, it must involve all those who have been most deeply affected by the conflict. . . . Egypt, Israel, Jordan and the representatives of the Palestinian people should participate in negotiations on the resolution of the Palestinian problem in all its aspects.

And the key provisions concerning the West Bank and Gaza read as follows:

> . . . in order to ensure a peaceful and orderly transfer of authority, and taking into account the security concerns of all parties, there should be transitional arrangements for the West Bank and Gaza for a period not exceeding five years. In order to provide full autonomy to the inhabitants, under these arrangements, the Israeli military government and its civilian administration will be withdrawin as soon as a self-governing authority has been freely elected by the inhabitants of these areas to replace the existing military government. . . .

> These new arrangements should give due consideration to the principle of self-government by the inhabitants and to the legitimate security concerns of the parties involved. . . . As soon as possible, but not later than the third year after the beginning of the transitional period, negotiations will take place to determine the final status of the West Bank and Gaza and its relationship with its neighbors and to conclude a peace treaty between Israel and Jordan by the end of the transitional period.

In the fall of 1978, negative Arab reactions to the Accords were such that Jordan declined to participate, and there has never been any progress in enlisting the participation of Palestinian representatives, because of three interrelated facts:

—It has not been possible to produce an agreed statement of the powers and responsibilities a Palestinian self-governing authority would exercise, so that the Palestinians in the West Bank and Gaza have never been able to commit themselves on whether they would stand for election. If they were given serious responsibilities, they could achieve general support from the Palestinian diaspora. If not, responsible leaders would refuse to serve as quislings.

—Israel has removed from office freely elected mayors in the West Bank and Gaza, and has taken an adamant position against any dealings with the PLO, irrespective of any PLO acceptance of Israel and of the specified Security Council Resolutions, on the ground that the PLO is basically an illegitimate "terrorist" organization.

—The PLO itself has declined up to now to declare openly and authoritatively that it accepts Israel and is prepared to pursue a negotiated settlement if Israel is prepared to do so.

The Camp David framework is not just "the only game in town." Its concepts of a transitional period, transitional authority, and two-stage negotiations may still be the only practical approach. A series of bilateral negotiations may also be more practical than any wider multilateral forum.

Having been ratified by the Israeli Knesset, that framework remains a solid foundation to build on. If other moderate Arab states wish to participate, this should not present insuperable difficulty. But, at a minimum, ways must be found to maintain Egypt's engagement and to enlist the participation of Jordan and of Palestinian representatives, which under present circumstances almost necessarily means a role for the PLO.

If attitudes can be changed so that each party will commit itself to a negotiated approach, then agreement must be reached on how the negotiation will be carried out. Questions such as these must be dealt with: To what extent must the big issues, such as borders or principles like self-determination or security and recognition for all, be agreed before negotiations begin? To what extent can agreements on limited issues be reached as building blocks and confidence-buildings steps toward larger agreements before final issues are resolved? Will the parties negotiate directly with one another? Or will they work through or with a mediator? Which parties will negotiate?

Large differences remain among Americans, Arabs and Israelis on these key points. Careful diplomacy would be required to iron these out, at least to the point where serious negotiations could resume.

Turning to the substance of such negotiations, the Camp David Accords did not resolve the key issue of the Palestinians' right to self-determination. The concept was that there should be genuine autonomy for the inhabitants of the West Bank and Gaza and withdrawal of Israel's military occupation and its civilian administration, as an *interim* arrangement before the final status of those territories was to be negotiated with full Palestinian participation. But that approach faltered when Begin indicated, by word and preemptive action, that he sees only Palestinian autonomy under Israeli sovereignty as the long-term Israeli-Palestinian relationship, while moderate Palestinians would accept a transitional period and an open relationship with Israel and Jordan, but only when they were assured that they could exercise their right of self-determination—which in principle could be a choice for a separate Palestinian state in the West Bank and Gaza, or conceivably for some form of federated association with Jordan.

It would of course be a major breakthrough if in the course of stating their respective commitments to a negotiated peace, the two sides implied understanding on the shape of a possible solution. But the obstacles to such an understanding are formidable.

In the 1960s and early 1970s, leaders of the Palestinian people proposed a binational state in Palestine with rights guaranteed for Arabs and Jews. Since Israelis insist on a separate state, however, the Palestinians in the last half of the 1970s began to take the position that they are prepared to accept a state of their own in the West Bank and Gaza in land from which Israel had withdrawn under Security Council Resolution 242. The latter position has not been stated unambiguously, but there is little question that it remains the mainstream view of the Palestinian people as endorsed by the Palestinian National Congress. The conflict in Lebanon seems to have reinforced this view—while the eviction of the PLO apparatus from Lebanon may also have led many in the

PLO, and in the Palestinian movement generally, to conclude that the objective must now be sought by peaceful political means.

The original option of a unitary binational state west of Jordan could now be renounced as part of a declared acceptance of Israel. But this would still leave what is presently Palestinian insistence on a separate state—a possibility rejected not only by the present Israeli government but by an overwhelming consensus of present Israeli opinion.

In short, it may be necessary—as at Camp David—that the two sides "agree to disagree" on the ultimate political structure of the West Bank and Gaza, and approach the problem—again as at Camp David—in two stages, looking to an interim period in which the situation could evolve so that the voice of Palestinians resident in the West Bank and Gaza would be clearly heard and they could participate in the second stage of negotiations, which would take up the final status of the territories.

An agreement which created genuine autonomy for a freely elected Palestinian self-governing authority as a transition device could not be dismissed lightly by the Arab world. The autonomy negotiations to date have achieved more than most realize, but they have yet to achieve these breakthroughs on key issues which would cause Arabs to question their current conviction that autonomy would only be a cover for long-term Israeli control of all territory west of the Jordan River.

The U.S. government has a choice between making a routine effort to achieve an agreement on autonomy and making a determined and sustained effort to achieve a real autonomy agreement that could launch the five-year (or other) transitional period in the West Bank and Gaza. A U.S. decision to help produce genuine autonomy would for the moment shift the focus of the autonomy talks from an Egyptian-Israeli negotiation to an Israeli-U.S. exchange. Such an exchange could be intense and difficult to sustain.

Moreover, it seems unlikely that the PLO or Arab governments will simply accept the Camp David framework (or an enlarged version) without some dialogue of their own with Israel or the United States on what the purposes of a negotiation would be. In Arab eyes, Camp David did not provide assurance that a transitional period would not allow Israel to complete its de facto annexation of the West Bank and Gaza. The U.S. strategy for an Arab-Israeli peace would not be complete if it did not now pursue an active dialogue with all Arab parties to the conflict, thus authoritatively establishing that they would negotiate peace with Israel. That position, to repeat, needs to be put forward publicly in a way that could force events as Sadat did when he went to Jerusalem.

Thus, it is apparent that the pursuit of a serious negotiating process will continue to have all the difficulties that have beset it for the past decade. The problem must in all probability be approached in stages, and with the hope that a base of trust and confidence can be created, and that over time the positions of both sides would evolve so as to permit the exercise of self-deter- mina-tion by the Palestinians and the creation of a political structure with full safeguards for the future security of Israel.

Generating Peace

In trying to launch a negotiation of this sort, the United States would be moving on four tracks simultaneously. It would work to resolve the Lebanese problem in such a way as to restore Lebanese integrity. It would attempt to restore the grounds of common purpose in the U.S.-Israeli relationship. It would try to develop a clear expression of Palestinian and other Arab readiness to make peace with Israel. It would try to achieve an interim first step on the ground in the form of genuine autonomy for the one million Palestinian inhabitants of the West Bank and Gaza while consulting with representatives of the large Palestinian movement.

Working on these four tracks is not a strategy to achieve a quick success. It is more like the strategy of a basketball team working the ball carefully back and forth across the court, forcing opponents to commit themselves, creating opportunities one at a time, and systematically building the score. It requires leadership, management, skill and grueling perseverance. Its objective is to begin changing the balance of forces, increasing the incentives to negotiate, and making the possibility of progress seem realistic.

In the garden of President Sadat's residence on the Nile just north of Cairo, I was talking with an Egyptian colleague during a break in one of the 1974 Kissinger shuttles. He was lamenting that the United States had not been decisively involved in the search for an Arab-Israeli peace between the 1967 and 1973 wars. "We're sure involved now," I replied. "Yes," he said, "but it took a war to get you here."

It is tragic when our nation, which aspires to leadership for peace, freedom, justice and human rights, cannot marshal the same energies and political courage to prevent war and to make peace that we seem to marshal after a war to put our shattered interests back together. It is dangerous in the wake of war if our nation has no larger vision of peace or strategy for leading toward peace. I know how hard it is to decide which way to move next, when there are so many uncertainties. I also know that drift underscores weakness and enlarges danger, while leadership and competence can increase strength and lead toward peace and security. War changes conditions, but peace follows only when leaders tirelessly pursue a strategy of building peace from those new conditions.

However the tragedy of Lebanon may rest on the consciences of responsible Americans, we have now had the 1982 Israeli-Palestinian War to "get us there." The questions in the wake of Israel's final withdrawal from the Sinai, Israel's accelerated program for dominating the West Bank and Gaza, and the Israeli-Palestinian War are whether and how an Israeli-Palestinian peace process can be generated and what the strategy of the United States and the quality of its leadership will be.

APPENDIX

TEXT OF UNITED NATIONS SECURITY COUNCIL RESOLUTION 242 OF NOVEMBER 22, 1967

Adopted unanimously at the 1382nd meeting

The Security Council,
Expressing its continuing concern with the grave situation in the Middle East,
Emphasizing the inadmissibility of the acquisition of territory by war and the need to work for a just and lasting peace in which every State in the area can live in security,
Emphasizing further that all Member States in their acceptance of the Charter of the United Nations have undertaken a commitment to act in accordance with Article 2 of the Charter,

1. *Affirms* that the fulfilment of Charter principles requires the establishment of a just and lasting peace in the Middle East which should include the application of both the following principles:

(i) Withdrawal of Israeli armed forces from territories occupied in the recent conflict;

(ii) Termination of all claims or states of belligerency and respect for and acknowledgement of the sovereignty, territorial integrity and political independence of every State in the area and their right to live in peace within secure and recognized boundaries free from threats or acts of force;

2. *Affirms further* the necessity

(a) For guaranteeing freedom of navigation through international waterways in the area;

(b) For achieving a just settlement of the refugee problem;

(c) For guaranteeing the territorial inviolability and political independence of every State in the area, through measures including the establishment of demilitarized zones;

3. *Requests* the Secretary-General to designate a Special Representative to proceed to the Middle East to establish and maintain contacts with the States concerned in order to promote agreement and assist efforts to achieve a peaceful and accepted settlement in accordance with the provisions and principles of this resolution.

4. *Requests* the Secretary-General to report to the Security Council on the progress of the efforts of the Special Representative as soon as possible.

TEXT OF UNITED NATIONS SECURITY COUNCIL RESOLUTION 338

Adopted by the Security Council at its 1747th meeting, on 21/ 22 October 1973

The Security Council

1.*Calls upon* all parties to the present fighting to cease all firing and terminate all military activity immediately, no later than 12 hours after the moment of the adoption of this decision, in the positions they now occupy;

2. *Calls upon* the parties concerned to start immediately after the ccase-fire the implementation of Security Council Resolution 242 (1967) in all of its parts;

3. *Decides* that, immediately and concurrently with the cease-fire, negotiations start between the parties concerned under appropriate auspices aimed at establishing a just and durable peace in the Middle East.

BIBLIOGRAPHY

An asterisk (*) preceding a reference indicates that the article or part of it has been reprinted in this book.

Books and Pamphlets

Abrahamian, Ervand. Iran between two revolutions (Princeton Studies on the Near East). Princeton University Press. '82.

Costello, Mary. Middle East transition. Editorial Research Reports, Vol. II, No. 21. D. 1, '78.

Curtis, Michael. Religion and politics in the Middle East (Special Studies on the Middle East) Westview. '82.

*Dayan, Moshe. Living with the Bible. Morrow. '78.

Dimbleby, Jonathan. The Palestinians. Quartet Books. '79.

Elazar, Daniel J. The Camp David framework for peace (Studies in Foreign Policy). American Enterprise Institute. '79.

Foreign Policy Association. Great decisions '81. The Association. 205 Lexington Ave., N. Y. 10016. '81.

*Foreign Policy Association. Great decisions '82. The Association. 205 Lexington Ave., N. Y. 10016. '82.

*Foreign Policy Association. Israel and the U.S.: friendship and discord. The Association. 205 Lexington Ave., N. Y. 10016. '82.

Greene, J. N. Jr. The path to peace: Arab-Israeli peace and the United States; report of a study mission to the Middle East. Seven Springs Center, Oregon Rd., Mount Kisco, N.Y. 10549. O. '81.

Gubser, Peter. Jordan (Nations of Contemporary Middle East Series). Westview. '82.

Herzog, Chaim. The Arab-Israeli wars. Random. '82.

An international law analysis of the major United Nations Resolutions concerning the Palestine question. Unipub.

Isenberg, Irwin, ed. The Arab world (Reference Shelf Series). H. W. Wilson. '76.

Johnson, Nels. Islam and the meaning of politics in Palestine nationalism. Routledge & Kegan. '82.

Lippman, Thomas W. Understanding Islam: an introduction to the Moslem world. New American Library. '82.

Mansfield, Peter, ed. The Middle East: a political and economic survey. Oxford University Press. '80.

McLaurin, R. and others. Foreign policy making in the Middle East: Domestic influences on policy in Egypt, Iraq, Israel, and Syria. Praeger. '77.

Metzger, Jan, and others. This land is our land (Palestine). Lawrence Hill. '82.

Rostow, Eugene, ed. The Middle East: critical choices for the United States. Westview Press, for the National Committee for American Foreign Policy. '76.

Said, Edward W. The question of Palestine. Random. '80.

Seibert, Robert F. and Anderson, Roy R. Politics and change in the Middle East: sources of conflict and accommodation. Prentice-Hall. '82.

Shoukri, Ghali. Egypt; portrait of a President: Sadat's road to Jerusalem. Lawrence Hill. '82.

Sinai, Anne and Pollack, Allen, ed. The Middle East confrontation states: the Hashemite kingdom of Jordan and the West Bank: a handbook. American Academic Association for Peace in the Middle East. '77.

Talal, Hassan B. Palestinian self-determination: a study of the West Bank and Gaza strip. Charles River Bks. '82.

United Nations. The question of Palestine. '79.

U.S. Central Intelligence Agency. Issues in the Middle East. U.S. Government Printing Office. '73.

U.S. Department of State. Egyptian-Israeli peace treaty, March 27, 1979. Bureau of Public Affairs, Selected Documents, #11, Ap. '79.

Yacobi, Gad. The government of Israel. Praeger. '82.

PERIODICALS

America. 146:142. F. 27, '82. How to blow up the United Nations (resolution of Israel's annexation of Golan Heights).

America. 146:202-3. Mr. 20, '82. A new voice in the Middle East (F. Mitterand).

Business Week. p 50. Ap. 5, '82. Behind the flare-up in Israeli-occupied lands. S. W. Sanders.

Business Week. p 49. S. 6, '82. Lebanon's next crisis; coaxing the foreign troops out. S. W. Sanders.

Christian Century. 99:196-7. F. 24, '82. The U.S. as Israel's godparent. D. M. Graybeal.

Christian Century. 99:555. My. 12, '82. Anti-Semitism and the Sinai withdrawal. J. M. Wall.

Christian Century. 99:857-9. Ag. 18-25, '82. The house that George and
    Salima built (ordeal of Kumsiya family, Palestinians on the West
    Bank). Orayb Najjar.
Commentary. 73:15-24. Mr. '82. The Middle East: a consensus of error.
    S. L. Spiegel.
Commentary. 74:19-30. O. '82. Lebanon: the case for the war. R. W.
    Tucker.
*Commonweal. 109:355-6. Je. 18, '82. The 'perfect logic' of Mideast war
    (editorial).
Commonweal. 109:457-60. S. 10, '82. Birth of a Zionist. A. A. Cohen.
Commonweal. 109:554. O. 22, '82. Framework for a Mideast future. J.
    B. Hehir.
Comparative Politics. 14:191-210. Ja. '82. Change and continuity in Zi-
    onist territorial orientations and politics. Baruch Kimmerling.
Current History. 81:1-4+. Ja. '82. United States policy in the Middle
    East: toward a pax Saudiana. Leonard Binder.
*Current History. 81:5-8+. Ja. '82. Egypt after Sadat. John G. Merriam.
*Current History. 81:9-13+. Ja. '82. The politics of extremism in Iran.
    James A. Bill.
*Current History. 81:14-7. Ja. '82. Iraq: pragmatic radicalism in the fer-
    tile crescent. Arthur C. Turner.
*Current History. 81:18-21+. Ja. '82. Israel's foreign policy challenge.
    Harold M. Waller.
*Current History. 81:22-5+. Ja. '82. Jordan and Arab polarization.
    Adam M. Garfinkle.
Current History. 81:26-9+. Ja. '82. Turkey's policy in flux. James
    Brown.
*Current History. 81:30-5. Ja. '82. Divided Lebanon. William H. Had-
    dad.
*Economist. 283:24. Je. 12, '82. Putting the Shias in their place.
*Economist. 284:9-10. Ag. 14, '82. The Habib opening.
Foreign Affairs. 59:756-80. Spring '81. Peacemaking in the Middle East:
    the next step. Shai Feldman.
*Foreign Affairs. 68:769-88. Spring '82. The foreign policy of Egypt in
    the Post-Sadat era. Boutros Boutros-Ghali.
*Foreign Affairs. 68:789-801. Spring '82. Israel's role in a changing
    Middle East. Yitzhak Shamir.
*Foreign Affairs. 68:802-13. Spring '82. Jordan's quest for peace. El
    Hassan Bin Talal.

Foreign Affairs. 60:1110-23. Summer '82. Why Begin should invite Arafat to Jerusalem. Joseph Alpher.

Foreign Affairs. 61:67-83. Fall '82. Begin's rhetoric and Sharon's tactics. Amos Perlmutter.

*Foreign Affairs. 61:103-21. Fall '82. An Israeli-Palestinian peace. Harold H. Saunders.

Macleans. 95:30. Ja. 18, '82. The Pope's PLO connection. R. Wright.

Macleans. 95:35-6. F. 1, '82. The 'Canadians' are moving again (Gaza stript town of Rafah). E. Silver.

Macleans. 95:26-7. F. 15, '82. Mubarak carries off a high-wire act. M. Posner.

MacLeans. 95:24-7. Jl. 26, '82. The future of the PLO (special section).

MERIP (Middle East Research & Info Project). Reports. 12:3-28. Ja. '82. Islam and politics.

Middle East Journal. 35:557-77. Autumn '81. Israel and the West Bank after Elon Moreh: the mechanics of de facto annexation. I. Lustick.

Middle East Journal. 36:22-47. Winter '82. Power and religion in revolutionary Iran. James A. Bill.

Middle Eastern Studies. 17:447-91. O. '81. Nationalism through localism: some observations on the West Bank political elite. S. Mishal.

*Nation. 233:597-600. D. 5, '81. Israel after Zionism. Boas Evron.

*Nation. 233:613-16. D. 5, '81. Notes on Jihad: Is Islam anti-semitic? Edward Mortimer.

*Nation. 233:616-19. D. 5, '81. International Law and the Israeli occupation. Michael Reisman.

Nation. 234:269-72. Mr. 6, '82. The two faces of the PLO. Robert Friedman.

Nation. 234:357. Mr. 27, '82. Desert fox (Israel's withdrawal from the Sinai Peninsula). Neil Barsky.

*Nation. 235:97. Ag. 7, '82. Mr. Begin's new friends.

*Nation. 235:100-1. Ag. 7, '82. Middle East comments. Yael Lotan.

*Nation. 235:100-1. Ag. 7, '82. Middle East comments. Henry Schwarzschild.

Nation. 235:333+. O. 9, '82. How democracy can be distorted (censorship in the West Bank). Matti Megged.

National Review. 34:250. Mr. 5, '82. Peace-lovers unite! (U.N. attacks on Israel). J. P. Roche.

*National Review. 34:253. Mr. 5, '82. The Israeli blues (Palestinian state question). William F. Buckley.

New Leader. 65:2. F. 8, '82. Between issues (J. J. Kirkpatrick's statement on Israeli annexation of Golan Heights).

*New Leader. 65:6-7. Ap. 19, 82. On Israel's border. Walter Goodman.

New Outlook. 24:21-5. Ja./F. '82. Prepared to pursue the cause of peace. Hussein I, King of Jordan.

New Republic. 186:9-10. Mr. 10, '82. A journalistic cover-up (issue of whether reporters in Lebanon and Syria have been intimidated in their work). M. Peretz.

New Republic. 186:8. Mr. 17, '82. Still stonewalling (intimidation of Western reporters by the PLO).

New Republic. 186:7-9. Ap. 7, '82. Begin at the end?

New Republic. 196:5-6. My. 12, '82. Brave retreat.

*New Republic. 187:7-9. Ag. 30, '82. Mideast ironies.

*New Republic. 187:7-8+. O. 4, '82. Good idea, bad start (Reagan peace plan vs. Arab plan presented at Fez).

New York Review of Books. 29:11-12. F. 18, '82. Begin and the Jews. Arthur Hertzberg.

*New York Times. A1+. Je. 21, '82. Arab inaction on Lebanon. T. L. Friedman.

New York Times. A1:4. Jl. 14, '82. Iraq, Iran and the U.S. Philip Taubman.

New York Times. A14:1. Jl. 14, '82. Iran-Iraq war at a glance.

New York Times. A14:4. Jl. 15, '82. Israel weighing impact of Gulf war. Henry Kamm.

New York Times. IV,1:1. Jl. 18, '82. From Beirut to Basra, Arabs squeezed hard.

New York Times. IV,1:5. Jl. 18, '82. Military defeat, political gain.

New York Times. A6:1. Jl. 19, '82. Resolving the crisis. T. L. Friedman.

New York Times. A1:4+. Jl. 25, '82. Lebanese tell of anguish of living under the PLO. D. K. Shipler.

New York Times. IV,1:1. Jl. 25, '82. West Beirut's future could settle the fate of all Lebanon. T. L. Friedman.

New York Times. IV,1:3. Ag. 8, '82. Beirut and after: Begin's dark vision. Henry Kamm.

New York Times. IV,1. Ag. 15, '82. What if the battle for Lebanon has just begun. T. L. Friedman.

New York Times. A1:1. Ag. 19, '82. Lebanon approves Habib plan. Thomas Friedman.

New York Times. A16:1. Ag. 19, '82. Refugees, hounded from one camp, live fearfully in rubble of another. Marvine Howe.

New York Times. IV:1. Ag. 22, '82. U.S. senses a Mideast role, if not a plan. Bernard Gwertzman.

New York Times. IV:2. Ag. 22, '82. Israeli-Palestinian future depends on use of war's lessons. T. L. Friedman.

New York Times. IV:2. Ag. 22, '82. Jerusalem is hardly in a hurry on autonomy. James Clarity.

New York Times Magazine. p 16-22+. Mr. 7. '82. Self-searching in Israel. Michael Elkins.

New York Times Magazine. p 26-31+. Jl. 11, '82. Has Israel altered its visions? Amos Oz.

Newsweek. 99:39. Ja. 25, '82. A stone wall on autonomy. Angus Deming.

Newsweek. 99:54. F. 8, '82. A civil war in the Sinai? Angus Deming.

Newsweek. 99:77-8. Mr. 1, '82. Who's afraid of the PLO? (charges of media bias against Western press are made by Z. Chafets of Israel). C. Kaiser.

Newsweek. 99:34. Mr. 15, '82. Mubarak's message (excerpts from interview). D. Pattir.

Newsweek. 99:49. Mr. 22, '82. Americans in Haddadland (Christian Lebanese warlord). Angus Deming.

Newsweek. 99:36-7+. Ap. 5, '82. The West Bank boils over. M. Whitaker.

*Newsweek. 99:61. My. 10, '82. Syria: a retreat into isolation. Angus Deming and Ray Wilkinson.

Newsweek. 99:24+. Je. 28, '82. The fragile truce in Lebanon (Israeli invasion). Angus Deming.

Newsweek. 100:20-7+. O. 4, '82. Israel in torment (after the Beirut massacre: special section).

Newsweek. 100:47-8. O. 25, '82. A window of opportunity? (meeting of Y. Arafat and King Hussein). Angus Deming.

Reader's Digest. 120:122-6. F. '82. Countdown in the Middle East. W. E. Griffith.

Senior Scholastic. 114:5-7. Mr. 5, '82. Golan Heights—aftermath of annexation. L. Edelman

Time. 119:35. Ja. 25, '82. The time is now—if ever (A. M. Haig joins Palestinian autonomy talks).

Time. 119:54-5. F. 1, '82. Islamic fervor (Islamic fundamentalist students opposed to the PLO on the West Bank).

Time. 119:46. F. 8, '82. "You spoil this naughty baby" (excerpts from interview with Y. Arafat). M. Gart and R. Suro.

Time. 119:28. F. 22, '82. Anyway, nice to see you (C. Weinberger's trip to the Middle East).

Time. 119:24. Mr. 1, '82. Sharon's plan (for proposed invasion of Lebanon).

Time. 119:30-7+. Mr. 1, 82. Years of upheaval. Henry Kissinger.

Time. 119:87. Mr. 1, '82. News gathering under the gun (Israel accuses U.S. journalists of suppressing stories).

Time. 119:32-4. Ap. 5, '82. Turmoil in the occupied lands. W. E. Smith.

Time. 119:24-5. Ap. 12, '82. Tension on the borders. W. E. Smith.

Time. 119:54. My. 24, '82. Mounting tensions on two fronts (Israeli attack on the PLO in Lebanon). W. E. Smith.

Time. 120:10-14+. Jl. 19, '82. Beirut (invasion by Israel; special section).

Time. 120:48-52. O. 18, '82. 444 days of agony (excerpt from *Keeping Faith*—Iranian seizure of U.S. embassy, 1979-81). Jimmy Carter.

Time. 120:44. O. 25, '82. Struggle for a compromise (Y. Arafat and King Hussein meet). T. A. Sanction.

UN Monthly Chronicle. 19:11-15. F. '82. Security Council declares Israeli actions on Golan Heights "null and void" (with text of resolution).

UN Monthly Chronicle. 19:54-5. F. '82. Israel denounced for refusing to allow experts into occupied lands.

U.S. Catholic. 47:18-23. Ja. '82. Fear never sleeps through Arabian nights (Palestinians in Jerusalem).

U.S. Department of State Bulletin. 82:46-7. Ja. '82. U.S. and Israel review MFO participation (Sinai multinational peacekeeping force: U.S.-Israel statement, December 3, 1981).

U.S. Department of State Bulletin. 82:60. Ja. '82. Security Council votes on Golan Heights situation (State Department statement December 18, 1981: with text of resolution).

U.S. Department of State Bulletin. 82:44-7. Jl. '82. Peace and security in the Middle East (address May 26, 1982). A. M. Haig.

U.S. News & World Report. 92:30-1. Ja. 25, '82. What U.S. has riding on Saudi royal family: even if Israel and Egypt reach agreement, success of America's pursuit of peace could rest on the king and princes of Saudi Arabia. Al Webb.

U.S. News & World Report. 92:31-2. F. 15, '82. Balance of Mideast power now with PLO: U.S., Egypt, Israel all are trying to reach accord; but in the end an unpredictable band of Palestinians will hold the key to a settlement. Al Webb.

U.S. News & World Report. 92:31-2. Mr. 15, '82. "The end is in sight for Camp David" peace process: interview with Jordan's King Hussein.

U.S. News & World Report. 92:33-4. Mr. 22, '82. Why Syria blames U.S. for its troubles. Dennis Mullin.

U.S. News & World Report. 92:33-4. Ap. 5, '82. As rift widens between U.S., Israel—. Dennis Mullin.

U.S. News & World Report. 92:25-6. Ap. 12, '82. Sinai pullout: a bitter pill for Israel. Dennis Mullin.

U.S. News & World Report. 92:27-8. Ap. 12, '82. Iran: a land of hardship and hatred. Al Webb.

U.S. News & World Report. 92:16-21. Je. 28, '82. Mideast nightmare: search for a way out (Special section).

U.S. News & World Report. 93:22-6+. S. 27, '82. Back to square one (effect of murder of B. Gemayel; with interview with C. W. Weinberger). W. A. Taylor.

U.S. News & World Report. 93:33-4. N. 15, '82. Hussein: missing piece in Mideast puzzle. Dennis Mullin.

World Press Review. 29:47. F. '82. Tinder in the Golan. H. Toledano.